ID0706963

The Lost Jungle

In the 1930s and the 1940s, in the US and elsewhere, cinema-goers saw not just a film but a programme that might include a double-bill, one or more shorts, and a serial. The latter, consisting of up to fifteen episodes shown at weekly intervals, were not confined to children's matinees but were part of the regular bill at numerous neighbourhood theatres. In some countries they were the main attraction.

Serials such as Flash Gordon and The Lone Ranger were extraordinarily popular; others provided a reliable return for the studios that produced them: Universal, Columbia, Republic, Mascot and a handful of other Poverty Row outfits.

The Lost Jungle will help revive and re-invigorate the study of 1930s and 1940s Hollywood serials. It examines the episodic structure and melodramatic nature of serials made in Hollywood during the Great Depression and the Second World War and their places within the American film industry and American culture.

Guy Barefoot is Lecturer in Film Studies, Director of Studies, History of Art and Film, and member of the Centre for American Studies at the University of Leicester

Exeter Studies in Film History

Published by University of Exeter Press in association with the Bill Douglas Centre for the History of Cinema and Popular Culture

Series Editors: **Richard Maltby,** Professor of Screen Studies, Flinders University
Steve Neale, Professor of Film Studies, University of Exeter

UEP also publishes the celebrated five-volume series looking at the early years of English cinema, *The Beginnings of the Cinema in England,* by John Barnes.

The Lost Jungle

Cliffhanger Action and Hollywood Serials of the 1930s and 1940s

Guy Barefoot

UNIVERSITY
of
EXETER
PRESS

First published in 2017 by
University of Exeter Press
Reed Hall, Streatham Drive
Exeter EX4 4QR
UK
www.exeterpress.co.uk

British Library Cataloguing in Publication Data
A catalogue record for this book is available
from the British Library.

ISBN 978 0 85989 887 4

Typeset in Caslon by
Short Run Press Ltd, Exeter

Printed in Great Britain by
Short Run Press Ltd, Exeter

Contents

Illustrations

Acknowledgements

My thanks to James Chapman for supporting my original idea back in 2006, to the University of Leicester for giving me study leave to pursue it, and to the British Academy for funding an initial research trip to the United States. That took me to Los Angeles and New York as well as to Brigham Young University in Utah. I am grateful for the help given to me at the USC Cinematic Arts Library, UCLA Special Collections, the Margaret Herrick Library, the Museum of the American West, the Howard B. Lee Library at Brigham Young and the New York Library for the Performing Arts. Thanks also to staff at the Library of Congress in Washington and at the British Film Institute, the British Library and the Public Records Office in London, as well as at the University of Leicester Library. Others have enabled me to do much of my research without travelling, notably the Media History Digital Library Team. The page reproduced from *Motion Picture Herald* is from their website. My thanks to Brian Patten for permission to quote from his poems, 'Where are you now, Batman?' and 'Where are you now, Superman?' I am also indebted to all those fans, collectors and suppliers who have kept the serial alive and have allowed me to watch serials that earlier accounts identified as lost, as well as others that somehow got missed off the film studies curriculum. An earlier version of Chapter Two appeared in the *Historical Journal of Film, Radio and Television*. I am very grateful to Anna Henderson for picking up on this and commissioning this book for University of Exeter Press, to Simon Baker for his subsequent editorial work, and to the series editors of the Exeter Studies in Film History. Thanks also to Anna Claydon, Phyll Smith, Luke Terlak Poot (even if we didn't manage to track down that elusive Sol Shor article on the cliffhanger) and to colleagues and students in the Department of History of Art and Film and the Centre for American Studies at the University of Leicester.

Introduction

Near the beginning of Mascot Pictures' *The Lost Jungle* (1934), Captain Robinson tells his daughter Ruth that unless lion-tamer Clyde Beatty agrees to marry her he will insist that she accompany him on his South Sea expedition. Clyde loves Ruth, but is preoccupied with his lions, and Ruth accompanies her father. Like earlier Robinsons, father and daughter find themselves shipwrecked. When Clyde learns of this, he joins a search party, but the dirigible chartered by the search party is struck by lightning. It crash lands on the very island where Clyde's fiancé and her father are sheltering. The lion-tamer encounters assorted wild animals, some of which he eventually takes back with him on the Captain's repaired ship, and discovers the treasure hidden in the buried city of Kamor. At the end of the film he turns his attention away from his lions. Clyde and Ruth embrace.

At least, they do in the feature-length version. Poverty Row studio Mascot specialized in serials but by 1934 it was also making features and releasing films in serial and feature versions. *The Lost Jungle* was released as a twelve chapter serial, as a feature followed by ten chapters, and as a 'straight feature'.[1] In the serial, Clyde and Ruth meet for the first time on the island. Romance is downplayed and more time is devoted to animal encounters and other life-threatening dangers. There is no closing embrace.

The serial itself survives in different versions. In one of these the second chapter begins with an explanatory voice-over:

> The lost jungle is an island where lions, tigers, bears and other wild animals are found living together. How did they get there? Scientists declare that Asia and Africa were once joined by land which has sunk into the ocean. Only the tops of a few high mountains remain above water as islands.

1. *The Lost Jungle* (1934)

The sequence is illustrated by an aerial shot of the island, a shot of animals fighting with a superimposed question mark that increases in size (Fig. 1), a map showing Asia and Africa joined together and an image of mountains above the sea. The crude stage prop waves provide a thin justification for the story's inclusion of so many of the Hagenbeck-Wallace Circus animals in the wild on a South Sea island. The sequence cuts off abruptly. The images are not repeated in later chapters, but in some the voice-over begins, 'The lost jungle is an island . . .' or just 'The lost jungle . . .' before being abruptly cut off.

The Lost Jungle did fair box-office business.[2] The feature received a run at the Criterion in New York and a *New York Times* review.[3] Yet away from the metropolitan centres it was the serial that attracted attention, particularly if the circus was in town. 'When the opportunity presented itself for us to buy and book the serial "The Lost Jungle," with Clyde Beatty [who played Clyde Beatty] and we found we could spot it just two days after the circus appeared here featuring Beatty, we got to work at once,' wrote the manager of the Ohio in Dayton, Ohio, who had gone for the feature followed by ten episodes option. 'We put on what we considered a very comprehensive campaign, considering the size of our theatre and were rewarded with a record-breaking week and several record-breaking days, including a new high for the theatre from the standpoint of receipts as well as attendance.' Beatty's local circus appearance, and attendance at a reception organized for him by the Ohio, as well as a free Saturday night preview that 'attracted city officials and so forth', helped make *The Lost Jungle* a civic event as well as a box-office success.[4]

It continued to reach audiences after its initial release. In 1939 *The Lost Jungle* became the first serial to be broadcast on television.[5] The lion-taming reputation of its star endured to the extent that he was name-checked in Errol Morris's *Fast, Cheap & Out of Control* (1997), which features material from Beatty's other serial, *Darkest Africa* (1936). But lion-taming has fallen out of fashion and film historians have not paid much attention to 1930s serials. The fate of the serial can seem like that of the mini-lecture delivered at the start of some versions of the second chapter of *The Lost Jungle*, surviving only as a trace of an antiquated practice. The serial itself is an example of a strand of film history that is either neglected or looked down upon: its history has been largely left to fans and collectors. It has had a limited place in a more established narrative that stresses the dominance of the feature film from the second decade of the twentieth century.

It deserves further exploration. Far more attention has been paid to *It Happened One Night* (also 1934), the screwball comedy that took the major Academy Awards and ushered in a new mix of sophisticated comedy and romance, but away from the downtown metropolitan first run cinemas there were other films on the programme. The film programme itself deserves further scrutiny. Audiences in the 1930s brought tickets not just to a single film but also to a double bill or a feature accompanied by other attractions. At many cinemas, serials continued to hold a place in the programme throughout and beyond the 1930s. The serial could provide the main attraction.

The film serial emerged when films were no longer limited to a single reel. This led to the multi-reel feature, viewed at a single sitting, but the instalment plan provided another means of extending narrative. It achieved a high profile in 1914 and the years immediately following, particularly but not only through serials made in the United States. It is a narrative format that has a long print history and that has been a mainstay of radio and television. In its own way it has returned to contemporary cinema, as franchises such as the Harry Potter (2001–11) and Marvel superhero (2008–) features have come to dominate the box-office. Earlier American serials relatively quickly came to take the form of weekly instalments each lasting twenty minutes or thereabouts. Serials became more marginal to the American film industry during the 1920s, and outside the United States their production was all but abandoned in the 1930s. But Hollywood (understood here to include major and minor studios with a production base in the Los Angeles area) continued to produce them well into the 1950s. Mascot specialized in serials until they became part of Republic Pictures in 1935, who in turn continued this line of film production up to 1955. Universal Pictures' first serial was made in 1914, its last in 1946. Columbia Pictures started to release serials in 1937, and continued in the serial business up to the production of *Blazing the Overland Trail* in 1956. In addition, selected minor studios made serials up to the late 1930s. In general disparaged (if noticed at all) by critics and those working within the film industry, they achieved sufficient success in the late 1930s for some to suggest that Hollywood's Big Five were considering competing for a share of the lucrative market.[6]

Hollywood made sound serials in significant numbers. Each one lasted between ten and fifteen chapters and thus had a total running length significantly longer than even a lengthy feature. One source lists sixty-nine Universal and twenty-four Mascot sound serials (including serials such as *The Ace of Scotland Yard* [1929] and *King of the Kongo* [1929] released in silent and part-talkie versions), sixty-six Republic serials, fifty-seven Columbia serials and fifteen independent serials.[7] Another includes the calculation that the sixty-six Republic serials had a total running time of 224 hours, ten minutes and fifty-two seconds, a figure that does not include the running time of features made from serials or serials re-released under different titles.[8] As well as being produced regularly and in quantity, serials continued to be seen in significant numbers. According to one report, in 1946 approximately 8,000 of the 18,765 cinemas in the United States regularly played serials, a further 2,000 played them on an irregular basis, while an average serial played to an audience of four to five million.[9] Serials continued to have a significant audience outside the United States into the second half of the twentieth century.

You would not gather this from most film histories. Just as American cinema in 1934 has tended to mean *It Happened One Night* rather than *The Lost Jungle*, the mid-1940s is far more likely to mean film noir rather than the film serial. David Cook does not mention the American serial in his *A History of Narrative Film*.[10] Jon Lewis's history of American film contains only a brief comment on *The Perils of Pauline* (1914) and

The Exploits of Elaine (1915), in which he suggests that 'each episode ends with a cliffhanger'.[11] 'The Brief Heyday of the Serial' in Kristin Thompson and David Bordwell's *Film History* is similarly devoted to the silent serial.[12]

Film historians have paid some attention to the silent serial. In particular, Ben Singer's work on the empowerment and imperilment of the serial queen of the 1910s has been followed by other discussions of the significance of the serial for female performers and audiences.[13] Little attention has been paid to later decades. Singer's entry on serials in the *Oxford History of World Cinema* remains representative, limiting consideration of the period after the 1910s to three closing paragraphs, beginning: 'In the United States, film serials lived out the 1920s, and survived to the rise of television, as a low-budget "B" product with limited distribution and an appeal primarily to hyperactive children'.[14]

Fans, collectors and those with fond memories of watching serials at Saturday matinees for children have written books, articles and even established periodicals devoted to the film serial in general and the sound serial in particular, while the internet currently hosts fan sites, forums and blogs devoted all or in part to the topic.[15] Their discussions can be informed by detailed knowledge; in particular, Jack Mathis's publications on Republic serials provide valuable source material on the topic.[16] All tend to be accompanied by a denial of its significance. W.K. Everson's introduction to Alan Barbour's *Saturday Afternoon at the Movies* includes the following disclaimer:

> With full regard for the skill of the serials, the money they made, and the entertainment they brought to millions, the serials have not added one iota of development to either the art or the history of the film. One could sweep them away, blot them out totally, and the blow to film history would not be a major one. Indeed, if the serial had never evolved at all, it is unlikely that the course of film would have been changed or diverted in any way.[17]

The authors of *The Great Movie Serials* are representative in describing their work as 'primarily intended as a book of nostalgic entertainment'.[18]

Seriality across media has come to attract increasing attention. A recent anthology on serialization in popular culture includes chapters on *The Perils of Pauline* and Ingmar Bergman's *Scenes from a Marriage* (1973), alongside others on *Mrs Beeton's Book of Household Management* (1859– 61), *Mad Men* (2007–15), *The Walking Dead* (2010–), the graphic novel, video games and Wikipedia; it is silent on the Hollywood sound serial.[19]

The serial's identification as children's entertainment provides one reason for this neglect and devaluation. The attention paid to the adult female audience for the serial queen melodramas of the 1910s has not been extended to later serials, associated as they are with Saturday matinees for children. There are exceptions here. Rafael Arnaldo Vela and in particular Scott Higgins have done important work on the nature of the sound serial and its appeal for children.[20] Yet the serial's adult audience was not restricted to the 1910s. Another reason for the neglect of the serial lies in its more general appeal outside the downtown first-run cinemas in major metropolitan centres. The fact that the serial does not fit the dominant view of film history provides an additional reason. The first serials can be fitted into a film history in which the 1910s exist as a transitional era, as exhibition moved from a collection of short attractions to the feature film. Beyond this, however, the model of the programme of regular instalments has tended to be linked to radio and television rather than cinema. Studies of studio-era Hollywood allow for continuation at the level of the studio, the genre, the star, the auteur, but discuss these in relation to the self-contained film. In addition, much recent interest in the television serial has been based on the perception that longer-form narrative allows for complexity and diversity. While it may be possible to make this case for either the soap opera or the HBO drama, it is less easy to do this for the Mascot, Republic, Universal or Columbia serial.

The fact that serials appealed to children is no reason to ignore them. However, it is important to pay more attention to the serial's different audiences: children and adults, after as well as before 1930. There are good reasons for understanding cinema-going in the 1930s and 1940s in terms of the programme of individual features but also regular added attractions. It is important to examine forms of entertainment and narrative that are based on repetition as well as variation and that emphasize transparent action rather than inner complexity. Audiences may have gone to see Clyde Beatty at the circus not because they wanted narrative development or complex characterization but because they wanted to see Beatty doing his lion-taming routine. The cinema and the circus brought with them different expectations, hence the marriage plot of the *Lost Jungle* feature and the story of hidden treasure common to feature and serial. But *The Lost Jungle* also points to the perpetuation of a form of film entertainment that diverged from the norms of 'classical Hollywood' while retaining an appeal for adults as well as children.

In what follows I examine evidence for this across a broad field.

My focus is on Hollywood serials made between the first 'all-talking' serial, *The Indians are Coming* (1930), and the last Universal serial, *The Mysterious Mr M* (1946). I focus in particular on the Hollywood serial of the 1930s. However, in attempting to understand the ingredients (what it is derived from as well as its components) and appeal of the serial it is also necessary to look beyond these dates and beyond Hollywood. In examining definitions and origins of the serial and the cliffhanger, the first chapter considers literature and theatre as well as cinema and the silent as well as the sound serial. In examining the serial audience, the second chapter continues this concern with the silent as well as the sound era while primarily focusing on the period after 1930. Here I look at adult, child and international serial audiences. I also address questions of regulation, with a view to assessing the extent that the film industry's concern to present the serial as suitable for children concealed a broader audience.

The third chapter examines the serial as a specific but not homogenous commercial strategy within the American film industry. Examining Universal's serial production again necessitates some attention to the silent era, though my focus is on that studio's serial production between 1930 and 1946. By ways of contrast, I examine Sherman Krellberg's involvement in the serial, through the production and distribution of *The Lost City* (1935) as well as the distribution of assorted Universal serials. In the final section of this chapter, my focus shifts to Republic, the studio established in 1935, when it took over the smaller scale Mascot's serial production. I examine the particular ways in which Republic streamlined serial filmmaking and developed a particular identity outside the Hollywood Majors while achieving its own pre-eminence within its specific field.

The next two chapters move on to the films themselves. In the first of these I examine the organization of material within the serial's second chapter. This focus will allow me to be less restricted in other ways. The serious discussion of the sound serial that does exist often concentrates on the Republic serial, in particular those directed by John English and William Witney. I address these films but as part of a broader survey of Hollywood serials made between 1930 and 1946. I also examine the cliffhanger alongside other features of the serial chapter. Looking at patterns across episodes, the subsequent book chapter provides more detailed analysis of four serials from the 1930s: Universal's *The Lost Special* (1932) and *Jungle Jim* (1937), Mascot's *The Whispering Shadow* (1933) (paying some attention also to the feature version), and Republic's

Daredevils of the Red Circle (1939). Thus here I examine a relatively familiar English and Witney serial alongside lesser known examples. The final chapter looks at the serial after 1946, not with a view to providing a detailed history of the period up to *Blazing the Overland Trail* but to give a perspective on shifting attitudes to the film serial, particularly when serials ceased to be produced but continued to be watched, on television, in cinema revivals and through fan networks. This chapter thus serves as an opportunity to consider the legacy of the film serial and to highlight my key conclusions.

This book does not attempt to provide a comprehensive history of the film serial and concentrates on some aspects more than others. I have undertaken more extensive research into Universal and Republic serials than I have into those made for Columbia, and into serials made before rather than after 1946. However, my concern is to be as comprehensive as possible in my study of serials made between 1930 and 1946. While this in effect covers the Great Depression and the Second World War, the aim is not to examine how the upheavals of these times were reflected in the film serial: that is for another study, if one that will also need to take account of how the serial combined aspects of modernity with resistance to reflecting the contemporary world. The purpose rather is to provide a study that is not limited to a small number of films that have been singled out as distinctive. Film history remains narrow in its focus on the main feature at the first-run cinema and even in its emphasis on what was new rather than in forms of cinema that remained rooted in earlier practices. In line with my concern to go beyond that, this is not a study of the serial that is restricted to even the better known examples of a relatively unknown form of cinema. *The Phantom Empire* (1935), *Flash Gordon* (1936) and the English/Witney serials, all have a place here, but as part of a regular, serialized production process, alongside *The Lost Jungle*, *The Lost Special*, *The Lost City*, *Lost City of the Jungle* (1946), and other serials that are not in fact lost.

In Britain, only a small number of serials have had a commercial VHS or DVD release, and it has been some while since serials have played at the cinema or on television. Yet through online platforms and individual suppliers it has become possible to see all but a small number of serials produced since 1930. The 233 sound serials identified by Alan Barbour include a few that can be discounted as part-talkies as well as some missing believed lost early sound Universal serials: *The Jade Box*, *Terry of the Times* and *The Lightning Express* from 1930, *Finger Prints*, *Danger Island*, *The Spell of the Circus* from 1931, *Detective Lloyd*, *The Jungle Mystery* and

The Airmail Mystery from 1932.[21] *The Voice from the Sky*, an independently produced serial released in 1930, remains unavailable, as does the serial version of another independent production, *Tarzan the Fearless* (1933).[22] The number of 'lost' serials was larger when I started this project, but rediscovered copies of several serials have since become available, up to and including the recent DVD release of (oh joy!) the first six chapters of *Clancy of the Mounted* (1933). A few other serials are missing chapters or include chapters without sound. The vast majority of the 2,000 plus serial chapters produced by Hollywood between 1930 and 1956 can be located in some form, if not always in pristine condition.

Even allowing for the decision to focus in particular on serials produced between 1930 and 1946, this has still left a significant body of material. While all studies filter their data to some degree, my starting premise was at least to watch all the available sound serials made up to 1946, and the early stages of my research consisted largely of doing that (as well as selected examples from both before and after). There are enthusiasts who insist that the only way to watch serials is at weekly intervals; as this would have taken me past my 100th birthday I adopted a more intensive viewing programme. I had to struggle to get through some serials, from the very long and often incoherent *The Black Coin* (1935) to some of the later Universal serials and even some of the more mechanical Republic films. Yet I also developed an admiration and affection for both the efficiency and pace of the Republic serial and the endearing absurdity of many serials of the early 1930s. Most importantly, I became increasingly aware of how little I knew of film history. Unlike the fans who write on the serial in order to recall childhood memories of Saturday matinee screenings, I did not grow up with the serial, and thus to watch *The Lone Defender* (1930) or *Pirate Treasure* (1934) was to encounter a new world. This was not limited to the serial: to look at the listings in local newspapers from a mid-west American town such as Oelwein, Iowa (see Chapter Three), was to realize the extent to which audiences were watching films (features and serials) that have barely left a trace.

Narratives about lost jungles, lost cities, or lost cities of the jungle, are of course narratives of discovery. The material discussed here has never quite been lost. But the acute neglect of the serial deserves rectifying, not just for what this can tell us about these particular films but also on account of the wider significance they have for our understanding of film history and American culture.

1

The Serial and the Cliffhanger:
Definitions and Origins

In 'College Hero', the opening chapter of *The Adventures of Frank Merriwell* (1936), Frank receives a telegram telling him that his mother is dangerously ill. His friend, Elsie Belwood, drives him and another friend, Bruce Browning, to the station, but just after their train has left she learns of a runaway engine on the track, heading straight for the train carrying Frank and Bruce. While she drives as fast as she can in an attempt to warn them of the danger, Frank makes for the front of the train. The trains collide. An announcement appears on the screen: 'See "THE DEATH PLUNGE" Chapter Two of "ADVENTURES OF FRANK MERRIWELL" serial to be shown at this theatre next week'.

The following chapter reveals that Frank and the train driver were able to jump to safety. After Frank has helped the wounded passengers, Elsie takes him and Bruce the rest of the way in her car. On reaching the family home, Frank learns that his mother has recovered. She remains disturbed by the nightly appearances of a ghost-like figure. She is convinced the figure is searching for a ring given to her by Frank's father before he mysteriously disappeared.

'The Death Plunge' thus replaces one pair of questions with another. It resolves the questions about the survival of Frank and his mother. It introduces the questions that provide the initial narrative impulse that will take us through its twelve chapters: where is Frank's father and what is the mystery of the ring? In this and other respects it is characteristic of the Hollywood sound serial in general.

Like many other serials, it tells of an athletic hero, his lost father and a sought-after object that will lead to both riches and the return of the father. As in other serials, the hero is accompanied by a trusted male friend and a woman with whom romance remains undeveloped. The better-known *Flash Gordon* (which Universal released later the same year) differs in having a father who is not lost but a helpless onlooker back on earth and a hero seeking to save the world rather than find wealth and his father. Both have a similar episodic structure, their twelve (in the case of *The Adventures of Frank Merriwell*) and thirteen (*Flash Gordon*) chapters lasting around twenty minutes each. Jean Rogers played the hero's female companion in both serials. Both serials have cliffhanger chapter endings, leaving the hero in danger of his life. This above all has been taken as defining the film serial, or the cliffhanger as it is often known. As Buck Rainey notes, 'we normally think of the serial as having a continuing story, continuing characters, and cliffhanger endings that leave the hero or heroine in jeopardy. Viewers are drawn back the following week to see how the hero or heroine manages to emerge unscathed from some near-death experience'.[1]

This is a very specific form of seriality. It differs starkly from the serials discussed in other accounts. Thus Robert C. Allen contrasts television serials to non-serial popular narratives, which 'tend to be organised around a single protagonist or small group of protagonists and to be teleological; there is a single moment of narrative closure (obviously involving the protagonist) towards which their plots move and in relation to which reader satisfaction is presumed to operate'.[2] The twelfth and final episode of *The Adventures of Frank Merriwell* ends with Frank, the single protagonist, having found his father and the treasure, escaping from the villains who have held him captive just in time to win the football game for Fardale, an act which balances the baseball game featured in first chapter just before he received notice of his mother's ill health. On Allen's soap opera-based criteria, *The Adventures of Frank Merriwell* is the very thing from which the serial is to be distinguished.

It contrasts also with the serialized Victorian novels discussed by Linda Hughes and Michael Lund as illustrating how, 'Victorians valued slow, steady development in instalments over time, seeds planted in spring leading to harvest in distant autumn', a process that was in sharp contrast to the speed of modern literature and thought.[3] An audience watching *The Adventures of Frank Merriwell* in weekly instalments would have seen the serial over a period of months, not quite spring to autumn but perhaps spring to summer. However, when Frank takes the train home he is after speed rather than steady development, in line with other film serials of the period such as *The Lightning Express* (1931), *The Hurricane Express* (1932) and *Burn 'em Up Barnes* (1934), which all emphasized modern modes of transport that raced and crashed.

In addition, as a serial, *The Adventures of Frank Merriwell* differs from other episodic forms. Alex Marlow-Mann has provided a useful taxonomy, identifying four main trends within the serial format. First:

> the true serial, in which key plot points remain unresolved at the end of each episode to be picked up at the start of the next (most characteristically in the form of a cliff-hanger); the true serial also shows a clear narrative progression across the individual episodes. Second, there is what I will call the semi-serial, which has an overarching progress and sense of progression and a consistent set of characters but which has clearly demarcated, self-contained chapters that contain the resolution to their own narrative goals. Third, there is the character-based series, which features recurring character(s) in a number of short films but with no over-arching narrative progression, made by the same production company and/or director and/or screenwriter. Finally, there is the thematically based series, which utilizes different characters and self-contained narratives but maintains strong thematic links and a sense of continuity between episodes.[4]

Yet if this identifies *The Adventures of Frank Merriwell* as a 'true serial' it is not one with a clear narrative progression. At the end of 'College Hero' Frank Merriwell is faced with the prospect of imminent death; at the end of 'The Death Plunge' Frank Merriwell, as the title implies, is faced with the prospect of imminent death; at the end of 'Death at the Crossroads', the serial's third chapter, Frank Merriwell is, as the title implies, faced with the prospect of imminent death . . . The progression of Frank Merriwell's treasure and father hunt is accompanied by repetition and return, in effect, a series of cliffhangers. The cliffhanger is part of the sequential process in that it provides a hook between episodes: in episode one, Frank and the train driver are about to be killed in the collision of train, in episode two, Frank and the train driver jump to safety just in time. But the cliffhanger does not offer the development and change identified in the television serial.

The Adventures of Frank Merriwell is not discussed here as an exceptional example of the serial. It 'looked creaky throughout for 1936' according to one account.[5] This in itself provides one reason for examining it as part of a study that looks beyond the familiar. It is more representative of the Hollywood serial than the better-known *Flash Gordon*, both in its earth-bound setting and its repetitive narrative. In addition, through its source material it provides a means of examining the roots of the Hollywood serial and the cliffhanger and thus also the relationship between the film serial and the serial in other media. The Hollywood serial had distinct characteristics but it remains important to understand it as part of a wider pattern of seriality. This importance is acknowledged in other accounts of the film serial which have emphasized what the film serial took from the stage.[6] In going back to the nineteenth and early twentieth century my account includes a consideration of stage melodrama but places greater emphasis on other media. Since Frank Merriwell first appeared in print it is worth taking this earlier version as a starting point.

Frank Merriwell Before Film

'Frank Merriwell, or, The First Days of Fardale' appeared in Street and Smith's *Tip Top Weekly* in April 1896. It was the first of what has been calculated as 777 Merriwell stories written by Gilbert Patten under the name of Burt L. Standish. Together with later contributions by others writing under the Standish name, these established Merriwell as, in the words of J. Randolph Cox, 'perhaps the most famous individual in all dime novel literature'.[7] As well as being significant on account of their extraordinary volume and popularity (if not long-standing reputation), 'The First Days of Fardale' and the subsequent Merriwell stories marked an important shift in the publication of popular fiction. For Michael Denning, *Tip Top Weekly* was a move away from the working class culture of earlier dime novels.[8] It also marked a shift towards an increasing emphasis on a teenage, often male readership, in contrast to the working-class women emphasized in Denning's account.[9] *Tip Top Weekly* was designed, as its sub-heading proclaimed, as *An Ideal Publication for American Youth*, and emphasized stories of male athleticism and heroism.

In addition, the publication demonstrated a new level of corporate control over the individual writer. As Christine Bold has described, one shift in popular publishing in nineteenth-century America came with the establishment of Beadle's Dime Novels in 1860. However, while Beadle introduced a standardized packaging and price and a regimented payment and contract of employment for authors, the 'principle of systematization penetrated much more deeply into the relationships between publisher, editor, author and audience in the firm of Street and Smith'.[10] This is illustrated in the instructions senior partner Ormond Smith gave to Patten when commissioning the series.

14

Smith asked for:

> a library containing a series of stories covering the class of incident, in all of which will appear one prominent character surrounded by multiple suitable satellites . . .
>
> It is important that the main character in the series should have a catchy name . . . The essential idea of this series is to interest young readers in the career of a young man at a boarding school, preferably a military or naval academy. The stories should differ from the Jack Harkaways in being American and thoroughly up to date. Our idea is to issue, say, twelve stories, each complete in itself, but like the links in a chain, all dealing with life at the academy . . .
>
> After the first twelve numbers, the hero is obliged to leave the academy, or takes it upon himself to leave. It is essential that he should come into a considerable amount of money at this period. When he leaves the academy he takes with him one of the professor's servants, a chum. In fact any of the characters you have introduced and made prominent in the story. A little love element would also not be amiss, though this is not particularly important.
>
> When the hero is once projected on his travels there is an infinite variety of incident to choose from. In the Island School Series, published by one of our London connections, you will find scenes of foreign travel, with color. This material you are at liberty to use freely, with our hero as the central character, of course, and up-to-date dialogue.
>
> After we run through twenty or thirty numbers of this, we would bring the hero back and have him go to college, say, Yale University; thence we would take him on his travels again to the South Sea or anywhere.[11]

As this indicates, the Merriwell stories were to roam over a wide territory but within the framework set out by Ormond Smith. Narrative elements introduced in particular issues were to be resolved within that issue but within an overarching 'links in a chain' structure.

Patten broadly adhered to this blueprint. Equipped with the catchy and characteristic name of Frank Merriwell, the honest, happy and healthy contemporary American hero of the *Tip Top Weekly* stories went from military academy to a series of adventures that took him as far afield as the South Seas but also to Yale. He had periodic romantic involvements, accumulated a succession of sporting achievements and took part in regular pranks while always maintaining his moral standing. In Ryan K. Anderson's description, each issue of *Tip Top Weekly* contained a 20,000-word story that 'could be enjoyed on its own or read as a mini-story arc of three stories that, in turn, tied into a larger twelve story arc'. There were four arcs running across what was 'known collectively as the Merriwell saga', that developed across the decades during which *Tip Top Weekly* was published. These followed Merriwell's growth from schoolboy athlete to fully-grown man, detailed a love triangle with Elsie Belwood and Inza Burrage, narrated the discovery and redemption of Frank's long-lost half-brother, Dick Merriwell, and, fourth and finally, told of the establishment of the Merriwell American School of Athletic Development.[12] There were also less extended narratives that ran across issues. Thus the seventh issue of *Tip Top Weekly*, 'Frank Merriwell's Mysterious Ring, or, The Man in Black', leads eventually to 'Frank Merriwell in Arizona, or, The Mystery of the Old Mine' (the sixteenth issue). This pattern was later used in the Universal serial, in a more truncated manner, the ring introduced in the serial's second chapter taking Frank Merriwell and others to the mine in chapter six.

In addition, issues of *Tip Top Weekly* included 'Applause'. In Anderson's description, this consisted of a 'literary community' in which readers and correspondents updated middle-class traditions of self-education and 'answered questions about how a boy should prepare for success in corporate America, what the proper gender roles in the new environment were, and how one could lead (or follow) as a man'—and repeatedly applauded the publication.[13]

With the exception of *Mr Frank Merriwell*, a novel published in 1941, George Patten's last Merriwell story was published on 7 September 1912. The contributions from other writers kept the story going for a few more years, if now more focused on Frank Merriwell Junior. In addition, the stories were collected, repackaged and republished in *Tip Top Quarterly*, in the *Medal Library* and *New Medal Library*, in *Merriwell's Baseball Stories* and *Merriwell's Football Stories*, in the *Merriwell Series*, the *Burt L. Standish Library* and *Merriwell Library*. Selected titles were issued individually in cloth or paperback editions. Appearances in other media included comic strip versions published in 1928, between 1931 and 1934 and the mid-1950s, and two radio series, broadcast in 1934 and 1949 respectively. The 1934 radio series starred Donald Briggs, who went on to star in Universal's *The Adventures of Frank Merriwell*.[14]

Individual *Tip Top Weekly* issues came with narrative resolutions rather than cliffhangers but bore many of the serial features others have identified. The 'Applause' section acknowledged audience response in line with Jennifer Hayward's argument that the serial has been based on an interaction between producers and consumers.[15] For Umberto Eco the serial, 'another term for repetitive art', was a synonym for the series, while the saga was 'a series in disguise', in which the deeds of the ancestors were repeated by their descendants, just as in the 'Merriwell saga' Frank Junior repeated his father's deeds.[16] The quantity of Merriwell stories, the contributions of different authors, and their hero's appearance in different media, links them to Ruth Mayer's observation that 'the lexicon of the serial mode in popular culture is replete with such terms as sprawl, growth, dispersion, and excrescence rather than exclusively relying on associations of linear unravelling, careful design, or microstructural complexity'.[17] At the same time the Merriwell stories were written to a plan, and were part of move towards corporate control: a process by which the American serial was defined in terms of regularity as well as continuation.

The regular distribution of the *Tip Top* publications, and the regular distribution of other publications such as Frank Tousey's *Work and Win*, was also facilitated by the particular circumstances of the time. The 1879 Mail Classification Act allowed for periodicals to be sent as second-class mail. In order to be classed as a periodical, items had to appear at least four times a year from a stated location, bear the stamp of their date of issue, possess a legitimate list of subscribers, have neither cloth nor board bindings, and contribute to either American intellectual life or the expansion of scientific and technological knowledge. It was in publishers' interest to fulfil these criteria as the cheaper second-class rate was calculated by bulk: books were liable to the significantly higher third-class rate, made even higher by the fact that this was charged by item.[18]

Objections to this situation culminated on 18 November 1912, when Justice Oliver Wendell Holmes passed judgement on the cases of Frank H. Hitchcock, U.S. Postmaster General, against Street and Smith and Frank Tousey, Publisher. Central to the ruling was the distinction between a periodical and a book. Justice Holmes observed that each issue of Street and Smith's *Tip Top Weekly* contained a:

> single story complete in itself, but the same character is carried through the series, and the reader is led by announcements to expect further tales after the one before him. Most of the stories are by the same author. The element of sequence may be indicated by a few of the titles in the Tip Top Weekly: Frank Merriwell in Arizona; or,

17

the Mysteries of the Mine. Frank Merriwell's Friend; or, Muriel the Moonshiner. Frank Merriwell's Double; or, Fighting for Life. Frank Merriwell Meshed; or, the Last of the Danites. Frank Merriwell's Magic; or, the Pearl of Tangier. Frank Merriwell in London; or, The Grip of Doom, etc., etc. There is nothing else in a number except a roll of honor or list of some of those who have endeavored to increase the circulation of the series, laudatory letters with insignificant comments, and a page or two of inquiries as to physical culture, purporting to come from readers, with short replies, all more or less incidental to the muscular tenor of the tales.[19]

On this basis he ruled that:

> It must be taken as established that not every series of printed papers published at definite intervals is a periodical publication within the meaning of the law, even if it satisfies the conditions for admission to the second class . . . neither do we find much weight in the identity of authorship, the retention of the name of the hero through successive tales, or the ever-renewed promise of further wonders in the next . . . generally a printed publication is a book when its contents are complete in themselves, deal with a single subject, betray no need of continuation, and, perhaps, have an appreciable size . . . From this point of view Tip Top Weekly and Work and Win are books. They are large enough to raise no doubt on that score; each volume is complete in itself and betrays no inward need of more, notwithstanding that, as in the highwayman stories of an earlier generation, further adventures to follow are promised at the end.[20]

For Anderson, it was this ruling that signalled the final death of the dime novel. Street and Smith had emerged in the space between established book publishers and the newly emerged magazine market. This particular strategy was halted by Holmes's approach to the law, based as it was less on precedent than on 'reading social and cultural practices that defined the differences between books and magazines' which had fundamentally shifted between 1879 and 1912.[21] Tousey found it most difficult to adapt to the changing situation. The publisher had already been struggling to survive. Established in 1878, it had first run into trouble with the postmaster general in 1883 when issues of its Wide Awake Library dealing with outlaws such as Jesse James were banned as incitement to murder. Subsequently faced with the Post Office's increasing reluctance to allow his publications to benefit from the second-class postal rates, between 1907 and 1913 Frank Tousey, in Bold's words, 'juggled with his novels, adding short stories, news items, editorial pages, and advertisements. He even cut up the main story into disjointed sections, to make it look like a serial'.[22] He succeeded only in losing much of his audience along with his mailing privileges. The company survived until 1925, when Street and Smith, better equipped to respond to legal and cultural changes, brought the rights to the last of the Tousey weeklies, *Secret Service* and *Wild West*, from Frank Tousey's widow. Subsequently, Street and Smith shifted attention to pulp magazines such as *Detective Story Magazine*, first issued in 1915, and, unlike *Tip Top Weekly* including an assortment of short stories and serials from different authors. New Merriwell stories continued to be produced during the 1910s but more attention was paid to repackaging this material in other formats.

From Print and Stage to Screen: Cliffhangers and Situations

Frank Merriwell made his screen debut in 1913. Few noticed: the only contemporary reference I have seen is an advertisement for the Welcome Theatre in Beaver, Pennsylvania, including *Frank Merriwell in Arizona*, 'A Big Feature of 3000 feet', promising that on the following Monday the cinema would be showing *Frank Merriwell's Schooldays*.[23] The lack of information on either film does not suggest any great success, and though intertitles on *Frank Merriwell in Arizona* identify 'Tip Top Films' what connection this had with the publisher of *Tip Top Weekly* is uncertain. In fact, the Merriwell film was only two reels and thus less than thirty minutes long. The term, 'feature', soon came to be reserved for significantly longer films. In 1913 the vast majority of American films were still a single reel but the number of two-reel films had increased significantly and there was already a move towards even longer films.

At this stage the film industry had itself moved towards regularized production and distribution, though not in the manner adopted later. Cinema was largely regularized in terms of the single reel film and thus lacked the serial's inherent multiplicity. With the emergence of the multi-reel film things began to change. In 1911, 2,016 single reel films were released in the United States, in contrast to only twelve two-reel films and seven three-reel films. The number of single reel films continued to increase up to 1915, when 3,608 were made, but in that year 1,176 two-reel films were made, as well as 389 five-reel films and three twelve-reel films.[24]

Screenwriting manuals give an indication of the response to this. In 1913, Epes Winthrop Sargent identified four ways in which the new format could be used. Instances 'where the single reel is capable of being used independently' were distinct from the

> series of reels with a continuous subject, each terminating with a minor climax with a grand climax at the end of the last reel. For this no better example can be given than the play of the stage. At the end of each act there comes a definite stoppage of the action at a point which leaves the audience eager for the continuation. At the end of the first act the villain declares that the heroine shall be his and the curtain falls on this situation, leaving the audience wondering how he is going to bring this to pass.

His third example was 'the disconnected series, such as the Vitagraph's Lambert Chase series [1912–13] in which each story is complete in itself, and yet employs a central figure, that of the detective'. While different writers might contribute to the disconnected series, Sargent's final example was what he called the 'serial series', introduced by *What Happened to Mary* (1912), and 'precisely the same as the monthly or weekly instalments of the published serial and must be written by the same author that the unities be presented'.[25]

Variations of this advice can be found in other screenwriting manuals. A British advice column linked the minor climax to publishing practices, asking:

> Have you ever taken the trouble to observe the construction of a multiple-reel film? If you visit the picture theatres recently (as you ought to) and study the photoplays from a writer's point of view, you have no doubt noticed how the interest is skilfully sustained from the beginning to end in these multiple-reel productions.
>
> Each reel generally ends at a most exciting point, like the 'to be continued' serial in the papers.[26]

Similarly, in the 1913 edition of *Writing the Photoplay*, J. Berg Esenwein and Arthur Leeds advised that, while the one-reel film should close 'with a single grand climax', '*each* reel of the multiple-reel photoplay must not only contain its own climax, like the end of each instalment in an ideal magazine story, but the end of each reel except the last—also like the serial instalment—must throw a strong forward look, so as to give the continued-in-our-next feeling of delightful suspense and interest'.[27]

At this stage the move to longer, multi-reel films and the emergence of the serial were as much identical as parallel developments. Two-reel films were advertised as being 'in two parts', as in Vitagraph's advertisement announcing that 'SPECIAL FEATURE PRODUCTIONS IN TWO PARTS Will be Released Regularly Every Saturday, Beginning Saturday 2nd August, in place of the one reel releases'.[28] For the exhibitor with a single projector this necessitated a break. However, as the multi-reel film became the norm rather than the exception, so did the two-projector cinema. The feature film thus moved away from the 'break', which was retained in the serial but as a break between performances rather than within a single performance. Esenwein and Leeds corrected their account in 1919, redefining the serial as

> a film totally, say, 30,000 feet in length, and divided into fifteen episodes, each episode being made up of two reels, or parts, 2,000 feet of film. The production covers one long continued story, each episode planned to end with a thrilling climax, with a 'To be continued in our next', so to speak, tail-piece. The climax comes only at the end of each episode (as the two parts released each week, taken in conjunction, are termed). Incidentally, it should be born in mind that, in all up-to-date picture theatres, two projecting machines are employed, so that no 'break' occurs in the showing of any picture. For this reason, 'feature' subjects do not necessarily have any special climax at the end of each reel, and, to repeat, serial photoplays, have the grand, forward-looking climax only at the end of each episode.[29]

'*What Happened to Mary*, the first of all screened continuous stories, was a series not a serial' insisted Alfred A. Cohn in 1917.[30] Others have disagreed, and initially little attempt was made to differentiate serial and series. An advertisement for 'Four New Edison Series' begins 'The phenomenal success of the "Mary" series proves conclusively that the public wants these serial films . . . There are four new series, in addition to "Cleek"': it listed *Dolly of the Dallies* (twelve newspaper stories), the *Wood. B. Wed* 'comic series', the *Andy* 'comic series', and *The Adventures of Octavius* 'comic series'.[31] The tendency to use the terms as if interchangeable continued, and some confusion remains as to whether particular serials had episodes that were 'complete in themselves' or with cliffhanging endings. The surviving version of the best-known serial of this period, *The Perils of Pauline* (1914), lacks cliffhangers. However it is incomplete and generally recognized as something of a travesty of the film, at least as it was released in the United States. Singer describes it as a 'transitional serial'.[32] *The Adventures of Kathlyn* (1913–14) was introduced as a film in which 'each subject is to be complete in itself, though it will end in such a manner that the person who has seen one of the series will instantly recognise that there is more to come, and will be on the lookout for the next picture of the series'.[33]

In fact, *The Adventures of Kathlyn* marked a significant shift. Writing of the initial, three-reel instalment, one reviewer complained that 'The trouble is that at the most interesting part we read that familiar sign "To Be Continued"'.[34] The fifth and sixth parts of *The Adventures of Kathlyn* provoked James McQuade to write of the increasing 'vogue of the Kathlyn series of pictures', but to continue:

> Contrary to the opinion of many, this serial photodrama has met with great success, but it must not be overlooked that to achieve this a unique, far-reaching and continuous campaign has been necessary to keep up public interest. This publicity campaign, clever as it is and ably and resolutely as it has been conducted, would have fallen short of the mark had it not been for the well constructed scenario, and the electrifying climax of every set thus far. These climaxes are almost exasperating, so eagerly do they leave us guessing and floundering when the 'To be continued' announcement flashes on the screen.[35]

Of the ending of the sixth part, the another reviewer wrote

> Handing over the three bags of silver as ransom money Umballah orders his men to seize Col. Hare and return him to Allahah as a prisoner. Turning to the chief of the bandits he suggests that Bruce and Kathlyn be fed to the tiger. Then, urging on his camel, he rides out of the picture.
>
> This being one of the most interesting and exciting moments of the story, it is quite natural that at this point we should behold the now familiar 'To be continued in two weeks' flashed on the screen.[36]

Bruce and Kathlyn to be fed to the tiger: we are surely on safer ground here. While *What Happened to Mary* was described as a 'serial series', each episode complete in itself, here at last we have a serial with the life threatening cliffhanger that was to become an almost essential element of the Hollywood serial.

This shift had emerged after the opening episode. The reviewer who identified 'that familiar sign "To Be Continued"' after the first episode of *The Adventures of Kathlyn* can only have been referring to the familiarity already established through the medium of print (the print edition of *The Adventures of Kathlyn* serialized in the *Chicago Tribune* or more probably the wider practice of publishing serialized stories). The reviewer who cited 'the now familiar "To be continued in two weeks" flashed on the screen' at the end of the sixth episode suggests familiarity established through this particular serial. Continuation was stressed while the cliffhanger was not named. However, the absence of the word did not mean that either the narrative danger or the audience response was absent. Indeed, it is at this point in time that the origins of the term 'cliffhanger' are regularly located.[37]

In fact, the term only achieved currency in later decades: the earliest use I have been able to discover is a 1930 reference to 'the revival of the serial, with Universal and Pathé leading the procession towards cliff-hanging heroines'.[38] A 1937 *New York Times* correspondent suggested that it was one of the terms invented by a contributor to *Variety*; in Britain in the following year it was identified as a broadcasting Americanism for 'adventure serials, now becoming popular over there', similar to calling jazz musicians 'cats', and likely to 'cause the immaculately-parted hair at Broadcasting House to stand on end'.[39] Until the late 1930s its use was largely confined to *Variety*, though not to films or even serials. Early references include: 'Coast radio stations, particularly hot at the moment for the crime thriller serial, are becoming the targets for the religious press and reform bodies and individuals. They claim the serial cliff hangers are inciting crime among children', and a reference to the crime feature, *Straightaway* (1933), as 'Sue Carol's Cliffhanger'.[40] However, it was most commonly used to designate a film serial. Thus a report that MGM might move into the serial business, chopping off reels at 'suspenseful points', speculated that the 'Biggest headache will be to keep reel from getting too corny and still give it that cliffhanger touch'.[41] Beyond *Variety*, an early definition has: 'Studio term for serial picture of melodramatic type: arose out of the fact that early serials featured players in thrilling action on high cliffs'.[42]

An emphasis on high tension before a break spanned stage and print a near-century before this. In Victorian Britain, in one account, 'It was the popular practice of serial publication that led the novel to strive for the strong scene-ending characteristic of the stage; novelists made it a point to close each instalment with an image or incident evoking strong interest'.[43] Thus the fourth, monthly part of William Makepeace Thackeray's *Vanity Fair* (1847) ends with Becky Sharp's response to Sir Pitt Crawley's proposal of marriage: 'Oh, Sir—I—I'm *married already!*[44] This provides strong interest but not of the about-to-be-fed-to-the-tiger kind. The serialized novel invokes the stage, and thus the break within the performance (as advised for the multi-reel film in the 1913 edition of *Writing the Photoplay*) even as it adopts breaks between instalments. Thackeray began *Vanity Fair* with a prologue titled 'Before the Curtain' and Kathleen Tillotson described Becky's line as 'perhaps the most magnificent curtain line of all'.[45] The novels of Charles Dickens in particular have been studied for their serialization and debt to the theatre. However, for Walter Phillips, as editor (and author) Dickens 'clearly demanded of the instalment fiction brevity and the capability of being divided so as to maintain interest', but with a view to 'unity of tone or action' rather than out of an insistence on 'the melodramatic climax or even incident'.[46] The serial publication of *A Tale of Two Cities* (1859) and *Great Expectations* (1860–61) were, 'notably free of "climax and curtain" endings for instalments'.[47] Yet Wilkie Collins and Charles Reade drew freely on the stage melodrama practice of the significant line immediately before the drop of the curtain at the end of the act, and exploited the specific nature of serial publication. Thus the third instalment of the *Cornhill* serialization of Collins's *Armadale* (serialized 1864–66) ends:

> 'The boat!!!' he cried, with a scream of horror that rang far and wide through the stillness of the night, and brought Allan instantly to his side.
>
> The lower end of the carelessly-hitched rope was loose on the water; and, a-head, in the track of the moonlight, a small black object was floating out of view. The boat was adrift.[48]

By the twentieth century such practices were in use on both sides of the Atlantic, and across the range of fiction production. 'In the boys' story-papers of a few years ago', advised one screenplay manual, '. . . the hero was frequently left hanging over the edge of the cliff, or tied to the railroad track, or waiting for the timed fuse to reach the keg of powder'.[49] While that comment seems almost to stumble on the term 'cliffhanger' (and then move on) others continued to refer to the 'curtain'. For instance, in *The Fiction Factory*, prolific writer William Wallace Cook outlined his technique of writing series fiction in the following manner 'Each chapter closes with a "curtain". In other words, the chapter works the action up to an interesting point, similar to a serial "leave-off", and drops a quick curtain'.[50] The relatively weak 'leave-off' did not catch on.

The other term often invoked was 'situation'. Esenwein and Leeds advised prospective serial writers that the end chapter climax should be 'a thrilling situation'. Bruner defined the serial in terms of 'Situations if they come along, yes, but never worked out!'[51] Situations were repeatedly emphasized in serial promotions. Every episode of *Zudora* (1914) was 'full of startling situations'.[52] *The Crimson Stain Mystery* (1916) was 'An Elaborately Staged High-Class Production Aglow with Tense Thrilling Situations'.[53] *The Hand of Vengeance* (1918) consisted of '10 gripping episodes, 20 reels, thousands of scenes—all crowded with interest-gripping situations, thrilling adventures, daring escapades, and beautiful photography', while *The Evil Eye* (1920) was 'THE FASTEST MOVING MELODRAMA EVER PRODUCED . . . Powerful Situations—blood-stirring thrills—hair-breadth escapes—furious fights —clever complications—baffling mystery and exciting suspense'.[54]

Again, this provides a link with the theatre. For Scott Higgins, in the production of serials, studios such as Republic:

> refined a formula for the quick and efficient production of situational stories that support modular action sequences based on physical problem solving. Long-range serial narratives meander incomprehensibly, but their main purpose is to provide a set of premises and a world within which each episode stages weekly chases, fights, and perils. In generating these plots, serial screenwriters tapped into the much older tradition of situational dramaturgy, which originated in 19th century melodramatic theater. In this mode, story creators conceived their task as assembling readymade pieces, of recombining proven elements rather than crafting original wholes.[55]

Singer had earlier invoked the notion the 'situation', referring back to Lea Jacobs' discussion of the situation distinguishing melodrama from classical dramaturgy. Singer qualified the concept as difficult to narrow down, but suggested that it could be defined as:

> a striking and exciting incident that momentarily arrests narrative action while the characters encounter a powerful new circumstance

and the audience relishes the heightened dramatic tension. Situation often entails a startling reversal or twist of events that creates a dramatic impasse, a momentary paralysis stemming from a deadlock or dilemma or predicament that constrains the protagonist's ability to respond immediately. Action might be temporarily suspended when characters are stunned by shocking news (the villain who has been trying to kill the heroine is really her uncle who has stolen her inheritance!), or faced with a deadly peril (the hero looks with alarm as the buzz saw draws ever nearer), or fixed in a deadlock among counterbalancing forces . . . The notion of situation also evokes the serial film's cliffhanger climaxes where narrative action is suspended not only while the wide-eyed protagonist assesses a grave peril but indeed for a full week until the next episode resolves the predicament.[56]

Singer highlights the saw-mill scene in Joseph Arthur's *Blue Jeans*, first performed in 1890, in which the heroine saves the hero from death by buzz-saw. It was an iconic enough scene for a reviewer of episode fourteen of the *Timber Queen* (1922) to describe the film serial as ending 'with a "Blue Jeans" smash in a mill, Ruth [Roland] unconscious on the endless carriage and moving towards the saws'.[57] Screenwriter Frank Leon Smith subsequently recollected that George Seitz referred to the serials he directed as having a 'Blue Jeans finish'.[58] Republic recycled the saw-mill situation as a cliffhanger at the end of chapters of both *King of the Royal Mounted* (1940) and *G-Men vs. the Black Dragon* (1943).

The film serial, then, emerged out of popular literature and theatre. Early serials were repeatedly associated with the dime novel, as in Frank V. Bruner's identification, in 'The Modern Dime Novel', of the film serial as 'the same thing that made you as a boy devour those Frank Merriwell and Nick Carter stories'.[59] Assisted in this direction by postal regulations that gave financial advantages to regular numbered publications, literature provided the volume (and volumes) necessary for regularized serialization. There were more direct links between the first film serials and newspaper and magazine publishing. Following the simultaneous publication (in *Ladies' World*) and screening of episodes of *What Happened to Mary*, *The Adventures of Kathlyn* was serialized by the *Chicago Tribune* syndicate, *The Perils of Pauline* and *The Exploits of Elaine* (1916) were released in conjunction with William Randolph Hearst's *Chicago American*, while *Lucille Love: Girl of Mystery* (1914) was published in conjunction with the *Chicago Herald-Record*. Such newspaper tie-ins were abandoned over time, though in the 1930s film serial production was again linked to the publishing industry when Universal's *Tailspin Tommy* (1934) initiated a series of film serials based on comic strips.

Theatre provided its own model of plot production on factory lines, as well as its sensation situations and narrative breaks. This is the link emphasized by Singer in his account of how sensational melodrama 'made the switch from stage to screen'.[60] Yet in important ways the serial was the one form of cinema where that switch was *not* evident. It certainly did not rely on direct stage adaptations. Throughout its history, the film serial has been based on a wide range of sources. Sound serials were adapted from comic strips, comic books, magazines, radio programmes, novels (including dime novels), short stories, television and even poetry.[61] The one source that was *never* directly used was the stage play. During the silent era stage plays were repeatedly made into films, both feature films and short films, but not serial films.[62] Film is a performance-based medium, but there are probably more direct links in terms of the circus rather than the stage play, providing as it did both serial settings from *Peg o' the Ring* (1916) to *King of the Carnival* (1956) and performers such as Betsy King Ross, Clyde Beatty, Dorothy Herbert and even one time circus bareback rider and stuntwoman, Pearl White.

Jacobs and Ben Brewster explain why stage melodrama moved into the feature film rather than the serial. They note that 'the brevity of most early films made it neither necessary nor possible to resort to the devices of the developed pictorial stage. The stories remained too simple to involve the peripeteia that gave rise to complex situations: actors did not have time to use attitudes in a way to punctuate and modulate the performance of a scene'. It was, they suggest, only with the rise of the multi-reel feature that films became more like plays (and were often adapted from the theatre) and it was in this new longer form that 'the pictorial theatre again became a model', allowing pictorialism (using pictorial effects to underscore narratively significant elements) to flourish 'in modified form'.[63] It is in this context that they discuss feature films such as *Alias Jimmy Valentine* (1915) and *The Whip* (1917).

Like the feature film, film serials extended narrative by moving beyond the self-contained single reel format, but not in a way that made them more like the stage plays discussed by Brewster and Jacobs. The particular case of *Blue Jeans*, highlighted by Singer and others for its sensational buzz-saw scene, is a revealing one in this context. Joseph Arthur's play was filmed in 1917, but as a seven-reel feature. The serial took the buzz-saw scene, and was still returning to it in the 1940s. For instance, the third chapter of *King of the Royal Mounted* ends with Sergeant Dave King on a conveyor belt taking him towards a buzz saw. This cliffhanger, however, points to differences between play and film serial. The closing section of the third Act of Joseph Arthur's play sees Perry, having been struck on the head by Ben, unconscious on a table moving towards the buzz saw (as Sergeant King would later find himself), but the Act does not end there. Perry is saved when June breaks down the door. Risener and Seth then seize Ben, and Risener asks 'What'll we do with him?' June rises up, seizes a coil of rope which she throws to the crowd, and exclaims, 'Lynch him!' The Act's final stage direction is 'MEN all rush BEN out of center door as curtain falls'. The Act ends not with the man about to be cut in half by a buzz saw but with the 'Lynch him!' curtain line.[64]

Different media worked out the buzz-saw situation in different ways. The curtain line was not the same as the cliffhanger. There was a shift from *Vanity Fair*'s 'I'm *married already*' (announcement) to *Armadale*'s '"The boat!!!" . . . The boat was adrift' (announcement and slow-motion event), and from *The Adventures of Kathlyn*'s 'he suggests that Bruce and Kathlyn be fed to the tiger' (promise) to *The Adventures of Frank Merriwell*'s train collision (rapid-paced event). The film serial operated within the realm of the latter two: the promise of being fed to the tiger (subsequently revealed as unfulfilled) or the fact of the train crash (subsequently revealed as not being fatal). Nineteenth-century cliffhangers could, true to the name, involve stasis, a pause within the narrative. Such pauses were different from those that separated instalments of the film serial.

There were initial variations within the film serial, though perhaps also between different screenings of the same serial. Examining a sequence from an episode of *The Perils of Pauline*, Shane Denson recounts how Pauline's descent from a hot-air balloon by rope is followed by her fiancé, Harry, scaling a cliff to come to her rescue, but falling when the villains cut the rope, writing:

> This is the principle of the cliffhanger, the serial's trademark device for segmenting ongoing narratives, demonstrated here on the face of a cliff. Indeed, the segmented line can be seen as the central form of the serial's overall narration. *The Perils of Pauline* is predominated by lines and linear segments, both narrative and visual: from the ropes that structure these images to the linearized chase sequences that lead inevitably to an episode's climatic peril.[65]

I don't think this scene illustrates the principle of the cliffhanger as it later came to be understood. As noted earlier, *The Perils of Pauline* survives only in re-edited form, suggesting different exhibition practices in America and continental Europe. However, the plot synopses that were published in American trade papers at the time do survive. Despite the idea that the cliffhanger can be traced back to Pearl White, most of these also indicate the absence of cliffhangers, though the episode featuring Pauline's escape from a hot-air balloon appears to be different. The *Motion Picture News* account runs as follows:

> Letting out the anchor she [Pauline] lands at the foot after a thrilling ride. Harry meets her, having followed the course of the balloon with his car. Getting a long rope, he slides down to meet her. The villains cut this and Harry is precipitated to the bottom. Undaunted by this, however, he starts the long climb to the balloon. This is a most daring feat. Arriving there he pulls the gas plug and on the balloon arriving at the ground takes the rope from its anchor.
>
> On making the long climb from the cliff they are assaulted by Owen's gang, and Harry is knocked insensible, while Pauline is carried away to a lonely hut. She is at last in the hands of her captives.[66]

This does leave Pauline imperilled (unlike the surviving version which includes a further rescue by Harry in the episode), and Denson's location of a cliffhanger on a cliff is neat. However, if there is a break here it would appear to come at the end of the reel rather than of the episode. The *Motion Picture News* report smoothes over the join marked by the cutting of the rope with its mid-paragraph 'Undaunted by this . . .' It provides the 'She is at last in the hands of her captives' curtain line that is not found at the close of the surviving instalment. However, at this stage cliff and rope-line seem to be central in that they are mid-chapter rather than belonging to a chapter end cliffhanger.

The Perils of Pauline does point to a shift in another sense. Esenwein's reference to the hero 'frequently left hanging over the edge of the cliff' in the boys' papers of a few years previous is illustrated by *Three Modern Crusoes, or Perseverance and Indolence*, serialized in 1879 in the *Boys' Sunday Reader*. In one instalment the persevering hero, George Merridew, lowers himself by rope in an attempt to get hold of a birds' nest which he intends to give as a present to Stella, the woman he loves. As the roots of the trees to which the rope is tied begin to give way, Ned

Conyers, George's rival for the affections of Stella, is tempted to cut the rope, but the indolent Ned does not need to act: the tree gives way and George falls. The instalment ends:

> A great cry—a shriek—rose from beneath; a cry which was echoed by one from Ned, who, leaping to his feet and covering his face with his hands, fled from the spot.
>
> He was free from his rival.
>
> But how?
>
> He had not hurled him to his death, certainly, but he had held out no hand to try to save him from his fate.
>
> He was innocent, but indeed in his conscience he felt that he was guilty,
>
> *To be continued.*[67]

The following week's issue ('The Fate of Our Hero') finds George clinging on, contemplating his death, but thinking:

> . . . of the bright pretty girl.
>
> Of how her eyes had brightened on his return; of her pleasure at his delight in the Union Jack she had made for them.
>
> Of what her grief would be when his body was found, if it ever were, at the foot of the rocks.[68]

Inspired by such thoughts, Ned's inaction is now contrasted with George's action, as he manages to make his way to safety.

Three Modern Crusoes provided a cliffhanger based on hesitation between action and inaction. That situational hesitation disappeared in subsequent serials. While Ned thinks about cutting the rope, in *The Perils of Pauline* Owen's henchmen simply cut it. While George acts after contemplating the girl he loves and the Union Jack, in *The Perils of Pauline* Harry acts without contemplation. Similarly, at the end of 'College Hero' Frank Merriwell has no time to thinks of Elsie Belwood, and no doubt as to the value of his actions: he simply jumps from the train.

In part the shift here is in the significance of character, not the character of psychological complexity but character as a value to be learnt. Published serials such as *Three Modern Crusoes* were couched in moral terms; they combined thrilling adventures with lessons about the values of perseverance over indolence. Similarly, *Tip Top Weekly* narrated a coming-of-age narrative (albeit a protracted one) in which the hero was repeatedly tested and repeatedly proved himself worthy. An element of that is retained in *The Perils of Pauline*, in so far as Pauline's adventures tested her and ultimately taught her the values of settling down with Harry. However Harry himself was of age already, his character established. In later film serials heroes and villains act without reflection. Further, in the sound serial cliffhanger the emphasis has shifted so far towards action and movement that characters are only very occasionally left hanging over the edge of the cliff. Chapters almost always end at a point of movement or collision: the train crash at the end of 'College Hero' or Tim Tyler falling off the cliff at the end 'Dead Man's Pass', the second chapter of *Tim Tyler's Luck* (1937).

Discussing the relationship between nineteenth-century theatre and the serials of the sound era, Higgins describes the latter as leaving

> the hero deadlocked with death in a runaway car or in an electrical trap, priming the viewer to return for next week's last-minute reversal of fortune . . . The sound serials may rely on an especially narrow set of situations, and they may offer the same solutions again and again (they are, after all, designed for children); but in their very obviousness, these films help us see how situational plot construction might work in the action genre'.[69]

The gap between episodes provides some justification for the apparent tautology of the phrase 'dead*locked* with death in a *runaway* car' (emphasis added): at the very point where the serial's emphasis on action is accentuated to the highest degree that action is arrested, in effect frozen for the week until the next episode. My own reference to 'cliffhanger action' is based on similar principles. However this also highlights differences. The film serial came to avoid situational dilemma and cliff-hanging contemplation, ending episodes with a mid-action break rather than a pause or a stand-off.

In the silent era there were close links between cinema and theatre. The stage play provided a model for cinema exhibitors encountering the multi-reel film, particularly those with only one projector. It has provided a longer-lasting model for the feature film, hence more recent debates on whether contemporary Hollywood operates on the basis of a three- or four-act structure.[70] In its serialized form cinema had closer links with publishing. The fact that the film serial was a form of melodrama provides a link with the theatre though by the beginning of the twentieth century melodrama had become a cross-media phenomenon, evident in

31

print as well as on the stage. The film serial's literary connections existed in direct form and in a more general sense. Film serials became popular through the practice of directly linking episodes to published versions of the story. In addition, the publication of serial episodes at weekly (or longer) intervals provided a closer model for the film serial than the division of a play into acts.

However, writers at the time also pointed out complexities and differences in the literary serial/film serial relationship. For one:

> The serial story appears in approximately equal instalments at regular intervals on printed pages. The reader thus has a choice of several different methods of reading it. If he absorbs one instalment at a time, he has a choice of several days—the number depending on the magazine's frequency of issue—and some sixteen hours each day, any one of which he may select for the reading. If he wishes, or is forced by circumstances, he may allow two or more instalments to accumulate unread, and then digest them at a single sitting. And finally, he may save all the copies containing the serial until it is completed, and then read the whole story without interruption.
>
> None of these methods is possible with the serial motion pictures. Each instalment appears at certain theaters on certain definite days—generally in the evening only. If an instalment is released every week, or every two weeks, the 'reader' must not only wait that period, but must be on hand at the proper time or he misses the instalment. Except within extremely narrow limits, he cannot select his own time to see any part of it; he cannot see but one instalment at a time; and he cannot by any possibility let the instalments accumulate and view them all in one day or evening.
>
> So the serial motion picture is handicapped; for many people cannot or will not 'tie themselves up' to a series of definite dates, missing any one of which would kill the value of those preceding and succeeding it.
>
> Several attempts have been made by ingenious exhibitors to get around this difficulty. For example, several exhibitors have tried showing a serial film in instalments corresponding with its regular release dates, and later when the series is finished, repeating the whole story in daily instead of weekly or bi-weekly instalments. By doing so, the spectator is given two chances to see each instalment, and consequently a choice between two different ways of seeing the whole story.

Some of the popular magazines are in the habit of running stories which are virtually series made up of a number of short stories, each complete in itself and quite satisfactory to the reader whether he reads only one, or all, or the last one first. Yet these stories, taken together and considered as a serial, constitute a connected series of adventures or episodes in the lives of the characters . . .

The serial story or scenario whose each instalment is complete and perfect by itself is really no more difficult to write than the ordinary form of connected serial. It has all the advantages of the connected serial; for the familiar story ending which leaves the observer 'up in the air' by breaking off at a critical point in the story is not so popular in the theater as it is in a magazine, and sometimes engenders actual ill-feeling. It has in addition the advantage of holding the irregular patronage by the independence of its instalments and the consequent independence of the theater patron.

Serial pictures have had considerable measures of success so far, but it has largely been by dint of vigorous campaigns of newspaper advertising, which may not always be secured on such advantageous terms. If there is any further development of the serial film, it may well make better progress along the lines we have explained—the series-serial, whose instalments are complete stories, each interesting enough to carry the observer on the next one, yet not giving him the feeling that he is being forced to come back.[71]

I have quoted this at some length because of its suggestion that the acceptance of seriality may be dependent on particular features of specific media. The theatre and other forms based on live performance have not tended to be organized sequentially, unless we extend the notion of the serial as repetition to include repeat performances of the same play. In contrast, print but also web-based media lend themselves readily to the serial. The time-tabled nature of cinema-going presented specific challenges for the film serial, though not absolute ones. Radio and television programming demands a similar commitment, but this has not prevented them from being home to soap opera or other forms of seriality. The key issues here are the flexibility of the serial (its ability to accommodate occasional as well as dedicated consumers) and the place that it takes in the lives of its audience.

One approach to the history of the film serial is to see it as gravitating towards the cliffhanging format evident in serials such as *The Adventures of Frank Merriwell* and *Flash Gordon*. However, this teleological perspective

33

irons out variations and alternative possibilities. The serial was a cross-media phenomenon but serial consumption differed in different media. Identifying *The Perils of Pauline* as a transitional serial combining a mix of self-contained and incomplete episodes, Singer goes on to state that subsequently virtually all film serials came to make consistent use of suspenseful cliffhanger endings. 'With this design, serials encouraged a steady volume of return customers, tantalized and eager for the fix of narrative closure withheld in the previous instalment.'[72] Things were not always seen like that at the time.

For some, the term 'serial' came with negative connotations. Advertisers were, in different instances, keen to differentiate their films from the serial. An advertisement for *The Plum Tree* (1914) entreated: 'Remember—THIS IS NOT A SERIAL. It is a complete story, a complete mystery, in three acts'.[73] Another promoted *The Hidden Hand* (1917) as 'some Serial!' but also *The Price of Folly* (1918) with the statement that 'Each chapter is a two reel drama, complete in itself, full of thrills and heart interest. It's not a serial but a series'.[74] Vitagraph's *The Goddess* (1915) was advertised with the statement: 'it is not a serial . . . it is not a conglomeration of stunts thrown together without rhyme or reason . . . *The Goddess* is a change in the order of things—sounds the death knell of the commonplace serial, and marks the era of a continued photoplay in chapters'.[75] Similarly *The American Girl* (1917) was 'A SERIES—Not a Serial' which would 'appeal to thinking Exhibitors because it contains all the elements of a successful SERIES and none of the drawbacks of a Serial' and *The Master of Beasts* (1922) was 'NOT A SERIAL, but the most daring undertaking ever accomplished for the production of hair-raising, heart-throbbing, and humanly diversified entertainment'.[76]

In part this highlights how the distinction between the series and the serial was significant to exhibitors and audiences of the time. The serial was a potentially reliable source of income at a time when the film industry was keen to develop cinema-going as a regular habit. It continued to be. However it came with risks. Josh Lambert notes that ending an episode in the middle of the action in whatever medium requires extraordinary confidence.[77] It demands a formal structure that allows audiences to link the part to the whole as well as an industry structure that allows for the regular production, distribution and exhibition of long-form narratives. This was a particular challenge for an industry just moving on from the one-reel film but presented its own problems when the feature film had become the norm. In addition, the word 'serial' could be avoided on account of its low status connotations ('a conglomeration of stunts thrown together without rhyme or reason'), and replaced by other descriptions ('a continued photoplay in chapters') that implied (whether or not they delivered) different ways of providing links in a chain.

The widespread adoption of the cliffhanger did not mean that the idea of the self-contained story was abandoned. In 1919 *The Fatal Fortune* was advertised as 'one of the Greatest Serials Ever Made . . . Every episode . . . a complete story in itself with a constant succession of breathless chapters'.[78] Even in 1945, Universal producer Morgan Cox was making the case for the use of new rather than repeat footage at the beginning of the serial chapter on the grounds that 'It seems to me that the great advantage in telling back story through new scenes, rather than by titles of commentation, lies in the fact that it makes each Chapter seem to any audience a complete story within itself, a small part of which is the climax of the previous chapter'.[79]

The Sound Serial Formula

This chapter has emphasized differences, changes, complexities and the polysemic nature of the serial. This did not disappear. However, in focusing on the film serial it is important to acknowledge its increasingly narrowly and rigid definition.

Reports on the film serial in the 1930s and after repeatedly emphasized its unchanging nature. In 1938 a writer on the sound serial invoked silent cinema and stage melodrama, commenting: 'The villain still pursues the virtuous damsel while the handsome hero dangles from crumbling cliffs or miraculously escapes from horrible fates to give to the villain that ultimate trouncing which he so richly deserves'.[80] Similarly, in 1946 William Roberts wrote that 'except for a few modern gimmicks, the perils faced by current serial heroes and heroines are precisely the same as when Pearl White was suspended over a vat of molten steel by unscrupulous individuals seeking to learn the whereabouts of The Papers'.[81] The rigid structure of the individual serial chapter was also emphasized from around this date. According to Roberts, in serials made by Republic:

> Between two and three minutes are devoted to titles and the 'take-out'—the rescue of the hero or heroine from the utterly hopeless situation in which they have found themselves at the climax of the preceding episode. Then you get around 12 minutes of new violence, ending in a thunderous climax wherein the hero or heroine is once

more hopelessly trapped and will obviously be burned to a crisp, blown to bits or ground to dust.[82]

Robert's account (or rather that of Republic producer Ron Davidson, quoted by Roberts) seems to have formed the basis of later versions of the screenwriting advice manual. 'The most important element of the serial plot is the "weenie",' wrote Roberts; in his *Practical Manual of Screen Playwriting* (first published in 1952 and reissued in 1963), Lewis Herman included a section on the serial in which he wrote that 'the first chapter must introduce the "weenie". This is the thing, the object, the papers, the will, the secret formula, the treasure map, the pearl of great value which sets the suave bad guy off on his trail of mayhem and arson against the good guy and his gal. It is the seesawing struggle to obtain this weenie which motivates the action of the serial'. Herman went on to break down the individual serial chapter as follows:

1. The recap, lasting two or three minutes, recounting 'the details of the previous episode's climatic point, in which the hero is left dangling over the cliff's edge while a cougar nibbles at his straining fingers'. The insertion of a 'cheap cut', introducing the means of escape absent from the close of the previous episode (the leap from the wagon before it crashed over the cliff or the de-activation of the death ray before it is to be detonated), enables the 'take-out' or rescue.

2. The few minutes after the take-out 'should be devoted to exposing the course the new action is to take'.

3. A couple of subsequent minutes of suspense, as 'we see the girl being stalked by the mobsters' or 'we yearn for the marines to arrive'.

4. The 'middle action' fight: 'a sadistic, knock-'em down, drag-'em out ruckus', which ends with the toughest tough knocking out the hero with a lucky punch.

5. 'The girl is then spirited away by the henchmen and the place is set on fire with our hero still unconscious in it.' He recovers in time, which leads into roughly seven minutes devoted to the chase, ending with the hero arriving at the henchmen's hideout.

6. After another two or three minutes of fighting, once again the hero should receive a lucky clout on the jaw. Once again he finds himself chin-deep in a manhole situation. Once again the girl is

whisked away as the water slowly fills the manhole, to kill off the hero for certain this time.

In Herman's account, throughout this pattern the key inflexible rule was constant movement. Dialogue needed to be kept down to a minimum of 700 words per episode. Characterization was to be 'sedulously avoided'. There must never be 'the slightest leer of sex to besmirch' the frail blonde heroine's relations with the clean-living, typical American hero. 'Stock film is a must: wild animals, train crashes, conflagrations, and the like'. Change was limited to replacement of death-dealing buzz saws and alligator pools by death rays 'and other such modern forms of civilized persuasion'. The aspiring serial writer who could 'think of a new weenie, and devise new methods of torture, new manhole situations, and new take-out devices' would be kept busy at Columbia, Universal-International or Republic.

> But your creative faculties should stop there. For from then on you must conform to the strict rules of serial-making. They are inflexible. Like the rigid, formalistic movements of a ceremonial dance, they must be adhered to with complete conformance.[83]

This is a description of serial organization to the extreme degree, a move away not just from the branded publication of Beadle's Dime Novels but also from the broad blueprint given to Gilbert Patten.

Was this an accurate description of actual film serials? No, at least when the second edition of the *Practical Manual* was published in 1963, since by this date serials were no longer being made in the United States. Even in 1952, only Columbia and Republic remained in the serial production business. Yet if the practical manual was out of date and based more on a *Los Angeles Times* report of 1946 than attention to actual films, its comments are in line with other accounts of the film serial, from the silent as well as the sound era. In particular, the notion of a struggle for possession of a valuable object is one that has been picked up by later commentators. Singer, for instance, described American serials as:

> an extraordinarily formulaic product. With few exceptions, the conflict between the heroine-hero team and the villain expressed itself in a back-and-forth struggle for the physical possession of the heroine (whom the villain constantly kidnaps or tries to kill)

as well as for the physical possession of some highly prized object —what Pearl White, Pathé's preeminent serial queen, called the 'weenie'[84]

Interviewed in 1919 by William Lord Wright, Hollywood screenwriter Bertram Millhauser claimed that there was 'no such thing as a serial *story* that is continuous through fifteen episodes'. He went on:

> This is what happens. At the end of the first five reels, that is, the first two episodes, the unsolved mystery is in some way associated with a material object—a block of wood, or a ring, or a piece of parchment—which is striven for by the two opposing forces—the hero, or heroine, and the villain. In episode three the hero has it. In episode four the villain gets it from him. In episode five it is again recovered, et cetera, et cetera, ad infinitum, or, rather, till your closing . . . the *story* does not progress. There are only exciting incidents in the recovery of an *object* to relate. And the only thread that ties these separate instalments together is the recurrence, in each chapter, or episode, of the principle characters of the preceding episode, in their same relative relationship.[85]

This is not the clear narrative progression of which Marlow-Mann wrote, or indeed the sort of narrative causality that has been seen as characteristic of Hollywood cinema more generally. It is closer to Higgins' 'modular action . . . to provide a set of premises and a world within which each episode stages weekly chases, fights, and perils'. It is also a variety of Eco's repetitive art. More specifically, it looks back to *Tip Top Weekly*'s 'Frank Merriwell's Mysterious Ring, or, The Man in Black' (1896) and forward to Universal's *The Adventures of Frank Merriwell*. Alerted to the importance of the ring, in 'The Death Plunge' Frank is able to stop the ghost-like figure when he returns in a further attempt to steal the ring. The 'hero of a thousand college stories' (as the credits described him each week) fights off the intruder, but at the end of the chapter one of his friends is tricked into giving the villains the ring. Chasing after them, Merriwell jumps into the villain's car, which goes off the road into the water. He dies . . . No, in the take-out at the beginning of the third chapter it is revealed that not only has Merriwell survived the death plunge but that he has reclaimed the ring. But the villains are still after the ring, and in 'Death at the Crossroads' . . . In line with Millhauser's account, there is little story progression here, both within the specific serial (which becomes a series of adventures) and across the film serial more generally.

The pattern evident in *The Adventures of Frank Merriwell* lends weight to the understanding of the film serial as structured around a back-and-forth struggle. Yet even this single example has other features: the struggle over the ring, and the attempts to decipher the message inscribed on it, takes up much of 'Death at the Crossroads', but the chapter still has room for an extended rumba dance performed by Carla Laemmle, niece of Universal studio boss Carl Laemmle. The serial provided different pleasures, was subject to different institutional and individual demands, and while formulaic was not quite as homogenous as Herman suggested. I will examine how this operated at the textual level in film serials made in the 1930s and 1940s in two later chapters, one focused on the structure within a single serial chapter, the other on individual serials and the pattern across chapters. Before that I will examine in more detail how the serial functioned in commercial terms and, first, the nature of its audience. The concern here is with how that audience was understood and the consequences this had for the regulation of the serial.

2

Thursday Night at the Ritz
Exhibition, Audiences and Regulation

Writers on the film serial have repeatedly assigned it to a specific location within the day and the week. If you are looking for material on the serial you can go to books with titles such as *Saturday Afternoon at the Movies*, publications such as *Those Enduring Matinee Idols*, book chapters with titles such as 'Perilous Saturdays', or web sites such as http://matineeatthebijou.blogspot.com.[1] Such publications are not necessarily limited to the serial but discussions of the serial have been clear as to its Saturday matinee home.

Nostalgia is central to this literature. It is relatively standard for books written by and for the fans of serials to start with an account of the author's childhood introduction to the world of the serial. William Cline begins one of his books on the serial with a description of how, one Saturday, he accompanied his older brother to his first serial.[2] Ed Hulse writes: 'My love affair with serials began in 1962, when I was nine years old'.[3] Based on his doctoral thesis, Richard M. Hurst's study of Republic (serials included) is a little different; it has no such introduction, but it ends with the following note on the author: 'Richard M. Hurst grew up in Central Indiana in the mid-1940s, where he was exposed to Westerns and serials on a weekly basis. It created an interest in these films, especially those of Republic, which remained into adulthood'.[4]

Academic interest in memory and childhood cinema-going can lead to a related, personal note, but when this is absent the association between serials and children's matinees remains.[5] Thus Yannis Tzioumakis has defined serials as 'particular types of pictures for the very specific audience of matinees'.[6] A different picture has emerged in recent work on the serial in the 1910s, but this has been used to reinforce rather than vary the image of the sound serial. For Jared Gardner, 'when thinking about serial film, we are likely to conjure images of *Flash Gordon* or the *Lone Ranger*—science fiction or western serials from the 1930s and 1940s, primarily directed to youngsters attending Saturday matinees'; he contrasts this to the very different 'serial queen' films of the 1910s.[7] Ben Singer's work on the film serial has emphasized the adult female viewer but he reports that by the sound-era they had become 'slapdash juvenile movies for "Saturday afternoon at the Bijou"', leaving 'little question that serial producers were after the nickels and dimes of America's children'.[8] Roger Hagedorn outlined a similar shift, writing: 'By the 1930s, however, women had become accustomed to regular movie consumption and, in the wake of the transition to sound, serial production companies turned their efforts to the exploitation of a new target audience, children'.[9]

Some accounts come with qualifications. W.K. Everson suggested different venues when he wrote that by the time of Republic's *Drums of Fu Manchu* (1940) 'serials had been dismissed as being of no importance save as fodder for action houses and kiddie matinees'.[10] Gardner allowed that serials were *primarily* directed at children's matinees. Often, however, acknowledgement of instances of wider appeal has served to emphasize the main point, as in the identification of *Flash Gordon* (1936) as 'so successful that it played evening performances at first run theaters, one of only a handful of sound serials to do so'.[11]

That serials were regarded (and often dismissed) as 'kiddie matinee' fodder in the 1930s and after is irrefutable. That children watched serials in numbers during this period is equally certain. Important work in this field dates back to studies on cinema-going in Britain by J.P. Mayer and Herbert Blumer's contribution to the Payne Fund Studies in the United States.[12] Both discuss the appeal of the serial for the child audience. However, Mayer and Blumer's studies, and the use that has been made of them, raise certain questions.

Writing of the serial, Mayer noted that there was 'tremendous excitement whenever the hero or heroine is in danger, or is rescued, and particularly when any kind of fight takes place. Groans accompany the success of the villain, and sighs of relief are heard when the peril is past'. He went on:

> The characteristic feature of the serial is that it stops abruptly when suspense is at its height, and instead of the child being left in a state of tranquillity it is keyed up during the whole of the subsequent week, and is brought to the same condition again by the next instalment. It is impossible to say definitely what permanent effects this

perpetual state of suspense may have on the child's mind, although it seems certain that these effects are of an important kind.[13]

Earlier, Blumer had reported on children watching serials by writing of 'their groans when the heroine or hero is in extreme danger, the din of their shouts when either is freed', and commented:

> It is interesting to notice that the thrilling serial picture has a peculiar relation to the excitement of the child. Contrary to the usual motion picture which finishes with a rounding out of the plot, the serial instalment stops abruptly at a high level of suspense. Instead of leading the excited feelings of the child to a state of quiescence or satisfaction, the serial ends at the point where they are keyed up to the highest pitch. The result is to put the youthful spectator under the spell of suspense, sometimes of frenzy or panic, which persists for a week, only to be renewed at the next instalment. Just what permanent effects come from this persisting expectancy or keyed-up state of the mind cannot be declared with any certainty from our materials—although there is no question but the effects are important, even though obscure.[14]

The similarities between these accounts have a clear cause: Mayer's study was based not just on his own observations but also on Blumer's earlier work. Others have returned to Blumer's research, and in particular to its richest material: the 'autobiographies' which include repeated accounts of watching serials as a child. For instance, in his discussion of the sound serial as 'play', Scott Higgins cites one autobiography identified as from a twenty-year-old male, who recollected that 'The serial was the sole object for going to the movies for me and most of the children in the good old days when I was seven or eight years old'.[15] Blumer collected these accounts immediately after 1929.[16] Someone who was twenty in 1929 would have been seven or eight in 1916 or 1917. Serials they watched at that date would have been those that Singer and others identify as appealing to adults. The implication is clear. Children did not need to become a new target audience at the beginning of the 1930s since they had already been part of the serial audience for years.

The size of that part was important for the serial's economic viability. An industry entirely dependent on Saturday matinees screenings would have made little economic sense. In Britain in the 1930s, exhibitors had a clear view on children's matinees. In 1936 the British Film Institute organized a conference on 'Films for Children', the report on which included the observation that 'Our first difficulty is the financial one. Children's matinees are not profitable'. In addition to the lower ticket price, 'Depreciation is quite a serious charge. The child is a destructive and untidy creature. Peanut shells, sticky sweets on expensive upholstery, even slashed arm pads and seats are common consequences of our performances'. Supply was a further problem: 'Films are not produced specifically for the children's market'.[17]

One answer to this was to subsidize the matinee. There could be commercial justifications for this. *How to Make Money with Serials*, issued by Universal to support their 1927/28 season of serials, includes the following:

> Kids? Of course they attract kids. Good business, that. The kids of today are the men and women of tomorrow—and you can bank their money just as easily as you can adult admissions. And once you get the kids along they drag the older folk along. It never fails.[18]

Again, this is at least ambiguous as evidence that serials were made for children. American producers wanted to appeal to as wide an audience as possible. However, it was precisely the suggestion that serials were watched by children but not produced specifically for them that troubled commentators such as Blumer and Mayer. A second answer was to subsidize not just the matinee but the production of films for the matinee. Thus in Britain, J. Arthur Rank put money into films, serials included, made specifically for children. In the words of Rank's biographer, 'That was the beginning of a pioneering enterprise—films made especially for children—which had never been attempted in Britain before (or anywhere else in the world, except for Soviet Russia)'.[19] Rank's involvement didn't last, but the initiative was picked up by the government-subsidized Children's Film Foundation, which again led to the production of serials such as the eight-part *Five on a Treasure Island* (1957).[20]

In 1931 *Variety* reported that for American exhibitors 'the dime matinees for kids don't bring in a profit anyway, and are only run as good-will builders'.[21] Whatever the extent to which good-will motivated cinema exhibitors, questions remain about the degree to which producers would devote themselves to such an apparently unprofitable section of the market. Fortunately, information on who watched serials is not restricted to recycled images of Saturday matinees at the Bijou. There is, for a start, an abundance of material on what films played where and even when. If we look beyond the first-run cinema and the feature films that headed the box-office list a slightly different picture emerges.

It is on this basis that I have titled this chapter 'Thursday night at the Ritz'. The Ritz I have in mind is the Ritz in Oelwein, Iowa, a town, about thirty miles north-east of Cedar Falls, with a population in the 1930s of a little under 8,000. The Saturday edition of the Oelwein *Daily Register*, 1 February 1936, carried advertisements for two cinemas, the Grand and the Ritz, as well as a report on the 'movie attractions' for both cinemas in the coming week. The Grand does not appear to have screened serials: at least it did not advertise them. On Sunday and Monday it was scheduled to show *Anything Goes* (1936), supported by *Whipsaw* (1935); Tuesday night was Bank Night, and included a screening of *The Murder of Dr Harrigan* (1936); *Dangerous* (1935) played on Wednesday and Thursday, while on Friday and Saturday the cinema hosted *Rose of the Rancho* (1936), with a 'Friday Nite Only' performance of 'Platts School of the Dance'. Over this period the Ritz operated a slightly different programming policy, with only one change in the week: *Freshman Love* (1936) played with *Another Face* (also known as *It Happened in Hollywood*, 1935) Sunday to Wednesday, while the Thursday, Friday and Saturday 'double show' consisted of Gene Autry in *Melody Trail* (1936) and *The Roaring West* (1935), a Buck Jones serial.[22] The newspaper preview of the feature and the serial included a quote from *The Roaring West* director, Ray Taylor, on how 'the attractiveness of the serial was founded on violent and almost constant action, and in this respect the present-day chapterplay differs little from its prototype'.

The promise of violent and almost constant action may have had a particular appeal for children, who may well have attended on Thursday and Friday as much as Saturday. However, the *Daily Register* gives no indication that the serial was for their particular benefit and it seems likely that there was an overlap between the appeal of Gene Autry (whose films have been identified as popular with women as well as men and boys) in *Melody Trail* and Buck Jones in *The Roaring West*.[23] An adult in Oelwein on Friday 7 February 1936 who chose not to go to Platts School of the Dance would not have had many other forms of public entertainment to consider. Oelwein cinemagoers of all ages are likely to have watched serials on a regular basis.

There are other sources of information on either who watched serials and how the serial audience was understood, including contemporary commentary from newspapers and the trade press, promotional material and other industry documents, and details of other cinema screenings.

My examination of this material is divided into three sections, the first focusing on the adult audience, the second on children and the third on the international audience. My concern here is with who watched serials but looking at the available evidence also raises questions of what was constituted suitable children's entertainment, and thus issues of supervision and regulation. My focus is on the 1930s and the 1940s, though in order to understand serial exhibition, audiences and regulation it is necessary to pay some attention to the silent as well as the sound era. In a broad sense my aim is to contribute to a film history that is limited to neither the major studios nor the top of the bill at the first run, downtown cinemas. While evidence does not support the claim that serials normally only played at matinees, it is true that they only very occasionally played first-run cinemas. However, this does not mean that they had a small audience. Film history has tended to concentrate on either the major box-office successes or films that differed from the norm in ways that chime with more contemporary perspectives, on the feature film rather than the short item, and on the tastes of those living in major metropolitan centres who could afford first-run prices. Other films and other audiences deserve attention.

Adults

The adult female audience was particularly important for the first film series and serials. *What Happened to Mary* was shown on screen in coordination with the serialization published in *Ladies' World*. *Our Mutual Girl* was promoted alongside *Our Mutual Girl Weekly*: exhibitors were advised to 'Make your women patrons happy by giving them a copy of OUR MUTUAL GIRL WEEKLY free'.[24] *The Adventures of Dorothy Dare* was promoted as 'A motion picture of thrills and excitement centred around a magnificent fashion display . . . A splendid fashion show and a vivid drama'.[25] While not strictly a woman's genre, notes Singer, the films went out of their way to appeal to women, as is evident both from the narratives of female power and peril and through the way in which they were promoted. *Runaway June* (1915) was promoted through a competition open only to women.[26] Developing this argument, Shelley Stamp has examined the ways in which 'Serials catered to their large female fan base with engaging portraits of plucky young women beset by harrowing adventures and blessed with unrivalled strength and bravado'.[27]

At this stage the serial achieved an extraordinary popularity and prominence. In 1915 *Variety* reported that North American's *The Diamond from the Sky*, was already breaking the records set by Thanhauser's *The Million Dollar Mystery* earlier that year; its thirty episodes were predicted to achieve rentals of $1,400,000.[28] The serial's popularity was matched by that of the serial queen. One source has it that, while Paramount struck an above-average 100 prints for Mary Pickford's 1917 *Pride of the Clan*, the same year Pathé issued 785 prints for a saturation release of Pearl White's *The Fatal Ring*.[29] Pearl White in particular became a major film star, at home and abroad, following her appearances in serials such as *The Perils of Pauline* and *The Exploits of Elaine*. Singer reports that in a 1916 *Motion Picture* popularity contest, Pearl White was top of the list of female stars, a point picked up in other accounts.[30]

While this slightly inflates Pearl White's popularity in 1916 (when Mary Pickford and Marguerite Clark received more votes) the fact that Pearl White retained her place in later polls testifies to her, and her serials', continuing appeal throughout the 1910s.[31] This picture can be contrasted with the marginalization of the serial at the dawn of the sound era. In a feature on the effect of the 'talkies' on cinema-going in a New York Jewish neighbourhood, H.A. Woodmansee described the odd cinema still doing 'business with wordless pictures'. In one:

> A cowboy epic flickers into nothing. It is replaced by a blood-and-thunder serial, another hang-over of the past. The Murder Mansion, the mysterious, mad barefoot man who prowls the dungeons. But even the children, in the new talkie era, don't shudder as ecstatically as formerly at clutching hands and horrible shadows. As episode No. 4 ends with a ten-ton weight relentlessly descending on the helpless hero's chest, a youthful critic remarks, 'Dese chapters go goofy, d'ya know it?'
>
> The scattering audience regards the screen apathetically. Shabby men slump in the rickety seats, nodding in the close atmosphere. Perhaps some of them are the old guard who have come because they don't understand or like talkies in English. Perhaps others are there because the admission is only ten cents, or because they want a quiet place to sleep. No Bowery flop house is so cheap.[32]

In the light of this it is unsurprising that historians have written of the decline of the adult serial. However, while there is no doubt that the adult serial audience was smaller in 1930 in comparison with 1914, and there was no longer a specific appeal to women, there are complications and qualifications to this picture of steady decline.

In their eagerness to make up for earlier neglect of the film serial as a woman-centred genre, film historians have neglected other audiences. The fact that serials were promoted to women is undeniable but the extent to which this was part of a broader appeal deserves further scrutiny. Attempts to attract a female audience are most evident in the promotions of films such as *What Happened to Mary* and *Our Mutual Girl*, which were based around self-contained episodes, and understood as series films as much as serials. *The Adventures of Kathlyn* is a clearer example of a serial but also of a subtle but relatively early shift in the location of its newspaper serialization: Richard Abel notes that the first instalment of the published version was featured in section six of the *Sunday Tribune*, 'an amalgam of women's interest stories, entertainment news, fashion updates, fiction (particularly romance), recipes, and sewing hints' though also of stories featuring pilots, motorcyclists, aerialists, and other 'adventurers, usually male . . . Further accentuating this juxtaposition of extreme femininity, early feminism, and overt masculinity was the *Tribune's* decision, in March 1914, to move *Kathlyn* to section three, 'The Sporting Section', which highlighted male athletic prowess and achievement'.[33]

The serial remained central to Hollywood production at least up to the end of the 1910s. Singer has described its commercial history in this period as 'erratic': the 1919 *Photoplay* article from which he quotes, was less ambiguous, citing the many producers who continued 'to specialize in serials and realize millions a year from this form of screen entertainment' and the following for Pearl White, Ruth Roland and Marie Walcamp 'from Oshkosh to Timbuctoo that surpasses with an overwhelming plurality, the vogue of any of Filmdom's feature stars'.[34] Yet Singer is right to point to differences of opinion. Serials continued to be booked by 'small-time vaudeville' chains such as the Loews and Keith circuits. From a relatively early stage, however, commentators saw the appeal of the serial varying in different markets.[35] In a 1915 US wide poll, the question 'Do Serials Continue Popular with Public and Exhibitors', was answered 'Yes' in ten instances, 'No' in fifteen, 'Increasing' or 'Picking up' in two, 'Declining' or 'On the wane' in nine, with two 'Cities, no; outskirts, yes' replies, alongside 'In the outskirts only', 'only in residential section' and 'Not in city proper'.[36] The same year a report answered the question of whether serials were falling out of favour by quoting a representative of the Detroit film exchange:

in the small towns and even in the neighborhood houses in the big cities, serials are very well thought of and in fact are in demand. But

serials are not good for downtown houses where the trade is more
or less transient, and the reason is easily explained. One chapter of
the serial means nothing to the person who had not been following
it up, but in the small cities and neighborhood house the trade is
steady, and the same crowd is able to come on the same night every
week. In the downtown houses the trade is more or less uncertain;
they come when they can and you cannot rely on them for any
certain night'.[37]

A similar case was made in *Wid's Daily* in 1919. This indicated that

the serial is still favoured in small houses, particularly in the West
and South; but that it does not fit into the style of entertainment
being developed for the larger theatres catering to audiences less
partial to screen melodrama.
    In many of the cheaper neighborhood houses, reports show
the management advertises a 'serial night'—the same night every
week, and on those nights the serial steals the show from the long
feature.[38]

Perhaps this downplayed the breadth of popularity of the serial at
this time. What is clear is that the serial remained central to the programming of many rural and small-town cinemas. Thus the records of
the Superba Theater, Freeport, Illinois, as set out by Raphael Vela, reveal
a cinema located in a community of around 5,000, fifty miles north-west
of Chicago, where in the late 1910s the serial was a regular part of its
programme, playing to a largely adult audience.[39]
    Serials faced a number of challenges in the 1920s. With the retirement
of the first generation of serial stars, and in particular of Pearl White,
they lost some of their drawing power. Radio was becoming increasingly
popular as a potentially alternative form of entertainment. Hollywood
Majors such as Fox and Paramount who had tested serial production
and distribution decided to abandon them and focus on the feature.
The film industry attracted increasing attention from state censors,
education and civic groups and parents' associations, the serial both
for its sensationalist material and for the fact that it was popular with
children as well as adults.[40] The ways in which those companies still
producing serials responded was unlikely to increase the serial's appeal.
Pathé, for instance, announced that 'in the view of the better class of
picture patrons, guns and gunplay have outlived their usefulness . . . In

two of the most powerful and entertaining serials in the long Pathé list
. . . gunplay is entirely supplanted by original dramatic devices and true
American athletic prowess'.[41] If this was ever intended as anything more
than a sop to pressure groups it was soon abandoned. The guns returned
while the search for 'the better class of patrons' continued.

The studios continued to stress the serial's adult appeal. In a reversal of
the view of the 1920s as a decade when adult serial viewers were replaced
by children, in 1922 one paper reported the claim of Joe Brandt, President
of Star Serial Corporation, that 'The old and unfounded prejudices
against serials, the old-fashioned belief that its appeal was exclusively
confined to children, the old idea that the chapter-play served only as
a "filler" to round out an entertainment, has disappeared'.[42] In 1925
Universal's Short Subject Sales Manager insisted on the importance of
the serial for stabilizing cinema attendance, as a way to combat the 'radio
menace', as consisting of exactly the same material found in feature films,
and as appealing to adults as much as children.[43] The lure of the serial
queen remained strong enough in 1924 for an exhibitor from Lamont,
Iowa, running a two day a week cinema, to advise other exhibitors to
'Get a serial with a woman star and one you know has lots of action, like
Ruth Roland's serials. Start it off on your week night, say Wednesday . . .
put your admission down to ten cents this night for everyone, play up the
woman star, and thereby get the women interested and in on the first
one'.[44] In the same *Exhibitor's Herald* issue, the 'What the Picture Did
For Me' column of reports from independent theatre owners, included
one describing Roland's *Haunted Valley* (1923) as 'great for the ladies,
men and children. I have two that drive twenty-four miles to see it and
haven't missed a number'.[45] In 1927 *Picture Play* reported on a poll in a
'farm paper reaching more than a million fans' on 'small-town patronage
inclining towards screen entertainment in this order: Melodramas, Farce
and Comedies, Short Comedies, Society Comedies, Serials, Society
Dramas, Newsreels'—suggesting a fall in the serial's popularity though
not to the depths of society dramas or newsreels.[46]

The picture in 1930 varied in different locations but was not only one
of decline. The account of a New York cinema given earlier can be com-
pared with another from Chicago in the same year:

> Numerous neighborhood houses here which draw a sophisticated or
> 'smart' audience, are booking a number of melodramas, westerns,
> serials and the like, with the result that independent product is
> getting its best play here in years . . . Audiences give the mellers a

big hand, the cheaper and more ludicrous the picture, the better it is liked . . . Recognition of this trend in popular taste, though naturally in a more modified vein, is being given even by circuit bookings. Publix, Warner and Fox theatres have booked independent product, largely serials and westerns. Originally the bookings were for kids' matinees, and did not show at evening performances. Adults, however, 'went' for the cheap product in such impressive numbers and with so much enthusiasm that it became a problem for a kid to get a seat at one of the matinees.[47]

A more sustained adult audience remained elsewhere. In the 1930s the clearest evidence for this exists in local newspaper listings such as those for Oelwein, Iowa cited earlier. The 7 September 1939 edition of the *Gazette*, Xenia, Ohio, illustrates different approaches to programming adopted by different cinemas in the same locality. It carried advertisements for three cinemas: the Xenia, the Ohio and the Orpheum. The Xenia does not appear to have shown serials: on the Thursday it was screening *Wuthering Heights* (1939), while on Friday and Saturday the programme consisted of *News is Made at Night* (1939) and *The Bill of Rights* (a patriotic Technicolor special, 1939). Thursday night at the Ohio was a double-bill of *Magnificent Fraud* (1939) and *Barbary Coast* (1935), while on Friday and Saturday the programme consisted of *Island of Lost Men* (1939), *Cattle Raiders* (1938) and an episode of *Daredevils of the Red Circle*. The Orpheum kept the same programme for Thursday, Friday and Saturday, made up of *Behind Prison Gates* (1939), *The Man from Texas* (1939) and an episode of *Oregon Trail* (1939).[48]

Such screenings were not restricted to rural or small-town locations. The 13 May 1939 edition of the Baltimore *Afro-American* carried numerous advertisements for serial screenings. In the week beginning 14 May the Carey Theatre was showing the twelfth chapter of *Red Barry* (1938) on Sunday, the seventh chapter of *Flying G-Men* (1939) on Tuesday and Wednesday, the first chapter of *The Lone Ranger Rides Again* (1939) on Thursday and Friday, and the thirteenth and final chapter of *Red Barry* on Saturday; the Lafayette was showing chapter six of *Red Barry* on Wednesday and Thursday, and both chapter twelve of *Hawk of the Wilderness* (1938) and chapter eleven of *Flying G-Men* on Friday and Saturday; the New Roosevelt Theatre was showing chapter five of *Flying G-Men* on Friday and Saturday; the Lincoln was showing chapter ten of *Scouts to the Rescue* (1939) on Tuesday and Wednesday, and chapter seven of *The Lone Ranger Rides Again* on Thursday, Friday and Saturday; the

Freemont Theatre was showing chapter six of *The Lone Ranger Rides Again* on Tuesday and Wednesday and chapter ten of *Flying G–Men* on Friday and Saturday; at the Dunbar Theatre, chapter six of *Red Barry* was showing on Wednesday and Thursday, chapter nine of *Flying G–Men* on Friday, and the first chapter of *The Lone Ranger Rides Again* from the Saturday.[49]

'What the Picture Did for Me' reports, which in the 1930s had become a regular section in *Motion Picture Herald*, provide further information, though most tend not to specify the audience age. In North Carolina, *The Wolf Dog* (1933) was 'A very good business getter and seemed to please the majority of our patrons'.[50] Elsewhere, the identification of the child audience was accompanied by a reference to a broader appeal. In Georgia, *Radio Patrol* (1937) was a 'Very good serial. Sure-fire for the kids. Grown-ups like it too', *The Adventures of Smilin' Jack* (1943) 'pleased more adults than most chapter plays of the past', in one Maine cinema, the exhibitor in another described *Rustlers of Red Dog* (1935) as 'now beginning to pick up speed and is attracting more of the older folks than did "Tailspin Tommy", which went over big with the kids', while another from New Mexico wrote of *Tailspin Tommy* that 'All patrons from 6 to 60 should like this even though transients'.[51] Others reported that *Jungle Jim* (1937) 'seemed to hold the serial fans' and 'Fans who like serials will go for' *The Fighting Devil Dogs* (1938).[52] *The Great Adventures of Wild Bill Hickok* (1938) provoked a rarer example of a more specific reference from Ontario, Canada: 'Personally I cannot stand serials but on interviewing our farm patrons they seem more than enthusiastic. I believe it does do us extra business'.[53]

Other reports point to the way in which individual serials could have a particular appeal, and in which the serial was not limited to Saturday matinees. In Kansas *The Lost Jungle* (1935) 'seems to be going over good. This pleases a lot of the adults that do not like serials on account of the wild animal acts' (Lebanon, Kansas).[54] Most of the audience at an Oklahoma cinema liked *The Red Rider* (1934) 'fine. It has plenty of action and thrills. We are playing this on 10 cents nights and they come back to see the serial regardless of the feature program'.[55] *The Painted Stallion* played in Utah 'with big business Thursday and Friday and turn-away business Saturday. The serial was filmed in southern Utah and has some local interest. It is well produced and has good sustained interest. Hoot Gibson always means something around this neck of the woods'.[56] In Minnesota, the same film was judged not so good, 'but I used it on bargain nite and it helped business a little'.[57] Some cinemas continued to screen more than one a week; *The Spider's Web* (1938) led one Ohio exhibitor to comment, 'With this serial on Friday–Saturday and "Great Adventures of Wild Bill Hickok" on Sunday, our weekend worries are nil'.[58]

Serials identified as having a particular appeal for children could also attract adults. 'And do the kids love this one', wrote an Iowa exhibitor of *The Lone Ranger*.[59] However the same film was described by one New York state exhibitor as 'a great deal of adult appeal' while another wrote:

> Ordinarily I lay off serials in order not to drive the sophisticates away and I've often been under the impression that the serial audience sometimes stops a patron from wanting to see a good feature, but with this serial I find that the tradition which serials used to establish in first run theatres is reversed, for instead of people coming in to see the feature and walking out on the serial I find that they stay to see the serial and then walk out on some of the features we showed with it. In eyeing the audience from the rear of the theatre to watch their reaction, I often see many of our intellectuals sneakingly sitting on the edge of their seats, oblivious to their surroundings, and enjoying the picture just as much as the kiddies. Played every Friday–Saturday.[60]

Such reports are valuable in providing a local perspective on individual films. By the 1930s reviews of serials had become sporadic even in the film industry trade press. Those that were reviewed were often identified as appealing to children, though on occasions to adults as well. 'There should be little difficulty selling this serial to youngsters' began the *Motion Picture Daily* review of *Flash Gordon's Trip to Mars*, while *Film Daily* suggested that it 'will not only have the kids whooping, but the older males as well', and *Motion Picture Herald* predicted 'an enthusiastic reception from the juvenile reading public of six and sixty years of age'.[61]

On occasions more general press reports appeared. The low regard for the serial, and its audience, at the beginning of the 1930s is indicated in a *Variety* report that 'Universal Studio, only major company making serials, said the kids provide the biggest audience for the continued-next-week films, but they are also made for the small Main Street type grind house and a general moron audience'.[62] Subsequent reports in local and regional newspapers can probably be attributed to publicity campaigns but at least give an idea of how the industry saw its market. In 1936 the *Rochester (NY) American*, 21 March reported, 'It's a far cry back to the days when practically every movie-bill boasted a serial attraction . . . But Universal haven't forgotten . . . Though they haven't played the downtown houses lately, serials have had their public ever since', while the *Newark (NJ) News* announced 'If there ever was a heyday of the serial, it's right here . . . The difference is that most urban moviegoers don't run into serials anymore. Twenty years ago the serial was a regular feature in almost every program. Now they are made for only certain types, selected neighbourhood and country district bills'.[63]

It was a theme picked up elsewhere. In 1938 *Washington Post* had it that:

> Serial addicts in cities furtively invade children's Saturday matinees to satisfy their craving . . . Neighbourhood theatres are cannily catering to this weakness in adults and showing cliffhangers on Friday and Saturday regular bills. Small town theatres make no bones about it, and many of them demand two episodes at a time, running them in the last four days of the week . . . Determined to bring adult quarters rolling in as regularly as children's nickels, producers of serials are now spurring their writers to make the continued-next-weeks more logical and with definite appeal to adult standards.[64]

In 1941 the *Hartford Courant* estimated that serials played in about seventy-five per cent of America's 20,000 theatres: 'In some places they run all week, in others on Saturdays only'.[65] According to a 1944 *Motion Picture Herald* report 'serials in low income neighborhoods are still well received'.[66] In the *New York Times* Thomas Wood wrote in 1946 that:

> serials are the life-blood of nearly half this country's approximately 21,000 theatres. Quality films with Bette Davis and Greer Garson may be fine for the big cities, but it's the serials, like 'Hop Harrigan' [1946], 'G-Men Never Forget' [1948] and 'Jesse James Rides Again' [1947] that keep the small town operators in business.[67]

The first book-length survey of American cinema audiences was based on research undertaken in the late 1930s. In it Margaret Thorp emphasized the continuing appeal of the serial for rural audiences, writing that 'the rural moviegoer likes to feel at ease with his art. That is one reason why the serial is so popular'. For Thorp, 'socio-economic classification' was far more important to the film producer than age, and the numbers going to the cinema before the age of fourteen was 'not large enough to make the manufacture of special films for their benefit a very profitable business'.[68]

Serial producers and promoters didn't want to limit their audience and did their best to keep their options open. Universal's *How to Make Money with Serials* included a section titled 'WHO STARTED THIS TALK ANYWAY ABOUT SERIALS BEING MADE FOR KIDS ONLY?' in which it was argued that 'Older folks have always enjoyed the serials. Many of 'em have been afraid to admit it', suggested that Friday night be 'reserved for the grown-ups who want to enjoy Universal's red-blooded, adventurous new types of chapter plays' and proposed that exhibitors stage 'a woman's matinee' and arrange for a local newspaper editorial commenting on how women 'no longer care for the wishy-washy type of fiction or plays and that they are showing their partiality towards virile he-man photoplays and serials'.[69]

The 1933 'remake' of *The Perils of Pauline* would, Universal claimed, 'bring back fond memories to our parents, who remember the motion picture in its infancy, and will bring new, modern thrills to the new generation'.[70] On the opening night of *Flash Gordon* at the RKO Majestic Theatre in Columbus, Ohio ('a big first-run house'), the serial apparently 'created so much enthusiasm among the adults as well as children that it was shown at every performance during the week'.[71]

References to the child viewer were regularly combined with at least a mention of adults. Mascot's entreaty that exhibitors of *The Galloping Ghost* 'go after the kids' was followed by an item headed 'And the Adults Too'.[72] The same studio's *The Lost Jungle* had, it was claimed, 'a particular appeal for men'.[73] Promotional material from Republic regularly emphasized the child audience, particularly for serials such as *Undersea Kingdom*, though even the suggested 'Young Explorer's Club' was presented as a way of using 'the kids to sell the kids—and their parents!'[74] The film was also promoted as 'a sample of the ultra-modern type of serial which holds all audiences spellbound, whether they be young or old, city slickers or rustics'.[75] 'Don't neglect the adults in staging your campaign', was the advice to exhibitors showing Columbia's *Overland with Kit Carson* (1939).[76] *Batman* (1943) was described as 'a timely, thrill-a-second chapter play that is bound to appeal to adults as well as the youngsters', and exhibitors were also encouraged to 'Utilize fashion shots for the tie-ups with women's apparel shops and department stores in town, and see that the woman's pages of local newspapers are supplied with stills'.[77] Suggestions for how to sell *The Desert Hawk* (1944) to children was followed by the observation that 'Many of the exploitation suggestions can easily be adapted to appeal to the more mature persons'.[78]

It is hardly surprising that the film industry would want adults as well as children to pay to watch serials if that was a possibility, and it cost studios little to add a comment to this effect in their pressbooks. However, evidence suggests a continuing serial audience that wasn't limited to children. In addition, there were occasional suggestions of a re-orientation of the serial towards older viewers, though this itself can be seen as part of a tradition of reports of a shift in the nature of the serial, generally unmatched by actual change.

Columbia's move into serial production was reported as with a view to making the serial

> palatable to adults rather than catering strictly to kids, as has been the habit in the past. If it can be done it is likely that all serials within the year or so will take that tangent, figuring on cleaving a line somewhere between the adult and kid mentalities but not beyond reach of either.[79]

Other reports had Columbia planning 'to distribute 4 serials with adult man and woman appeal, with Louis Weiss on production end with Adventure Serials, Inc.' and the studio's *Captain Midnight* (1942) 'designed to achieve the same "adult" appeal as the recently completed "Holt of the Secret Service"'.[80] Similarly, Universal's *Riders of Death Valley* (1941) and *Gang Busters* (1942) were said to be 'geared for adult appeal in an effort to attract the radio and serial fans to the theatre'.[81]

Republic succeeded in promoting *The Lone Ranger* to adults as well as children. George Trendle's *Lone Ranger* radio series has been identified as 'targeted to children, in particular fourteen and fifteen year-olds' though some publicity emphasized the programme's adult appeal and specific appeal to women.[82] One item in Republic's pressbook for their serial version states that 'Serials are written primarily for children', while another has '"The Lone Ranger" is excellent film-fare for adults, as well as children'. One of a series of single and double page *Motion Picture Herald* spreads promoting Republic serials in general and *The Lone Ranger* in particular, announced that: 'The nationally-famous radio program with the largest listening audience known to broadcasting—17 million weekly—becomes a Republic serial with the greatest *adult* audience possibilities. Truly a serial for *every* situation' (Fig. 2). *The Lone Ranger* achieved an unusually wide release for a serial, including screenings

2. *Motion Picture Herald*, 2 October 1937, p. 93

at the 1,700 seat Criterion Cinema on Broadway. Republic were particularly pleased with a letter they received from Charles B. Moss, of the Criterion, which described *The Lone Ranger* as 'one of the finest shows we have had at the Criterion in months', referred to 'two elderly gents, one about sixty, the other about five years younger, who presented their tickets to the doorman with a merry "HEIGH-YO, SILVER" as they passed into the house', and concluded: 'I don't yet know whether the kids brought the parents or vice versa'.[83] The letter perfectly fitted Republic's aim to present the serial as having an appeal for both children and adults, and the studio continued to use variations of it in promotional material. Thus the pressbook for *Perils of Nyoka* (1942) included an item on an 'exhibitor who had successfully run a Republic serial', and who had reported: 'I can't tell whether the adults are bringing the kids to see this serial, or whether the kids are bringing the adults . . . Republic officials put their heads together and decided that any type of entertainment with such a universal appeal was strictly their dish'.[84]

'Serial episodes . . . outshow any other type of films used' to relax and stimulate war plant workers, claimed one 1942 report, while it was after the Second World War that Republic began to develop the market for serial screenings at Army camps.[85] Assessing the extent to which a broader adult appeal lasted through the 1940s and 1950s needs further research. The picture in the 1930s and early 1940s is clearer. Aside from a 'smart' interest in the cheap and ludicrous, serials continued to play on the regular programme in a significant number of neighbourhood cinemas, promising violent and continuous action to audiences of different or unspecified ages. They were successful enough to attract increasing attention, part of which was focused on the serial's adult appeal. Identifying this was itself an acknowledgement of the extent to which the serial had become associated with children, though this itself can be traced back to the serial's early history.

Children, Regulation and Promotion

The post-1930 adult serial audience has been increasingly forgotten but so has the child viewer of the 1910s. At one point in her discussion of the serial's audiences, Stamp speculates that a cardboard 'crolette' used to promote Pathé's occult serial, *The Mysteries of Myra* (1916) 'suggests a targeted appeal to young, unmarried women romantic enough to thrill at the prospect of a darkened, occult encounter with a young man of their acquaintance'.[86] That may be, but the only reports for the film that I have seen breaking down the audience don't do this by gender. One noted that 'Frank D. Stanton, manager of Franklin Park Theater, Boston, filled his theater to capacity through a unique method of advertising the "Mysteries of Myra". Suspended above the playhouse was a huge balloon kite, with the title of the feature showing on all sides, and souvenirs in the form of toy balloons were distributed to all the children'.[87] Another announced that:

> Manager George N. Shorey, of the Gay Theatre, Knoxville, recently handled one of the keenest advertising stunts on record, for the purpose of getting a serial well started. Mr Shorey sent out ten thousand copies of Charles W. Goddard's fascinating story 'Myra' and announcement was made to the effect that every boy and girl bringing one of these copies to the theater would be admitted free of charge on Saturday, to see the story continued in pictures . . . It is needless to say that the house was packed by eager youngsters who will undoubtedly force their fond parents into furnishing the necessary coin with which to see the rest of the serial.[88]

The emphasis on the appeal that serials had for children is evident at an early stage, providing a different perspective on the serial's reception. Commenting on the 'extraordinarily successful film serial', *The Exploits of Elaine*, in Britain at the beginning of 1916 the writer of the 'Young Picturegoer' column:

> I went into a cinema early the other evening where children always form a big portion of the audience, and was astonished to hear the reception they gave the sixth episode of the story. Just before the film commenced the chorus of the 'Elaine' song was flashed upon the screen, and I don't think a single child failed to join in singing it.[89]

A report from the same year on a class of children in Toronto who, 'acting purely from memory, staged a synopsis of the serial story, "The Broken Coin" [1915] on their school platform, under the supervision of their teacher', included the observation that the 'children, ranging in age from eight to twelve, and including both boys and girls, have been constant visitors at a neighbourhood theatre, where they have been following for many weeks the adventures of the heroine in the great story'.[90]

Similar links between the serial and children were made within the

United States. According to B.F. Barrett's report on a 1916 Board of Education survey of the films likes and dislikes of 400 Chicago school-children, 'Travelogues' (35) were most popular, followed by 'serials' (32) and 'adventure and thrills' (31) (Charlie Chaplin received 27 likes but with 12 dislikes toped the poll of the films children didn't want to see).[91] The following year Barrett quoted a Nebraskan exhibitor as saying that 'The child's mind is more able than people think. They take a delight in serials and have no trouble at all to follow them from week to week'.[92]

In part this indicates continuity. Sound serials were watched by children in numbers but this was also true for the 1920s and for the 1910s. It also indicates a more mixed serial audience than is commonly acknowledged, in the 1930s and before. Gardner discusses films that he notes 'are often termed "adult serials," to differentiate them from the Saturday matinee serials of the 1930s and 1940s', pointing out that such 'adult' serials were formally not that different from the multi-reel features of the time.[93] The danger here is that the term 'adult serials' neglects what was an important part of the serial audience from an early stage just as the Saturday matinee label hides a broader picture for a later period.

Different interests were at play. Publications such as *Motography* and *Moving Picture News* were aimed at the film industry and provided a forum for the industry's interests, which lay in expanding the cinema audience while limiting external interference. The Nebraska exhibitor identified in *Motion Picture News* as 'one of the pioneers of the children's matinee in the state', was quoted as saying 'I don't favour these women's clubs interfering with children's matinees': the interests of those who saw themselves as guardians of children's welfare did not necessarily match the interests of the film industry. Yet this was not a simple battle between the film industry and the moral guardians. There were different views as to how matinees should be organized, varying from those who campaigned for highly regulated screenings designed to edify their audience to those who 'advocated play and tolerated more action oriented titles'.[94] To a significant degree the film industry acted in coordination with different pressure groups, soliciting their approval to avoid censorship and using this to gain wider acceptance.

Children's attendance at screenings of serials existed in shifting contexts. The supervised re-enactment of *The Broken Coin* in Toronto in 1916 contrasts with the complaints (in 1921) of Pennsylvania censor Ellis Oberholtzer that

The story of sixteen or seventeen episodes, two reels of which are shown on a Tuesday evening, leaving the hero or heroine, as the case may be, under a crushing machine, or in the track of a stream of acid, or confined in a sewer amidst serpents, to be rescued on the Tuesday following only to be hurled in turn into some similar predicament, is an achievement on the part of our picture men of which they are frankly ashamed . . . Frequently we are asked if there is not a film which is made for children 'movie' fans. This is it.[95]

For Oberholtzer serials were both made for children and unsuitable for children. He was an extreme advocate of a stance others shared. Like the Nebraska exhibitor complaining of interfering 'women's clubs', trade press reports could present this in gendered, indeed sexist terms. 'After the studios temporarily satisfied the club women by desexing serials for the benefit of the kids', claimed *Variety* in 1931, 'the girls are now jumping on the continued-next-week films as being material fit for morons only'.[96] 'Serials Tossed Out of All W-FC Houses at Instigation of Femmes' it announced later the same year, reporting that eight Fox Leader's Junior groups had substituted shorts for serials at Saturday matinee screenings at the request of women's clubs, school organizations and church groups who say serials are exaggerated, inconsistent, not true to life, and abnormal.[97] Fox Theatres were still worrying about serials towards the end of the decade, when the Production Code Administration received a telephone call from the Theatre's Public Relations Department, reporting complaints at screenings of Columbia's *Jungle Menace*, *The Secret of Treasure Island*, *The Great Adventures of Wild Bill Hickok* and in particular Republic's *The Fighting Devil Dogs*. The serials were described as 'too strenuous: at times the children were so terrified that they wouldn't stay in their seats and either ran out or were found hiding behind the curtains'. As a consequence, further bookings of the Republic serial were cancelled at Fox West Coast serials, at least temporarily.[98]

Evidence on the cancellation or direct censorship of serials is relatively rare. The most direct confrontation between the film industry and censors occurred in the early 1920s. One industry response (adopted by Fox and Paramount) was to keep clear of serials, given that they had come to depend on the very things that pressure groups felt they shouldn't contain. Another was to adapt them to meet the immediate demand, hence the Pathé 'gunless' serials. A third, related approach was to promote such serials as containing the very values which objectors said they lacked.

In 1921, head of the newly created serial Exploitation Department Fred J. McConnell, described Universal's new policy of serial exploitation as 'not only a welcome innovation in the serial field, but it is also censor proof. It is the company's intention . . . to create serials which fulfil entertainment requirements and at the same time afford wholesome amusement for the children'.[99] Evidently providing wholesome amusement was secondary to the need to be to be seen to be doing this, though Universal did change the nature of their product in some ways, responding to objections by producing 'historical' serials such as *With Stanley in Africa* (1922) and *In the Days of Buffalo Bill* (1922). Their reception was mixed. While exhibitors contributing to 'What the Picture Did for Me' were often favourable on the latter film, less enthusiastic comments included 'Too much history stuff to please the kids', 'Not quite enough action to suit the kids', 'Kids kick about too much history' (though adding 'but they always come back for more'), 'the only good one in the last five or six of the "historical" stuff' and 'Too much history', and 'Started off big but falling off. Too much history. Won't producers ever learn that people don't go to shows to be educated'.[100] The fear was clearly that children would be put off by the very changes designed to make serials more acceptable for them.

Promoting serials as suitable for children remained a comparatively safe proposition and could be effective in the right context. Despite the persistence of some objections, at the beginning of the 1930s the idea of serials for children had become more acceptable. The crushing machines and streams of acid that Oberholtzer had fumed about had been replaced by less graphic forms of peril (though some of them would return). Much of the anxiety about unsuitable material had passed to more 'sophisticated' forms of cinema. It was in this context that the serial took on a new importance for the film industry at the time of the release of *The Indians are Coming*. The film's pressbook included 'details for forming a kiddie club, holding a boy scout demonstration, making an Indian tepee and an Indian street ballyhoo. There is also a series of school tie-ups, a drawing contest for children'.[101] As had happened almost a decade earlier, there was an appeal to the historical. *The Indians are Coming* was 'A serial of twelve episodes which proves highly entertaining for the children as it concerns exciting happenings in the days of the Wild West'.[102] *Educational Screen* found it 'unusually satisfactory as a "western" serial . . . a notable production of its kind in that it retains the vigorous and wholesome thrills without the exaggerated elements that have made most serials objectionable fare for the youngsters'.[103] A report on children's matinees run in Macon, Georgia described an example programme as follows: 1) Community Singing, 2) Serial—*The Indians are Coming*, 3) Prologue—short pageant presenting replica of first [United States] flag raised, 4) Feature—*The Social Lion* [1930].[104] *The Indians are Coming* and nine other serials were later included in the National Board of Review selection of 'Junior Matinees, Special Book Tieups, Timeliness of Screen Story, Exceptional Artistry in Production, and Foreign Product'.[105] *Motion Picture News* identified it as 'Great for Youngsters'.[106] It was cited in a report on 'the decision to resume the making of serials on a big scale. It is generally felt that this will do more than anything else to restore kid patronage, or even build it up to new high marks, and at the same time catch a considerable number of grown-ups as well'.[107] On a broader level, for John Balaban of Paramount Publix, child attendance had diminished 'because a majority of talking pictures hold no particular appeal for juveniles . . . But talking serials, which they understand and enjoy, have the ability to transform scantily attended children's matinees into packed houses'[108] According to the sales officials cited in another report, the chief reasons were 'the desire of exhibitors to book material suitable for kid patronage, and an equal urge for a product that will induce consistent attendance by a greater number of patrons'.[109]

This was a theme taken up in subsequent publicity. Universal promoted *Clancy of the Mounted* (1933) as approved by 'representatives of women's organisations . . . as splendid entertainment for all members of the family, with especial appeal to children'.[110] 'I recommend it strongly for juvenile entertainment', was one of the reports listed, though others had 'I would recommend it for Junior Matinees. (And equally interesting to adults)', and 'I believe that "Clancy of the Mounted" would appeal to adults who enjoy serials as well as to children'.[111] 'The movement to bring the kids back to the theatre is more pronounced than ever', announced the pressbook for the studio's *Danger Island* (1931); 'mothers . . . parents' clubs . . . child welfare organisations are more concerned than ever with movie entertainment for children . . . Universal talking serials are recognized by all these as the best, clean entertainment'.[112]

Film producers made a concerted effort to get pressure groups on their side. When Nat Levine proposed that Republic make a serial based on the *Dick Tracy* comic strip he wired

> I am of the opinion that even tho we would have bad reaction from womens clubs and churches on Dick Tracy cartoon that it still represents a good investment for us . . . granted that this reaction exists

today we shall create the story for a serial with the thought in mind
of getting it approved by womens clubs and churches . . .[113]

Republic went on to use the external scrutiny paid to its serials as a
form of promotion. While *The Lone Ranger* was promoted as having 'the
greatest *adult* audience possibilities', the pressbook stressed that 'Serials
are written primarily for children. Therefore, they must not only be
approved by the Motion Picture Producer's Censorship Board, but by the
National Parent-Teachers' Association, as well as various local women's
clubs and other groups in the cities where the serial happens to be
showing'.[114] 'Since the juvenile audience is the largest a serial will reach,
nothing is put into the screenplay which might conceivably introduce
wrong notions into young minds,' reassured the *Dick Tracy vs. Crime Inc.*
(1941) pressbook.[115]

There were even serials featuring children. The serials that were made
in post-war Britain specifically for children's matinees placed children in
the leading roles. In contrast, Hollywood serials tended to have an adult
cast. A shift took place in the 1930s, as adult heroes were accompanied
by hero-worshipping young boys in serials such as *Undersea Kingdom* and
Dick Tracy.[116] *Radio Patrol* not only had Pinky Adams (played by fourteen
year-old Micky Rentschler) in a significant role but began each chapter
with a shot of a child reading a copy of *Radio Patrol* (Fig. 3), suggesting
that this was Universal's imagined audience. In *The Phantom Empire*
Frankie Darro (born 1917) played alongside Betsy King Ross (born
1922, and previously featured as the sole significant female in Mascot's
Fighting with Kit Carson) in a serial in which the idea of the young fan
was inscribed into the film's narrative. In the years that followed children
or young adults were featured in a number of serials. *Young Eagles* (1934)
and *Scouts to the Rescue* (1939) took the Boy Scouts as their subject.
Boys featured in hero worshipping roles in early Republic serials such
as *Darkest Africa*, *The Painted Stallion* (1937), *Dick Tracy Returns* (1938),
The Adventures of Red Ryder (1940), *Jungle Girl* and *Daredevils of the Red
Circle*. Similar juvenile roles can be found in Victory's *Blake of Scotland
Yard* (1937) and Columbia's *Overland with Kit Carson* (1939). At Universal
there was a tendency to emphasize adolescence rather than childhood,
evident in the studio's first comic book adaptation, *Tailspin Tommy* as
well as the Dead End Kids, Tough Little Guys serials and *Sky Raiders*
(1941).

There were, however, limits to this trend. Serials continued to assign
leading roles to adults and regularly featured no children at all. When

3. *Radio Patrol* (1937)

Columbia purported to adapt the radio series *Chick Carter, Boy Detective* (1943–45), it became *Chick Carter, Detective* (1946), with the title role played by Lyle Talbot (born 1902) a cast of adults and a plot similar to B-crime features of the period. Of the ten serials released in 1946 only Columbia's *Hop Harrigan* and *Son of the Guardsman* feature named non-adult characters.

The emphasis on the serial's suitability for children led to the use of the scrutiny it received as a means of promotion. Yet even that scrutiny can give a varied picture. In the final years of its serial production, Universal relied on the Southern California Motion Picture Council to view serials and produce reports, including a comment on 'audience suitability'. The comments generally served as a form of approval, but were not homogenous. Comments on the 1945 version of Universal's *Secret Agent X9* included: 'Entertaining for all ages', 'entertaining for any age . . . holds the attention of either young or old', 'especially for children', 'Over fourteen', 'For the more mature audience . . . or for those accustomed to seeing mystery films . . . or listening to exciting radio serials', 'Should be enjoyed by any age . . . Children particularly will enjoy this serial and find it harmless', 'entertaining for young and old', 'Only for those that enjoy the constant mounting excitement of hair raising incidents of adventure and intrigue', 'children and adolescents'.[117] *Jungle Queen* (1945) was identified as suitable in different reports for 'all ages and all degrees of intelligence', 'old teens', 'adolescence', 'adults that like mystery', 'probably more suited to adults and young people, rather than children', 'Children and all adults who enjoy serials', 'For young people and adults . . . the theme and development are of more interest for those capable of understanding the activities of enemy agents and the methods for dealing with them'.[118]

The *Film Daily* reviewer put it differently: 'Nazi business once more is thriving in a serial full of the stuff that captures juvenile imagination. The story, preposterous beyond the usual, is crowded with the sort of action that excites and thrills the simple souls.'[119] When they took notice of the serial, most press reports from this time characterized its audience as juvenile, though 'juvenile' or 'simple souls' was not always a reference to children.

Serials Worldwide

'Although aimed primarily at juveniles', reported *Variety* in 1940:

> the peril-packers are said to be attracting increasing numbers of adult devotees who get a kick out of the phoney thrills which the kids take seriously. However, special Saturday morning shows and Saturday matinees are still, by far, the best market . . . In the United States, the south constitutes the biggest market for the serials. They were never big in Europe, but South America has always been an important market and growing.[120]

Six years later, William Roberts identified 'the Saturday-afternoon kiddie trade' as most important, followed by the 'rural audience', and went on 'But if serials are hot in the rural areas, they are a sizzling item in Latin America'.[121]

The serial's international following was recognized from an early stage. Pearl White in particular was a global star. In 1917 John Ten Eyck wrote that:

> In France French soldiers on furlough idolise her in 'Les Mysteries de New York—The Exploits of Elaine'. In Porto Rico she crowds the theatres. In Bombay she features frequently in the newspapers. A Scottish newspaper runs her life on its front pages. Five Australian managers make fortunes presenting her pictures. In South Africa they name babies after her, and in Tokyo they give her name to theatres.[122]

Where the Pathé star's serials were not shown, for instance in Germany where Universal was the main supplier of American serials, other American stars such as Marie Walcamp and Eddie Polo gained a significant following.[123]

Noting the global, wartime popularity of Pathé serials, Kristin Thompson goes on to say that long-term international success was reserved for those countries which concentrated on features.[124] Yet American trade press reports continued to highlight the importance of the international market for serials in the years immediately following the war. In 1919 it was noted that

> One admitted peculiarity of the foreign market . . . is its abnormal fondness for serials. Serials are the easiest sold pictures which American exporters can find to handle, despite the fact that the market for serials of the average type in the United States is a tough one. So desirable, indeed, have serials become in the foreign market that the man with the rights to a good serial is often enabled to get action on a great many of his slow moving features by hanging a serial up as a reward or bonus.[125]

Americans south of the Rio Grande were identified as having a particular fondness for this form of cinema. In 1917 Universal reported great demand for its serials 'all over Latin America'.[126] In 1920 a discussion of Universal's arrangements for distributing their films in South America noted that this would assure South American distributors of 'a complete serial program . . . This is especially important in the South American market, where serials are more sought for than almost any other kind of film output'.[127] The 1922–23 *Film Daily Yearbook* identified the serial as having a particular appeal in Mexico, where the serial was most popular among 'all classes', but also China, which was 'a little slow on features, the demand there being for serials and action pictures rather than high-class dramas', India, Burma, Ceylon and Portugal, where 'melodramatic serials are especially popular'.[128]

Stephen Hughes's study of cinema-going in the Madras area of India in the 1920s provides further details on the size and nature of the serial's audience within one area. Hughes suggests that in the south of India, 'along with Indian films, serials were the most consistently profitable, reliably popular and dominant film category to be screened throughout the 1920s.[129] Exhibitors identified the appeal of serials as strongest among, but not restricted to, the poor, the uneducated and the young:

one confidently pronounced that the serial audience was seventy per cent wage earners, twenty per cent middle class and semi-illiterate and ten per cent rich and literate.[130]

International demand for serials declined over time, though in the Indian south silent serials remained 'the most consistently popular film attraction offered by small-time and remote exhibitors into the 1930s'.[131] *Film India* carried advertisements for serials such as *S.O.S. Coastguard* (1937), sold as 'a bag of thundering dynamites to please every class of audience!', and Columbia, Republic and Universal serials were distributed in India in the 1940s through the Victory Film Exchange.[132] In 1926 James P. Cunningham reported that in China 'screen comedies had superseded, to a large extent, to former demand for serials'.[133] Yet in 1937 there was still 'a small but profitable demand for good serials' in China.[134] A 1938 report on cinema-going in Syria identified, 'as expected', two classes of native audiences: the educated class had tastes 'similar to that of the higher European classes', while the uneducated preferred 'serials and adventure films'.[135] The following year *Variety* commented that 'Serials are big grossers in three major foreign markets, Brazil, Philippine Islands and India'.[136] The year after that the story was that 'Brazil . . . offers a good market for American films . . . In the interior and in many neighborhood houses, Westerns, action pictures and serials are in demand', while in the British West Indies the most popular films were 'action and Westerns, musical comedies and serials'.[137] A 1941 report singled out the popularity of serials in the 'neighborhood houses and provinces' of Peru.[138] 'Cliffhangers, the wilder the better, get preferential treatment over ordinary feature films in the Philippines . . . Three chapters are usually run off at a showing as bill-toppers' noted *Daily Variety* in 1942, suggesting that Universal's *Overland Mail* (1942) would get a more favourable reception than most of the studio's features.[139]

Individual serials could receive extensive international distribution. *The Lone Ranger* was described as 'getting heavy play in South America'.[140] Jack Mathis suggests that the foreign market accounted for approximately sixty per cent of the aggregate gross taken by the serial. Thomas Wood reported that it was translated into French, Dutch, Belgian, German, Spanish, Portuguese and Chinese and only flopped in Great Britain.[141] In fact it was shown at London's Shaftesbury Avenue, in a programme at the Gaumont News Theatre, initially alongside the Paul Lorentz documentary, *The River* (1938). In her review, C.A. Lejeune wrote that 'London audiences for the next fourteen weeks can share in an experiment that was the hit of fashionable New York last winter, the exhibition in a West-End Cinema of a real, full-blooded, old-time film serial'.[142] The 1939 British Film Institute Annual Report noted a 'growth in dignity of two Cinderellas of the screen—the Western and the serial . . .' commenting that it was interesting that for the first time in many years that a serial 'has been showing with success in a West End cinema, while at a University town another was strongly recommended by the film critic of the leading undergraduate paper'.[143]

The British, West End release of *The Lone Ranger* was something of an exception. From an early date children in Britain were watching serials in numbers, and they continued to do so into the post-war period; at least at the beginning of the 1930s some cinemas retained the serial on the regular bill, but there is little evidence of subsequent adult attendance at screenings of serials.[144] The situation appears to have been different in parts of continental Europe: in France, Germany and Netherlands the serial retained its adult associations into the 1920s; rather than the weekly, two-reel chapter that became the norm in the United States, longer serials were screened at irregular intervals.[145] To at least some extent this continued into the 1930s. Censorship records indicate that American serials continued to be screened in three-part versions in the Netherlands in the 1930s: the initial ruling for one (*Jungle Menace*) was that it was suitable for all, twenty-one were deemed suitable for those fourteen or older, six as for those eighteen or older, and one (*Red Barry*) was initially banned.[146] Serials identified as children's films in one country could be adult only in another.

Where the serial became the feature an adult audience appears to have been assumed. In his account of cinema-going in Trinidad, V.S. Naipaul wrote:

> And there are the serials—*Daredevils of the Red Circle, Batman, Spy Smasher*—which are shown in children's programmes in their countries of origin but in Trinidad are one of the staples of adult entertainment. They are never shown serially but all at once; they are advertised for their length, the number of reels being often stated; and the latecomer asks, 'How much reels gone?'[147]

Elsewhere the practice was to combine episodes but to retain an element of seriality. A cinema-goer in Kingston, Jamaica in the week beginning 15 June 1936 would have been presented with the opportunity of watching episodes 1 to 6 of Mascot's *The Whispering Shadow* at the Tivoli on the Tuesday, episodes 10, 11 and 12 at the Spanish Town on Wednesday, episodes 7, 8 and 9 at the Brown's Town on Thursday, or episodes 4, 5 and 6 at the Port Maria on Friday.[148]

Evidence of a different kind, location and time is provided in Hortense Powdermaker's anthropological study of the African mining town of Luanshya in what in the 1950s was Rhodesia. Describing how films were brought as a package by the mine Welfare Department, she notes that screenings invariably consisted of: a cowboy film (old and grade B), *British News*, *The Northern Spotlight* (Northern Rhodesian News), an animal cartoon (*Kadoli*), *The African Mirror* (incidents of African Life), an adventure serial such as *Superman*, and, occasionally, a very old American slapstick comedy.[149]

Her estimate was that

> 58 per cent of the adults on the township have attended the movies at some time, and of these, 39 per cent were going now. Among the latter, 53 per cent went once a week; 3 per cent, once in two weeks; 6 per cent, once a month; and the remainder, less frequently. There was usually one showing a week on the mine township; and the audience averaged twelve to fifteen hundred people, about half of whom were children under sixteen. The audience was diverse: old and young, men and women, educated and uneducated'.[150]

The cowboy films were the most popular, though some preferred the Superman film (presumably the 1948 Columbia serial of that name), and the reasons for the preference for the cowboy films could easily have been applied to many serials. For Powdermaker, the repetitive quality was similar to African folk tales and:

> popular stories and movies over the world. The African audience often anticipated what was going to happen in their comments to each other. The struggle is between good and bad people. The brave hero, always on the side of the good people, fights hard, sometimes infatuates a girl, and always triumphs through his manly strength. The symbols are clear, the emotions direct. The drama is acted over and over again, somewhat like a ritual, and offers release and hope. The catharsis was different from that of the radio songs of individual loneliness, love, joys, and troubles in town. Through the cowboy films, pent-up aggressions were played out in a group; and the African became free and triumphant.[151]

In his more recent account, Charles Ambler differentiates this experience from North American cinema-going, noting that:

> few moviegoers had sufficient knowledge of colloquial spoken American or British English to comprehend the dialogue—even if it had been audible in the noisy atmosphere that characterised these film shows. In any case, censors had cut films shown on the Copperbelt to ensure that African audiences were not exposed to images or story lines that they imagined might inspire challenge to the white supremacist colonial order—a tall order given the violent rituals that characterised the plot in a typical western. The resulting celluloid butchery apparently left more than a few movies devoid of discernible narrative'.[152]

In the light of this it is perhaps unsurprising that the audiences seem for the most part to have ignored or dismissed plots, watching films for their stock scenes, and taking particular delight in the regular fights.[153] 'I like the movements of the picture', reported one woman in Powdermaker's survey.[154] Another, described as 'a relatively well-educated (secondary school), law-abiding young man in his early twenties, who held a responsible job', commented 'I always want to see how strong Jack is and whether he can be knocked out early. But I expect the hero, Jack, to beat everyone and to win every time . . . I like the way they ride and fight with their hands'.[155] As Ambler observed, such audiences understood these films in their own particular context. They also illustrate how well films can travel, even if they are shown in worn-out or (through accident or design) incomplete copies, but particularly if they are based on action rather than dialogue.

This takes us some distance away from the Saturday matinee screenings with which this chapter started, even if the noisy atmosphere shares something with accounts of children's matinees. As Ambler noted, the Coppertown audience responded to the western and the serial in the context of their own experience. More generally, the film serial's emphasis on uncomplicated action, as well as the experience of waiting for and watching each serial episode, had an undoubted appeal for large numbers of children. Yet that appeal was already present in the heyday of Pearl White and in the sound era remained accompanied by adult interest in the serial, within and beyond the United States. The evidence here is clear. The balance between the child and adult viewer, and the degree to which this shifted over time, is more difficult to ascertain. Contemporary reports do not suggest a rapid or even steady decline in adult interest in the film serial after 1930. In the 1930s the serial proved to be remarkably resilient, even undergoing something of a revival among adults as well as children. The reasons for this lay not just in audience taste but also in the commercial history of serial production.

3

The Economy Chapter

The survival of the film serial in the sound era was based in part on keeping costs to a minimum. While box-office takings for serials were not limited to children's pocket money, the serial's market remained largely restricted to the cheaper houses. The overall length of the format meant that even the cheapest serial involved a more substantial outlay than a relatively low-cost feature. There were ways of economizing on footage. The practice of starting each chapter with a recap from the previous chapter meant that recycling was built into the format. Along with other low-budget films, in the serial heavy use was made of stock footage. In addition, some serials, particularly those made by Mascot and Republic, used what was sometime called an 'economy chapter': an instalment a high proportion of which was made up of repeat footage from earlier in the narrative. This was justified as a reminder of plot developments that might have been seen a month or more before but commonly recognized as a cost-cutting device. The danger with such practices was that they could alienate their audience. Thus, following a screening of chapter seven of Republic's *The Fighting Devil Dogs*, regular contributor to the 'What the Picture Did For Me' column of *Motion Picture Herald* Sammie Jackson commented: 'Chapter Seven was the weakest so far. Nothing but scenes from previous chapters. I call it very "false economy". Other chapters good. Many complaints on Chapter Seven'.[1] Similarly, Mascot's *Fighting with Kit Carson* (1933), which came with multiple 'economy chapters', attracted complaints such as 'The entire first reel of the chapter sent was a rehash of preceding events' and 'entirely too much repetition of scenes'.[2]

This chapter of this book is not intended *as* an 'economy chapter': it does not recycle material that has already appeared, a practice unknown within academic publishing. It is *about* the 'economy chapter' and the importance of recycling in the serial but also more generally about the different commercial strategies adopted by filmmakers aiming to make a return on films that could play to sizeable audiences but where the ticket prices tended to be lower and the serial tended to take up a relatively small proportion of a programme's full running time.

Investigating this demands making distinctions within Hollywood's production base while exploring the connections that operated across such distinctions. Low-budget Hollywood filmmaking in the 1930s and 1940s is sometimes grouped together under the B-film label but more precisely seen as a combination of films produced by the B-units at the Hollywood Majors and the products of the so-called 'Poverty Row' studios. Ben Taves identified four categories within 'Hollywood's other half': in order of prestige, 1) major-studio 'programmers', sharing the characteristics of the A- and B-film, 2) major-studio B-films, 3) B-films made at smaller companies such as such as Republic and Mascot, and 4) 'the quickies of Poverty Row'.[3] For Yannis Tzioumakis, a fundamental distinction existed between the first and last of these: between the Majors and Poverty Row. Thus even Universal, a studio that lacked the prestige, resources and the cinemas of Hollywood's Big Five (Paramount, MGM, 20th Century-Fox, Warners and RKO) operated in a different world to Republic, who appealed to audiences 'interested in action, thrills, pace and adventure, spectacle, stunts' and

> tended to emphasise these elements often to the detriment of classical cinema staples such as 'coherence, mood and characterisation' that exemplified studio-produced A's and the majority of B's. This is particularly noticeable in comparisons between serials (particular types of pictures for the very specific audience of matinees) made by Republic/Mascot and its rival Universal. According to John Tuska, on the one hand the serials produced by Mascot were characterised by relentless action (as much as possible per episode), while not being very 'long on [narrative] logic'. On the other hand, Tuska argues, Universal's chapter plays 'tended to stress story as much as action', making them more suitable for a more sophisticated audience that could appreciate narrative pleasures as well as thrills.[4]

For Tzioumakis, Republic may have been 'the most successful financially and "artistically" Poverty Row studio in the 1930s and 1940s', but it was still a Poverty Row studio.[5]

We can go lower. Eric Schaefer distinguishes between the films of the Majors and Poverty Row studios on the one hand and on the other hand the 'exploitation' films of the studio era: the latter disregarded Holly-wood conventions and instead emphasized nudity, drug-taking, child-birth or other forms of 'forbidden spectacle'.[6]

The serial existed in a territory distinct from both the prestige of the Big Five and the forbidden spectacle of the exploitation picture. There were, however, links between these different varieties of filmmaking, at least at the level of personnel. The Mascot serial, *The Phantom Empire*, was co-directed by B. Reeves Eason, whose other work included directing the chariot race for *Ben-Hur* (1925) and the burning of Atlanta for *Gone with the Wind* (1939). Ralph Berger worked as art director on Universal serials including *Flash Gordon* but also on *The Lost City*, a 'quickie' directed by Harry Revier and produced by Sherman Krellberg. Revier went on to direct the exploitation film, *The Lash of the Penitentes* (1936), while Krellberg went on to distribute a number of Universal serials, including *Flash Gordon*.[7]

In order to examine these differences and connections, and the different commercial strategies adopted in film serial production, this chapter is divided into three sections. First I look at Universal, a company whose first serial, *Lucille Love, The Girl of Mystery*, was released in 1914, and who continued serial production up to the release of *The Mysterious Mr M* in 1946. Sherman Krellberg's company, Super-Serial Productions, operated at the other extreme from Universal in terms of resources and longevity: *The Lost City* was its sole production. Yet in the mid-1930s several such companies looked to the serial as a business opportunity; my second section is thus devoted to Krellberg and *The Lost City*. Finally, I examine Republic, the company established in 1935 which took over the serial production of Poverty Row studio Mascot, and went on to make some of the most commercially successful serials.

This will not provide a comprehensive industrial history of the serial; for a start it does not include Columbia, the other significant provider of serials from the late 1930s. It will indicate different commercial approaches to the serial from the lower reaches of the Hollywood Majors to filmmaking closer to exploitation cinema. It will also trace some of the ways in which these were inter-connected, complicating the Hollywood hierarchy.

Universal

While Universal was a Major studio it retained a commitment to the low-cost and short film that differentiated it from other Hollywood Majors.

'The serial, or chapter play, go on and on, a perennial staple product', claimed John Hall in 1932. '. . . Like Henry Ford, with his big Lincoln for the affluent and his famous "Lizzie" for everyman, the Laemmles have their high-class features heading the list for consistent quality, and the serials and westerns, all with the Universal brand, recognised as a guarantee of quality'.[8] Carl Laemmle himself later wrote of his realization 'that the basic principle of motion pictures and Mr Woolworth's innovation were identical . . . a small price commodity in tremendous quantities'.[9] Later commentators have picked up on the Woolworth analogy. For Douglas Gomery, if Paramount's Adolf Zukor 'wanted to be the US Steel of the movie industry', at Universal Carl Laemmle 'offered a Woolworth five and dime store'.[10] The Laemmle regime at Universal included periods when particular producers set out to make prestige films: Irving Thalberg before he went to MGM in the early 1920s, Carl Laemmle Jr with *All Quiet on the Western Front* (1931), *Sutter's Gold* (1936) and a handful of other big budget productions. However at this time the studio was more consistent in its regular output of low-budget westerns, short films and serials. With limited exceptions it avoided investing in cinemas. While Hollywood's 'Big Five' acquired cinema chains and came to dominate the first-run, downtown circuit, Universal specialized, as Richard Ward puts it, 'in the secondary, largely rural, independent theatre market'.[11]

The studio presented itself as the friend of the little man. This image is dramatized in the final chapter of *Tailspin Tommy*, one of the last serials of the Laemmle regime. Unusually, rather than ending with the death of the film's villain, the second half of 'Littlefield's Big Day' deals with the premiere of Venture Picture's *The Midnight Patrol*. However the star of the film within the film, Tailspin Tommy himself, is not at the 'Gloman's Mandarin Theatre' premiere in Hollywood, choosing instead to go back to his hometown of Littleville, where they have organized a reception for him and where he arranges an alternative premiere at the local Gem Theatre. Thus *Tailspin Tommy* ends by contrasting the Gloman premiere, announced as 'the greatest event Hollywood has ever witnessed', and that held at the Gem Theatre, where the guests are not major stars and producers in evening dress but locals such as the postmaster, and where the crowd wanting his autograph consists of the postmaster's slightly scruffy daughters. Receiving a wire from Hollywood asking where Tommy is when his public is waiting for him, the hero's answer is to turn to his girlfriend, Betty Lou Barnes, and his mother, and say 'Tell them . . . this is my public'.

Within two years the Laemmle regime was over and Universal was under the control of J. Cheever Cowdin's Standard Capital Company. However, Universal continued to produce serials as part of a mixed programme made up of shorts as well as features. A report on the studio's planned programme of releases for the 1933–34 season lists 'Two road show specials, six westerns, 42 feature productions, five serials, 52 two reel subjects and 59 one reelers'.[12] Four of the serials listed, *Gordon of Ghost City*, *Pirate Treasure*, *The Vanishing Shadow* and *The Perils of Pauline*, were directed by Ray Taylor, whose directorial debut was Universal's 1926 serial, *Fighting with Buffalo Bill*; the fifth, *The Adventures of Anne*, promoted as 'The First Musical-Mystery-Thrill-Serial Ever Produced!' was never made.[13] The similar 1945–46 programme consists of fifty-five features, including five 'specials' from outside productions, seven westerns, fifty-eight shorts (thirteen Walter Lantz Technicolor cartoons, fifteen Person-Oddities, fifteen Variety Views, thirteen Name Band Musicals and two special featurettes) and four serials (*Secret Agent X-9*, *The Royal Mounted Rides Again*, *The Scarlet Horseman* and *Lost City of the Jungle*).[14] Directorial responsibilities had changed by this date only to the extent that serial veteran Taylor was now listed as co-director with Lewis Collins.

The following year brought a more fundamental change when Leo Spitz and William Goetz took over production at Universal and it was decreed that the studio would henceforth only produce films lasting seventy minutes or more. 'Universal finds no further room for serials,' had one report, 'because 1) they no longer fit into the new and broader horizon and 2) because increased labor costs in Hollywood make them an unprofitable operation'.[15]

One of the ways in which Universal retained its commitment to the serial for such a long time was through selling them as part of a larger package. In 1925 it introduced its 'Complete Service Plan', a contract designed to supply independent exhibitors with a regular, mixed product. It excluded the studio's most prestigious 'Super-Jewel' productions, and its newsreels, but included a selection of western and other features, as well as shorter 'Century Comedies', 'Hysterical History' comedies, Western featurettes, Baby Peggy specials, 'Fast Stepper' two-reelers, the 'Leather Pushers' series, and serials.[16] It received mixed but often positive responses from exhibitors. Some resented it as another form of block booking while others welcomed it as an affordable way of allowing them to screen a programme of features and shorts.[17] There was enough support for Universal to launch later versions, including, in 1929, the Complete Sound Service Plan.[18] Again, serials were included within the package, in this instance *The Ace of Scotland Yard*, *Tarzan the Tiger*, *The Jade Box*, *The Lightning Express* and *Terry of the Times*.[19]

As a more substantial organization than other serial producers, Universal was able to draw on its network of exchanges as well as the production resources that differentiated it from Poverty Row. The studio generally avoided the sort of recycling evident in the *Fighting with Kit Carson* or *The Fighting Devil Dogs* 'economy chapters' and in its final serials made an effort to reduce the use of repeat footage at the beginning of each chapter. This still left *Lost City of the Jungle* (1946) with a total running time of three hours and five minutes excluding credits, introductions and chapter recaps, and four hours and twenty minutes including these.[20] It kept costs down by recycling sets, music and other films. *Flash Gordon* used sets from *Bride of Frankenstein* (1935), *The Invisible Man* (1933), *The Mummy* (1932) and *Just Imagine* (1930).[21] It included music from *The Invisible Man*, *White Hell of Pitz Palu* (1929), *The Black Cat* (1934), *Bombay Mail* (1934), *Destination Unknown* (1933) and *Werewolf of London* (1935).[22] Universal made extensive use of its newsreel library for stock footage, for instance inserting footage of the destruction of the Hindenberg into the final chapter of *The Phantom Creeps* (1939). Footage shot for the 1931 feature, *East of Borneo*, resurfaced in different Universal serials with 'jungle settings', such as *The Perils of Pauline* (1933) and *Call of the Savage* (1935), while the studio's distribution of European films was used to provide spectacle and running time in different serials: much of the second chapter of *The Great Alaskan Mystery* (1944) is taken from *S.O.S. Iceberg* (1933), *Flash Gordon Conquers the Universe* makes extensive use of *The White Hell of Pitz-Palu*, and some of the same footage from that film reappears in *Lost City of the Jungle*.

Having made so many serials, Universal could reuse footage from them in subsequent serials: stock footage in *The Master Key* (1945) included material from *The Green Hornet Strikes Again* (1940) ('coups & touring cars runby and accident at Draw Bridge'), *The Phantom Creeps* ('train runbys, and Signal Tower sequence'), *Gang Busters* (1942) ('Police Cars runbys, accident at bridge, Ambulance and Taxi runbys, black sedan in city streets etc.'), *The Adventures of the Flying Cadets* (1943) ('Airplane Flights and crash before passenger train'), *Junior G Men* (1940) ('Black sedan runbys'), *Flash Gordon Conquers the Universe* ('mob scenes and ambulance runbys') as well as footage from different Universal features.[23]

Universal also used footage from films made by other studios. Following a screening of the 1945 version of *Secret Agent X9*, sales manager E.L. McEvoy wrote to Morgan Cox to complain 'that even ten and twelve year old children are laughing at some of the climaxes that are put into Serials'; he highlighted sequences featuring a truck which at the end of chapter four is shown to be destroyed beyond recognition, but where the beginning of the following chapter reveals the truck and its driver to have suffered only minimal damage.[24]

Cox replied:

> Actually, the scene was one continuous shot, made by Warner Bros. for 'THEY DRIVE BY NIGHT' [1940]. The truck turns from the road, crashes through the railing, starts down the bank, comes up on end, spewing boxes, cans and crates in all directions, rolls over and comes up on its wheels, with a driver still behind the steering wheel. What I did was to cut this scene for the climax thrill at the point where the truck comes up on end. Apparently, the speed of the action creates an illusion of destruction which is not on the film. The pay off is the audience reaction—so you can chalk up an error to me.
>
> I am wholly in accord with the opinion that the take-out should always be plausible. It is, however, sometimes most difficult to achieve. Usually, this occurs when the climax is Stock, and it is necessary to gloss over the probability of the method of the escape in order to use the film. In such instances, it is a choice between reality and a sensational pictorial climax. If the take-out is not too far-fetched, I think it is good showmanship to sacrifice a modicum of reality for the thrill.

Cox went on to defend *Secret Agent X9* in terms that fit the narrative of Universal serials appealing to a relatively sophisticated audience (in comparison with Poverty Row serials) and providing something closer to classical Hollywood:

> . . . each week I look at the same chapter, numerically, of the current Republic and Columbia releases, comparing them with our own . . . There is no comparison. Our product, serial by serial, is superior in Production, Story, Cast and Direction. In addition, our chapters hold up after the first three with a consistency wholly lacking in the others, and we give full footage of new material.[25]

Cox took over Universal's serial production in 1944. Henry MacRae was his most significant predecessor. MacRae joined Universal in 1912, and in the silent era had an active directing career that appears to include the first werewolf film and the first Thai feature film.[26] He co-directed his first serial, *Liberty*, in 1916, and continued to direct serials and other action films up *The Lost Special* in 1932. In the silent era he worked as the Director-General at Universal, and in the sound era he went on to supervise serial production at the studio. There were occasions when he lost some of his authority (for instance in the period initially after the end of the Laemmle regime), or when his departure was announced (as in 1934 when it was reported that he was leaving Universal to produce westerns for Buck Jones). However, he had a knack of returning and regaining at least something close to his former position. He finally retired in 1944, and died shortly afterwards.

Jon Tuska refers to MacRae as 'a very limited director', adding that 'as a production supervisor he had great difficulty maintaining uniformity and quality in his serials at Universal'.[27] For Kalton Lahue the silent serials personally directed by MacRae 'were for the most part undistinguished and reflected his concept of the two-reel short . . . The fact that he was responsible for Universal's serial program may help to explain why other Universal serials were of an average calibre . . . Although he held important positions at Universal during the thirties, the picture business passed him by. He had become married to the way in which he had always produced pictures and didn't seem to comprehend that passing time brought with it new techniques of story telling'.[28] Yet Lahue also contributed to the reputation of the man elsewhere labelled the 'serial king'.[29] Describing how MacRae persuaded Laemmle to make *The Indians are Coming* as a sound film, Lahue wrote:

> With the studio promotion force behind it, the serial netted nearly $1,000,000 and was the first picture of its kind to open for a Broadway first run at the Roxy, turning the trick in mid-September, 1930. McRae had proved his point and had opened the doors for many great talking serials to come. By this time, silent pictures provided only 7 per cent of the over-all gross, and extinction was near. Will Hays wrote Laemmle: 'The entire motion picture industry owes you a debt of gratitude for *The Indians are Coming*. It brought 20,000,000 children back to the theatre'.[30]

This story has been repeated by others, the present writer included.[31] However, Hays's letter to Laemmle has proved elusive. The phrase 'Bring Back the Kids' was used in 1930, in advertisements for *The Indians are*

Coming.[32] It was more clearly evoked in 1936 *New York Times* and *Los Angeles Times* articles which reported that Will Hays identified *The Indians are Coming* as 'worth $20,000,000' to the film industry for bringing the young back to the movies.[33] The story was repeated in a 1941 *Showmen's Trade Review* article which identified *The Indians are Coming* as 'one of Universal's big money-makers for that year . . . [which] created a new market for chapterplays. For his work in bringing about this situation MacRae was commended in a letter from Will Hays, who expressed the thanks of the industry for bringing millions of children— today's adult movie patrons—back into the theatre'.[34] In Frederick C. Othman's account the figures had shifted to 'The Indians are Coming netted almost $1,000,000 and resulted in Will Hays, the movie czar, writing Laemmle, "The entire motion-picture owes you a debt of gratitude for The Indians are Coming. It brought 20,000,000 children back to the theater"'.[35]

Thus reports (a little over five years after the event) of the calculation that in encouraging cinema attendance among the young, *The Indians are Coming* was worth $20,000,000 to the film industry became (a little over twelve years after the event) a claim that the film brought 20,000,000 children back to the cinema, and that the film made a net profit of almost $1,000,000. The claim has been echoed in more recent accounts. The source for the net profit figure is unclear: it would have made *The Indians are Coming* one of the most profitable films of the time.[36] But Othman did not limit his claims to *The Indians are Coming*. In his words:

> Mr Mac makes his own rules. He's been manufacturing serials since 1914, without regard for what is known as the art of cinema. And serials, in case you didn't know it, are Hollywood's greatest money-makers. A *Gone with the Wind* [1939] comes every decade or so; MacRae makes four serials every year and every one of them earns around $500,000, net. Can a David O. Selznick match that? Or a Samuel Goldwyn? Or a Cecil B. DeMille? The answer lies in the fact that MacRae is the only man in all Hollywood who holds a life contract, without option, to make movies as he sees fit.[37]

In arguing for the importance of the film serial it is tempting to appeal to Othman's figures but they are reliable only in indicating efforts to promote MacRae's importance. Othman was not alone in making this case. In 1932 one trade publication included a poem dedicated to him.[38] The announcement of MacRae's funeral in another was followed by the statement that he was 'credited with introducing many innovations in production' including artificial light, wind machines, double exposure and shooting at night' and a list of honorary pall-bearers that ranged from key figures in the history of the serials such as Eddie Polo, Francis Ford, William Desmond, Ray Taylor and Breezy Eason, to those better known in other fields, including Carl Laemmle Jr, Frank Lloyd, Robert Z. Leonard, John Ford, Frank Borzage, King Vidor and Allan Dwan.[39] 'Si Laemmle es el *cerebro* de Universal City, Henry MacRae simboliza la acción', announced *Cine Mundial* in 1933.[40]

The innovations credited to MacRae appear also in the *Showmen's Trade Review* article that discussed *The Indians are Coming* in addition to praising MacRae for directing such 'outstanding chapter plays' as *The Perils of Pauline* (he produced the little known 1933 version but had nothing to do with the better known 1914 film), *Liberty* and the first airplane thriller, as well as for fostering careers including those of Lon Chaney, Rudolph Valentino, Tom Mix, Janet Gaynor, Ruth Roland, John Ford, Frank Borzage, Alan Dwan and King Vidor. Yet while the film industry trade press regularly referred to MacRae up to his death and funeral, he was subsequently all but forgotten. This indicates someone who was a skilled and influential operator within the film industry but also a shift at Universal, which only maintained a commitment to the serial for a further two years. Our subsequent reliance on figures such as those Othman gave for the net takings of *The Indians are Coming* highlights the general difficulty of assessing Hollywood profits as well the particular scarcity of information on the serial.

More information is available on budgets, though here also there are gaps and myths. One account has estimated the average cost of a 1930s Universal serial to be around $200,000 and identified the cost of the first *Flash Gordon* serial as 'reportedly $350,000', meaning that the budget of $182,000 for the second *Flash Gordon* serial was 'about *half* the original's cost'.[41] Other reports suggest a lower average serial cost but echo the point about *Flash Gordon*. Raymond William Stedman has it as 'reportedly $350,000', Wheeler Winston Dixon gives a 'rough' budget of $350,000, while Tuska suggests $360,000.[42] The star of the film, Buster Crabbe, later said that the money Universal put into the project came to $750,000 (though this included promotion costs), and also that the film was the studio's second most profitable film of the year, out-performed only by the Deanna Durbin picture, *Three Smart Girls* (1936).[43] Jim Harmon and Donald Glut claimed a budget in excess of a million dollars.[44]

The $182,000 *Flash Gordon's Trip to Mars* figure seems close to the truth. A studio memo identifies the cost of that serial to be 'about $170,000', adding that Barney Sarecky 'feels that it will be reduced to somewhere around $150,000'.[45] It was not: total cost was later given as $192,594.34.[46] All budgets I have seen for 1930s Universal serials are under $200,000. The twelve-chapter *The Indians are Coming* was budgeted at $179,760, a higher than usual figure due to the additional cost of sound recording.[47] Serials produced in the years immediately following were made for significantly less: $110,300 for *Finger Prints* (1930), $125,376 for *Heroes of the Flames* (1930), $120,900 for *Battling with Buffalo Bill* (1931), $104,370 for *The Spell of the Circus* (1931), $132,056 for *Heroes of the West* (1932), $146,556 for *Rustlers of Red Dog* (1934), $97,813 for *The Vanishing Shadow* (1934), $110,100 for *Ace Drummond* (1936), $120,927 for *Jungle Jim* (1936), $127,689 for *The Phantom Rider* (1936) ($25,000 of that was paid to its star, Buck Jones) and $133,530 for the 1937 version of *Secret Agent X-9*.[48] The unavailability of equivalent figures for *Flash Gordon* means that a higher figure is possible. However, if it had a budget so much higher than other serials it would have been in character for Universal to have used this in their promotion. Instead it highlighted the more modest *Hollywood Reporter* claim that 'Universal splurged over $200,000 on the 13-episode picture's budget'.[49] According to *Variety*, Universal 'upped the figure on "Flash Gordon" to a serial top of $200,000.'[50] *Flash Gordon* was a relatively expensive serial, but it is unlikely that it was much more expensive than its longer sequel.

The overall pattern seems clear. In the 1930s Universal occasionally made a serial for less than $100,000 and even in the latter half of the decade succeeded in keeping costs for some serials closer to $100,000 than $200,000. Some of its serials were more expensive productions. Costs rose more significantly in the 1940s. *Riders of Death Valley* (1940) was labelled Universal's 'million dollar serial': according to *Variety* it cost a more modest $325,000, though this was still 'a record sum for an episoder on that lot'.[51] *The Great Alaskan Mystery* (1944) had a budget of $199,500.00 and costs that rose to $216,020.26, the budget for *Jungle Queen* (1945) was $215,000 and for *Lost City of the Jungle* it was $258,750, final costs rising to $320,316. Universal's last serial, *The Mysterious Mr M*, had a budget of $250,000: $261,401 had been spent by 18 June 1946.

If one narrative has characterized the sound serial as a matter of nickel and dimes, with barrel-scrapping budgets matched by pocket-money takings, another has emphasized profits and even costs that could reach seven figures. The contradiction here fits the image of Universal up to and in the period immediately following the Laemmle regime: a

Hollywood Major specializing in low-budget films but remaining distinct from Poverty Row in its average budgets and ability to muster relatively lavish productions in specific instances, and with an interest in promoting its serials as distinct from its rivals. In fact, in the late 1930s Republic was able to make serials on at least the same scale as Universal (see below). However, Universal's overall average budgets were higher than those of its sound serial competitors, and the final serials made by Universal were markedly more expensive than Republic's serials of the same period. The studio did what it could to keep costs down. 'You can't gamble on making a pot of money,' Morgan Cox told a journalist during the production of *Lost City of the Jungle*. 'Rates are set to a dime and distribution is known. Therefore we know how much money we can spend and still make the necessary profit, and we have to budget exactly.'[52] Budgeting exactly seems to have been precisely what Universal failed to do in this instance, though this may have been partly because of the death of Lionel Atwill (who played the lead villain) during the production. In general, the production of even Universal's more expensive serials was done on as tight and economical basis as possible. Thus the working schedule for *The Mysterious Mr M* outlines a remarkably tight shooting programme between 23 May and 19 June 1946 for the thirteen-chapter serial, with breaks only for Sundays and the 30 May holiday. The number of set-ups a day ranged from twenty-seven (on the final day's shooting) and 111 (achieved on 1 June through first and second unit filming).

A further tension at Universal was between innovation and the reliance on longstanding practices. MacRae was both innovator (from wind-machines to werewolf movies) and the man left behind by the picture business. A similar case can be made about Universal more generally at this time. MacRae directed the first 'all-talking' serial (as well as earlier part-talking serials such as *The Ace of Scotland Yard* [1929]). With *Tailspin Tommy*, Universal was the first studio to use a comic strip as the basis for a film serial. Yet, an innovation in some respects, *The Indians are Coming* was also a return to the past and not just in its historical setting. One contemporary report had it that the title had 'been on every yearly schedule for the past eight years, and 1930 is no exception'.[53] That seems to be an exaggeration, but the title goes back at least as far as 1925, when it when it was announced as Universal's latest 'Jewel', directed by Edward Sedgwick.[54] Exhibitors were subsequently given a choice of titles: *The Indians are Coming* or *Flaming Frontiers*.[55] In 1926 Ray Taylor directed a serial, *Fighting with Buffalo Bill*, which credited William Lord Wright's adaptation of 'The Great West That Was' by William F. Cody, the same source credited in the 1931 serial, *Battling with Buffalo Bill* and *The Indians are Coming*, for which William Lord Wright also has a writing credit. No more averse to recycling titles than it was to using stock footage, in 1938 Universal released a serial titled *Flaming Frontiers*: chapter twelve was titled 'The Indians are Coming'.

It is perhaps not so surprising that Henry MacRae's funeral was such an event. It marked not just the death of an individual but of a phase in the history of the American film industry. After 1946 Republic and Columbia continued to make serials for a little over a decade but Universal effectively drew a line under this phase of its history.

Sherman Krellberg, Super-Serial Productions and *The Lost City*

In the years following 1946 the *Flash Gordon* serials continued to be distributed, within and beyond the United States, though generally not by Universal. Rights to distribute them, as well as *Ace Drummond, Buck Rogers, Don Winslow of the Navy, Don Winslow of the Coastguard, Radio Patrol, Red Barry* and *Tim Tyler's Luck*, were sold to Filmcraft, one of a number of companies operated by Sherman Krellberg and Joseph Harris. Filmcraft also purchased rights to distribute *Rocket Ship* and *Mars Attacks the World* (feature versions of the first two *Flash Gordon* serials), as well as other features including *Meet John Doe* (1941). It turned *Buck Rogers* into a feature, under the title *Planet Outlaws* (1953). The extent of its ownership remained the subject of some dispute.[56] However, Filmcraft and later Goodwill (another Krellberg and Harris company) persisted with the distribution of the Universal serials, serials made into features, and other features. As late as 1977, shortly before his death, Krellberg was still in correspondence with Universal about his plans for a re-release of *Mars Attacks the World*.[57]

This link between Universal and Krellberg highlights differences. Universal made a total of 144 serials. The company operated on the basis of a regular schedule of production as well as distribution, with the emphasis on the return that could be made from new releases. Only occasionally (for instance with the *Flash Gordon* serials) did Universal attempt to extend the life of individual serials through the release of a feature version. In contrast, Krellberg's assorted companies (including but not limited to Filmcraft and Goodwill) were designed to get the maximum return from a limited range of films.

At the same time Krellberg's interest in the entertainment industry was longstanding and wide-ranging. His involvement in the serial went back to the fifteen-chapter *The Fatal Fortune*, starring Helen Holmes, which he produced in 1919. However, his activities were weighted towards distribution, exhibition and financing. His interests in New York cinemas included the Astor, the Belmont (operated through Paradise Pictures) and the Bijou (through Joan of Arc Pictures). He specialized in importing films from overseas, and was not averse to showing these in abbreviated and doctored versions: his screening of Carl Dreyer's 1928 silent classic, *The Passion of Joan of Arc* (hence Joan of Arc Pictures), was in a sixty-one minute version with the intertitles replaced by what was advertised as 'The Magic Voice of David Ross, well known to radio millions'.[58] He had interests in 'legitimate' theatre: at one point his Goodwill Pictures co-owned the Belasco Theatre, and he was a producer of stage productions as well as films.[59] Initially working with his brother, Alfred Krellberg (attorney to the entertainment industry until his death in 1939) he was President of Amusement Securities Corporation, which financed films such as Sol Lesser's *Tarzan the Fearless* (1933) and the Halperin brothers' *White Zombie* (1932); the latter was the subject of a lengthy law suit in which Amusement Securities claimed ownership of the word 'zombie', with some initial success.[60] His other companies included Coronet Pictures, Krellbar Pictures Corporation, Principal Film Exchange, Regal Distributing Corporation, Regal Talking Pictures Corporation, Super-Serial Productions, Theatre Securities Syndicate, Ultra Film Distributors, and Ultra Pictures Corporation.[61]

The production of *The Lost City* came at a time when Mascot had demonstrated that if costs were kept down the serial remained a potentially viable form of film production even for those lacking the resources of the Major studios. It was a lesson picked up by other companies such as Sam Katzman's Victory Pictures, which in 1936 announced plans for 'four exploitation pictures, two musicals and two serials'.[62] *The Lost City* was similarly presented as part of a slate of serials and features.

It was initially announced as a Sol Lesser production, though nothing else suggests Lesser's involvement.[63] Krellberg's subsequent statement that Amusement Securities Corp. was financing six melodramas, two serials and four features with Lightning the Dog was later amended to three Lightning the Dog features and two serials, the latter to exist in different formats: as twelve two-reel episodes, a feature version of their first four episodes followed by eight two-reel episodes and a feature version of the complete serial.[64] The second, underwater, serial which Krellberg was to produce was later identified as *Despots of the Deep*. A further, Krellberg-produced serial was announced in 1940. The fifteen-chapter *Sign of the Zombies*, 'for presentation in both white and colored houses', dealing with 'G-Man activities in routing out racketeering gangs who prey upon negro communities', was to feature world heavy-weight champion Joe Louis in a leading role.[65] The initial twelve film production slate never materialized, and neither *Despots of the Deep* nor *Sign of the Zombies* got off the ground, though Lightning the Wonder Dog did appear in the Regal production, *When Lightning Strikes* (1935). A further Regal production, *Thunderbolt* (1935), featured Lobo the Marvel Dog.

The incorporation of Super-Serial Productions (the company identified in the film credits) was only announced in June 1934, with capital of $20,000 and Alfred but not Sherman Krellberg listed as one of three stockholders.[66] *The Lost City*, in its different versions, proved to be its sole production. Shot on the former Mack Sennett lot in San Fernando Valley then being used by Mascot and later used by Republic, its twenty-one day shooting schedule, with three crews working simultaneously, was apparently an attempt to complete the film before Mascot's *The Phantom Empire*.[67] Speed was clearly the main priority. Editing was completed by mid-January, and both serial and feature versions were reviewed in February.[68] It only came to the attention of the Production Code Administration in April 1935, when some concern was expressed at the extent to which Joseph Breen would allow 'brutal and gruesome scenes in pictures of this type known as horror pictures, similar to the Frankenstein pictures', and how many cinemas were showing films without a proper PCA certificate. Yet the feature was passed with only three minor deletions; the PCA does not appear to have viewed the serial.[69]

Daily Variety's verdict was 'All in all, feature cannot get far, but producer apparently figures to nab a few bookings in isolated spots and trust to sale of the feature in those foreign countries where he cannot dispose of the serial rights'.[70] In fact, the feature proved to be a remarkable success when it played at the Globe in downtown New York; it took $14,683 in its first week in comparison to the $2,200 taken the previous week by *Hei Tiki: A Saga of the Maoris* (1935), and was still playing at the cinema after six weeks.[71] Its very shortcomings may have been part of its appeal. At the Orpheum in Lincoln, Nebraska, where the feature played a four-day run with *I've Been Around* (1935), the exhibitor reported that 'Patrons figured "City" was a comedy and biz. held up well'.[72] An exhibitor in Indiana wrote: 'We showed the first four chapters and discovered this was the worst piece of hokum ever to be presented on the screen, so we brought the feature and cancelled the remaining eight chapters and put an end to our misery'.[73]

Some reviews were more positive. *Film Daily* described it as possessing 'thrills, novelty, suspense and continued interest' and even claimed that it was 'well-produced and well-performed in its principle roles'.[74] One 'What the Picture Did For Me' contributor had: 'No doubt the dizziest plot ever filmed, but our patrons eat it up and keep coming back for more. If your crowd likes action pictures, you can't miss'.[75] However, as others have pointed out, Krellberg's expertise lay in his knowledge of the exhibition and marketing sides of the industry rather than the niceties of filmmaking.[76] He succeeded in selling *The Lost City* at home and abroad before shooting had begun.[77] The process continued in the year of its release. A report that the feature had been booked by RKO for its metropolitan houses accompanied the announcement that United Artists would be handling distribution of serial and feature versions in Cuba, Central America and South America.[78] In fact, United Artists seemed to have only dealt with the feature, as part of a package of 52 features and around 30 shorts, but there were separate agreements to distribute the serial in Puerto Rico, Santo Domingo, Haiti, Peru, Bolivia, Ecuador and Venezuela.[79] The Krellberg papers at the Library of Congress also include distribution agreements for screening serial and feature versions in Atlanta, Charlottesville, New Orleans, Memphis and Washington DC (20 September 1946) but also China, Hong Kong and Macao (3 July 1946), Greece (2 December 1946), Singapore, Straits Settlement, Federated and Non-Federated Malay States, Siam, Dutch East Indies (including Sumatra) (16 June 1947), Chile and Peru (11 August 1948) and the serial alone in the Philippines (dated 26 September 1945), Venezuela, Curacao and Aruba (4 June 1947), Cuba (3 September 1947), Puerto Rico and Dominican Republic (13 October 1947).

Krellberg, however, did not limit himself to one serial and one feature version. *The Lost City* was initially announced in three versions: as twelve two-reel episodes, as a feature made up of the first four episodes followed by eight two-reel episodes, and as a single feature: some subsequent accounts refer to three 1935 versions.[80] None of the sources I have consulted from this year refer to more than one feature version, but Krellberg did release a further feature version in 1943, retitled *City of Lost Men*.[81] He even recycled footage from *The Lost City* in his feature version of *Buck Rogers*: additional footage at the beginning of *Planet Outlaws* includes scenes from the beginning of *The Lost City*, alongside sequences in which Krellberg himself is shown, justifying the fantastic nature of the adventures of Buck Rogers with lines such as 'Jules Verne once dreamed of exploring the ocean depths, and in time we have the submarine'.

The practice of recycling was common to the serial, but it was also to other, even less-reputable forms of filmmaking. Thus Eric Schaefer cites *The Lash of the Penitentes* (1936) as an example of a commercially successful exploitation film that combined documentary footage of the secretive sect, Los Hernanos Penitentes, with a semi-fictionalized drama about the murder of a man investigating the cult. It was directed by Harry Revier, who, in Schaefer's words, 'peddled the film under the title *The Penitentes Murder Case* for a year before selling the feature to Michael J. Levinson, who kept it in circulation for decades.[82] The promise of 'adult' material in *The Lash of the Penitentes* might suggest a significant gap between such exploitation films and the film serial, associated as the latter is with the child audience. Yet in key ways Krellberg functioned like Levinson, working with material that was part-recycled and generally held in low-regard, and making money by keeping that material in circulation for decades. While Universal had its own exchanges for film distribution, serials such as *The Lost City* were sold through the 'States Rights' system, which involved selling exclusive distribution rights for a territory for a set period of time, a practice common to Poverty Row and the exploitation trade.[83]

There are more direct links. As well as directing *The Lash of the Penitentes*, and continuing his association with the exploitation film with *Child Bride* (1941), Harry Revier's career went back to the origins of Hollywood (the Burns and Revier Studio was where Cecil B. De Mille directed *The Squaw Man* in 1914); it also included directing both *Planet Outlaws* and *The Lost City* for Krellberg.[84] Zelma Carroll's film credits were more limited: she wrote the original story for *The Lost City* and the screenplay for *The Last of the Penitentes*. Roland Price, who shared *The Lost City* cinematography credits with Edward Linden, also went on to work on *The Lash of the Penitentes*, as cinematographer (he is credited as 'Roland C. Price, the vagabond cameraman'), and shared the writing and directing credits on that film, which the Internet Movie Database lists as produced by Roland C. Price Productions.[85]

In part this highlights the diversity of the personnel working on *The Lost City*. Revier provides a link with the exploitation film. *The Lost City* art director Ralph Berger's work at Universal included serials such as *Tailspin Tommy* and *Flash Gordon*. Ken Strictfaden provided the electrical effects for *The Lost City*, Universal features and serials (including *Frankenstein* [1931] and *The Vanishing Shadow* [1934]) as well as on

Stage and Screen's *The Clutching Hand*. Edward Linden, Price's fellow cinematographer, has credits that include other serials (such as *Jungle Menace* [1937]), exploitation films (*Assassin of Youth* [1937]) and *King Kong* (1933). There were, however, particularly strong links between *The Lost City* and *The Lash of the Penitentes/The Penitentes Murder Case*.

The film itself appeared in different forms and contexts and under different labels. Identified as 'for juvenile audiences', at one cinema the initial feature version found a place alongside *What Becomes of the Children?* (1936) as one of '2 first-run features ... an adult show'.[86] As *City of Lost Men* it appeared in a double-bill with Fritz Lang's *M*, the latter now named *M—The Kidnapper* and promoted with an image of Peter Lorre as 'M—the lust murderer' alongside that of one of the 'giant men' of Krellberg's film. For a producer such as Krellberg one of the attractions of the serial was clearly its adaptability. One reviewer of the initial feature version identified it as offering 'the greater appeal via the serial route, since its makeup is of the sort to find best reaction from the youngsters and those adults who, not particular as to performances and the ring of authenticity in situations, like their screen fare in the action tempo of melodrama. Here is week-end material'.[87] Another described that version as 'good fodder for the ballyhoo grinds ... Probably will show up better in chapter form'.[88] Its commercial success in its different formats cut across the children's matinee, the products of the Hollywood Majors, adult exploitation and art-house cinema. According to Tuska, the money it made enabled Krellberg to purchase the rights from Paramount to six Hopalong Cassidy features.[89] It presumably also helped him purchase the *Flash Gordon* films and other serials.

Krellberg's interest in the serial lasted well beyond the 1930s but the particular circumstances that led him to serial production did not. Other independent production companies had abandoned the serial by the end of the decade. In 1937 Sam Katzman's Victory made *Blake of Scotland Yard*, its final serial. By that year Louis Weiss, producer of *The Clutching Hand* (1936) was making serials for Columbia. Though Weiss had his own company, Adventure Films, the film serial was now essentially in the hands of Columbia, Universal and Republic.

Republic

Republic was established the same year that *The Lost Jungle* was released but Republic adopted a very different strategy from Krellberg in its search for economic return. While it did not have the resources of the

Hollywood Majors in some ways it exemplifies the studio system. It operated through regular and regimented production and distribution while its serials were based on regimented exhibition.

The key figure at Republic was Herbert Yates, whose Consolidated Film Industries had been incorporated in 1924 and had quickly become established as the major film processing company in the United States. Consolidated also provided much of the finance for the serial specialist studio, Mascot. Republic was formed in 1935 through the amalgamation of a number of small studios that specialized in low-budget films: Monogram, Mascot, Liberty, Majestic, Winchester and (in 1936) Supreme Pictures.[90] The amalgamation brought together different specializations, and in particular the production facilities that Mascot had been using and Monogram's distribution exchanges. Initially the new company was run by key individuals from the different companies that had been combined: W. Ray Johnston and Trem Carr from Monogram, Nat Levine from Mascot, as well as Yates. However, within a short period of time first Johnston and Carr and then Levine left, leaving Yates in control.

The subtitle of Richard Maurice Hurst's study of Republic, 'Between the Majors and Poverty Row', accurately locates the studio outside the Hollywood oligopoly while distinguishing it from the companies it took over.[91] Republic only joined the Motion Picture Producers Association in 1941. Universal had differentiated their 'Jewel' and even more expensive 'Super-Jewel' productions from their low-budget 'Red Feather' westerns. Similarly, Republic films ranged from 'Jubilee' westerns with a budget no higher than $50,000 to (in the post-war period) 'Premiere' pictures with named directors and costs that could run into seven figures.[92] However, even the latter tended to be westerns or action films. In a variation of Universal's strategy, Republic identified its market as lying outside the first-run downtown cinemas in the major cities, and to a large extent aimed its films at small-town cinemas in the American Midwest and South (in addition to the overseas market). It set out to develop efficiency of production and distribution within those limits.

Emphasis was placed on technical expertise. Once established at the old Mascot Studio, Republic set about developing the facilities. It gained a particularly high reputation for its sound recording facilities, winning an Academy Award in 1946 for its music auditorium. While Universal recycled music from other films, Republic tended to use specially composed scores. The special effects department run by Howard and Ted Lydecker could, Hurst argues, result in sequences that were superior to many other productions of their time or later.[93]

In the 1930s, Universal's investment in the serial was extended through the purchase of the rights to comic strip stories such as *Tailspin Tommy* and *Flash Gordon*, a practice continued in the 1940s in Columbia films such as *Terry and the Pirates* and *Batman*. In contrast, Poverty Row studios, notes Tzioumakis, were only likely to adapt material from other media when rights were cheap or in the public domain.[94] However, in the late 1930s Republic showed its competitive intent in the newly invigorated serial market, purchasing the rights to popular comic strip and radio characters such as Dick Tracy and the Lone Ranger. It developed plans to bring Superman to the screen, though these were never realized and the alleged similarities between Superman and Republic's *The Adventures of Captain Marvel* led to a lengthy legal battle.

Republic's challenge to Universal and later Columbia was based on streamlined efficiency.[95] Serial production was regimented, a process begun at the writing stage. Taking either a subject for adaptation or simply a title given to them by head office, screenwriters had three months to develop the story, working a regular nine to five week plus half days on Saturdays. Individual chapters were divided between a team of writers prior to conferences to discuss the different drafts. Producers and directors became involved on completion of the full draft. Filming schedules were tight. As at Universal, out of sequence shooting not only helped cut down the length of footage but also allowed for the employment of second rank name actors as villains at a relatively higher rate but for a limited period of time: in the case of *Spy Smasher* (1942) this meant that 1,773 scenes were shot over thirty-two days.[96] Mathis notes that:

> Editing was accomplished at the rate of one episode per week, and, after additional intervals for sound-effects compilation, music-scoring, dubbing and printing, a National Release Date was set according to the availability at exchanges of the sixth or seventh episode depending on whether it was a 12-chapter or 15-chapter opus . . . . By the time a backlog of half the number of episodes comprising a given serial had been accumulated, Republic began making release prints of the first chapter available to exchanges even though the editing had not been completed on the final chapters.[97]

Budgets were generally, but not always, lower than those at Universal. Costs ranged from the $82,616 budget and $87,655 negative costs of *The Vigilantes are Coming* (1936) to the $182,623 budget and $222,906 negative costs of *Captain America* (1944): Mathis estimated that in addition distribution costs (including publicity) would come to around $30,000 for a serial, while print costs would be upwards of $50,000 for 100 prints or more.[98] Republic invested significant funds into *The Lone Ranger* (1938, budget $160,315, negative cost $168,117) and *The Lone Ranger Rides Again* (1939, budget $193,878, negative cost $213,997). Both were more costly than Universal's 1938 western serial, *Flaming Frontiers* (budget $150,000, negative costs $159,193). Universal's *Sea Raiders* (1941) was kept to a negative cost of $150,145, while the negative costs for Republic's 1941 serials was $145,588 (*The Adventures of Captain Marvel*), $177,404 (*Jungle Girl*), $139,701 (*King of the Texas Rangers*) and $175,919 (*Dick Tracy vs. Crime Inc.*). However, the first half of the 1940s saw costs steadily increase at Universal but not at Republic. Aside from *Captain America, Secret Service in Darkest Africa* (1943), *Tiger Woman* (1944) and *Haunted Harbor* (1944), also had negative costs over $200,000, but subsequent Republic serials were kept below that figure. Republic serials released in 1946 cost $138,924 (*The Phantom Rider*), $137,320 (*King of the Forest Rangers*), $140,146 (*Daughter of Don Q*) and $161,174 (*The Crimson Ghost*), significantly less than the Universal serials of that year. Republic's final serial, *King of the Carnival*, was made for $177,050, less than some of its serials from the 1930s.

While Universal responded to rising costs by spending more before abandoning serials entirely, Republic persisted with serial production for a further decade but was able to do this by keeping costs down. This was achieved partly through shorter chapters and smaller casts. Over time it reduced the number of serials it produced, switching from four new serials a year to three and one re-issue and then two new serials and two re-issues. While Universal showed little interest in the serial after 1946, Republic (like Krellberg) did its best to make money from its serials years after their initial release, through reissues and feature film versions.

One strategy that Republic came to adopt was to reissue old serials under new titles: *Darkest Africa* became *King of Jungleland*, *Haunted Harbor* became *Pirates' Harbor*... The 'economy chapter' discussed at this chapter's beginning provided a means of recycling material within the serial, while individual shots could also be repeated throughout a serial: in *Daredevils of the Red Circle*, for instance, the same establishing shot of the Granville House appears in the first, second, fifth, sixth, ninth, tenth and twelfth chapters.

Recycling was not cost-free and the need to keep costs down had to be balanced against other considerations. Costs were not necessarily limited to the $2.50 to $7.50 per foot Republic itself charged in the 1940s but could include fees payable to individuals not under contract to the studio.[99] While later Universal serials moved to filming additional scenes for chapter recaps, Republic persisted with the use of repeat footage, though often in relatively brief sequences. It made significant use of stock footage. However, at least in the late 1930s and early 1940s it did its best to avoid the combination of ill-matching footage evident in serials from Serial Attractions' *Queen of the Jungle* (1935) to Universal's *The Phantom Creeps* (1939). When stock was used in his films, 'We used it better than the original picture did!' claimed William Witney.[100]

Questions over the rights to particular films could also complicate issues. In 1952 Saul Rittenberg cautioned that footage from *King of the Royal Mounted* (1940) could be used as stock

> provided that the amount taken and used, in any instance, is not so extensive as to constitute a substantial part of the new picture. Otherwise, it might successfully be contended that the new picture is a remake or a new picture based on the 'KING OF THE ROYAL MOUNTED' material, which you have no authority to make.
>
> Furthermore, in my opinion the stock material used by you must not be such as to be identifiable with 'KING OF THE ROYAL MOUNTED'. For example, it should not identify any of the 'KING OF THE ROYAL MOUNTED' characters, nor should any incidents taken from any of the comic strips or portraying any distinctive part of the 'KING OF THE ROYAL MOUNTED' material or formula be identifiable.[101]

Overall, serials proved to be highly lucrative for Republic, at least into the 1940s. Mathis estimates that every serial Republic made in its first seven years made a profit. Figures are more difficult to establish after this date, owing to the practice of diverting costs from over-budget features. Over time serial production, and the production values of serials, decreased. Yet while serials became less profitable, the financial problems that Republic encountered in the mid-1950s were primarily caused by its big budget, feature productions. At an earlier date the weekly edition of *Variety* (a publication that had tended to ignore serials) claimed 'Cliffers Bring Biggest Profits'.[102] Serials were heralded as the only form of filmmaking offering 'secure profit-grabbing possibilities', their fixed market providing grosses of between 100 and 200 per cent 'over and above the lensing outlay'. Citing the profits of *The Lone Ranger* and *Dick Tracy*, the article quoted Yates as saying: 'Show me the feature made on an equal investment that can equal those figures'. Some of the figures quoted in the article (such as the $1,350,000 profit attributed to *The Lone Ranger*) don't match those found in other sources, but the key point holds: at this moment in time the serial was seen by some as more financially reliable than the feature film. Republic had particular success with this form of film production.

Conclusion

The business of American filmmaking in the 1930s and 1940s is normally understood in terms of a mature oligopoly in which five major companies dominated the production, distribution and exhibition of feature films, augmented by three companies who acted as producers and distributors and a small number of high-end independents. This picture is incomplete in different ways. Alongside the feature film of an hour or longer, production companies continued to make short films and serials, and this was notably the case at Universal up until 1946. Alongside the Hollywood Majors and the films made by Selznick, Goldwyn and Disney, a significant number of smaller companies regularly produced films that differed from those of the Hollywood Majors in varying degrees. Lumping these together under the label 'Poverty Row' obscures significant distinctions. At one point the resources of Republic approached and in some respects exceeded those of Universal. For other companies the label Poverty Row was more appropriate. Their limited resources were matched by their limited lifespan.

The film serial only formed part of the production policy of a small number of companies. After 1937 that number was reduced to three, after 1946 to two. In the 1930s and 1940s, Universal, Mascot and then Republic and Columbia operated on the basis of producing a regular number of serials each year. This wasn't possible for less well-established producers. However the success of Mascot demonstrated that in the 1930s it was possible for a minor company with limited resources to make money from serials. The cost of most sound era serials ran into six figures; one way of keeping down the cost of a B-western feature was to reduce the running time to an hour or less, but even when Republic reduced chapter length to thirteen and a half minutes their serials remained longer in total than even a lengthy feature film. Some of the lowest production values can be found in the longest sound serial, *The Black Coin* (1936), made for the Weiss Brothers' Poverty Row Stage and Screen Company. It has a total running time of 323 minutes.

The serial shared with the exploitation film two key strategies for minimalizing cost: padding and recycling.[103] In the middle of chapter six of Metropolitan's *The Sign of the Wolf* (1931) there is a cut to a saloon bar, a call of 'Rose, how about a little dance', followed by a dance performed by a woman otherwise only glimpsed in the background. The scene ends when the dance is finished. It has no narrative function and no link to the narrative but it has filled the time at relatively low cost. However, this was not a practice distinct to the minor studios. More than any other serial producer, Universal had a tendency to pad out serial chapters. Much of the third chapter of *The Adventures of Frank Merriwell* is taken up with the different acts of a college show while chapter five includes several minutes of wood felling stock footage lacking any narrative purpose. At Republic, in contrast, shorter chapter length and a tight structure left little room for padding, and while the often extensive fight scenes did little to advance the narrative they clearly functioned as one of the primary attractions.

Recycling was common to all serials, in different ways and to varying degrees. It defines the serial, and was both a commercial and aesthetic strategy. Stock footage was used in serials from *The Lost City* to *Lost City of the Jungle*. The latter's use of footage from *The White Hell of Pitz-Palu* that the studio had already inserted into *Flash Gordon Conquers the Universe* amounted to recycling what it had already recycled. In the first ten years of its existence Republic tended to use stock in relatively brief segments and to take more care integrating stock and new footage.

The serial was a form of filmmaking particularly dependent on regularity of production, distribution and exhibition, and thus on a studio system of some kind. In the 1930s a number of smaller companies with an interest in the serial re-emerged. In some instances these set out to produce serials on a regular, medium term basis, though such plans were invariably cut back or abandoned, and in all instances such companies relied on the commercial framework of distributors or exhibitors. The overall length of a single serial, and the difficulties of making a one-off sale of a film that needed to run between ten and fifteen weeks, made this form of filmmaking a challenge to newcomers. However, attempting to compete at the prestige end of the market could be an even greater challenge. In the mid-1930s there remained enough demand at home and abroad to attract companies such as Burroughs-Tarzan Enterprises, Victory Picture, and Super-Serial Productions to this strand of filmmaking.

That situation didn't last. The last 'independent' serial was made in 1937, leaving the market for Universal (until 1946), Columbia and Republic. With a regular schedule of serial production and a distribution network covering significant territory in the United States and other countries even during the Second World War (when Latin America took on even greater significance), these companies were able to make money from serials up to 1946. After that date Republic and Columbia continued to produce serials but in decreasing numbers, on a more parsimonious basis and with smaller return. The general exclusion of serials from first-run cinemas deprived them of the most lucrative end of exhibition but the number of American cinemas that were showing serials in the 1930s and 1940s, and the size of their audience, meant that they could bring in significant revenues. In 1947 it was estimated that around 8,000 of the 18,765 cinemas in the US still regularly showed serials, a further 2,000 showed serials on an irregular basis, while the average serial was seen by an audience of between four and five million.[104] Serials such as *Flash Gordon*, *Dick Tracy* and *The Lone Ranger* demonstrated that the serial could take significantly more than the few dollars indicated in some accounts. Even a low-budget serial such as *The Lost City* could play relatively widely (if often as a feature rather than a serial), while other serials provided reliable if not spectacular revenues.

When *Variety* claimed in 1940 that the serials of Universal, Columbia and Republic had become the most reliable form of film production it added that Paramount, Metro, 20th Century-Fox, Warners and RKO, were 'understood to be gazing at the trio's cliffhanger takes with envious eye'.[105] The Big Five may have looked to the serial for reasons beyond the financial viability of individual productions. In the 1930s the Hollywood Majors set up their own B-film production units, concerned that Poverty Row studios might be making in-roads into their box-office dominance through cheaply-made films that could form part of a double-bill. While this helped the Majors retain their dominance, the double-bill remained. The potential of a fuller programme could represent one means of countering the expense of this; a move towards the single feature supported by a programme of shorter items, a serial included, could lessen the pressure on feature film production that was driven by the prevalence of the double bill. In the words of Thomas Doherty: 'Shorts served as the main defence against a programming practice the Majors vehemently opposed: the double bill'.[106]

Ultimately, however, it remained the *series* that appealed to the Big Five, as to other players in the American film industry. This illustrates the gap between Hollywood studios as much as it illustrates their

96

relationship. MGM's production schedule included *relatively* low budget titles and films that could be fitted into a programme alongside a longer feature. It was possible for an actor such as Ann Rutherford to move from a 1935 Mascot serial (*The Fighting Marines*) to a regular role (from 1937) in the Andy Hardy films, and for Nat Levine, the man in charge of Mascot and later of serial production at Republic, to end up (briefly) working for Louis B. Mayer at MGM. Yet both Mascot and Republic were a world away from MGM.

The serial represented a distinct commercial strategy. Like the studio system as a whole it was based on regularity of production and standardization of product, indeed, it took these far further than the feature film. It perpetuated a form of cinema that had emerged in the 1910s: it was rooted in the past but could be adapted to the present. The continuation of serial production well into the sound era illustrates how different business frameworks could co-exist, alongside different film styles.

4

The Second Chapter, 1930–46

The serials themselves are seemingly obvious. At the most basic level they are cliffhangers. The cliffhanger became more than a device used in almost every serial chapter but the final one. It was itself almost always restricted to situations that placed the hero in mortal danger. It also defined the overall serial structure, with each episode leading up to this climatic moment.

William Roberts in the *Los Angeles Times* and Lewis Herman in his *Practical Manual of Screen Playwriting* explored this a little further. They broke down the serial structure, identifying patterns within and across the serial chapter, emphasizing more than the end-episode cliffhanger but only adding weight to the point that this was a formulaic product. Jack Mathis described a similar pattern in his discussion of Republic serials. In his words, after an opening chapter that was relatively long due to the initial exposition it had to provide in addition to the standard serial elements:

> All subsequent episodes abided by a more regimented format beginning with the 'overlap' or repeat footage from the end of the preceding chapter, which culminated in the 'takeout' or escape from the previous peril. Exposition then moved the story along to the 'middle action', or a chase or fight segment that occurred approximately midway through the episode, followed by more exposition leading up to the 'cliffhanger', or predicament imperilling the principles that ended the chapter.[1]

This is useful and relatively accurate as far as it goes but deserves further scrutiny. That is, the pattern mapped out for Republic serials provides a useful starting point for a closer analysis of the serials themselves, including those made by Universal, Columbia and other companies. Republic serials have tended to dominate what discussion there has been of the sound serial structure. This is an attempt to provide a broader picture while maintaining a concern for the detail of the individual serial.

Of course, any study will be selective. This is the basis of research. In Tzvetan Todorov's words:

> One of the first characteristics of scientific method is that it does not require the user to observe every instance of a phenomenon in order to describe it: scientific method proceeds rather by deduction. We actually deal with a relatively limited number of cases, from them we deduce a general hypothesis by other cases, correcting (or rejecting) it as needs be.[2]

Or, as Steve Neale noted, it is impossible to write about film genres without being selective. Yet Neale went on to point out the problem of using pre-established and unquestioned canons of films as the basis for selection, and to quote Alan Williams' call for a study of genre based in part on 'studying all films, regardless of perceived quality'.[3] To study the serial is itself to move beyond the filmmaking canon. This study is concerned also not to limit itself to a canon of film serials.

My strategy is to use this book chapter to focus on the serial's second chapter. The often more extended opening chapter has to set-up the serial's overall pattern and therefore has its own distinct structure: the second chapter is more representative. This will allow me to examine a relatively wide range of the serials made at Republic, Universal, Columbia, Mascot and smaller companies such as Stage and Screen Productions, and to examine the cliffhanger but also other serial chapter features. In addition, in the interest of providing as comprehensive picture as possible, at the end of this chapter I have included an Appendix with a full list of the cliffhangers used at the end of the second chapters of available serials made between 1930 and 1946.

Picking up on the model outlined above, my chapter is divided into two parts: the first examines how the second serial chapter is framed (in Mathis's terms, the opening overlap/takeout and the closing cliffhanger, though I also consider the introduction), the second the material within that frame (the middle action, here including all material from the instigation of the new line of action to the closing section, in effect in most instances examining the movement from one cliffhanger to the next). In two places I refer to chapters other than the second: when discussing the 'death' of the hero in *Robinson Crusoe of Clipper Island*

(1936), *The Desert Hawk* (1944) and *The Phantom Empire* (1935), and in the concluding section. Otherwise my comments here are limited to the second chapter of the different serials. I will use the next chapter of this book to examine the narrative as it runs across the serial as a whole, where I will need to limit the discussion to more detailed examination of a smaller number of serials.

At the heart of this is a concern with close observation and analysis. This is particularly important for the current study given the dearth of critical material on many of the films I am discussing. The material that has been published on the sound serial has tended to avoid analysis, while film analysis has tended to avoid the film serial. There are signs that this is changing, but as yet little scholarly work has been done on *The Lone Defender* (1930), *The Vigilantes are Coming* (1936) or *The Mysterious Mr M* (1946).

Introduction, Recap, Take-Out and Cliffhanger

Serial chapters do not begin with a recap. Like other films they have credits, though credits that are distinctive in the way in which they function also as introductions to the leading characters and/or recaps of the story so far. Thus the pattern of overlap followed by take-out can be better described as one of introduction, recap and take-out.

The credits for Columbia's 'Trap of the Wasp' (*Mandrake the Magician* [1939]) include short filmed sequences, preceding the introduction of the rest of the cast), introducing 'Warren Hull as MANDRAKE', 'Doris Weston as BETTY HOUSTON', 'Al Kikume as LOTHAR' and 'Rex Downing as TOMMY HOUSTON', 'Edward Earle as DR. ANDRE BENNETT' and 'Forbes Murray as PROFESSOR HOUSTON', 'Kenneth MacDonald as JAMES WEBSTER' and 'Don Beddoe as FRANK RAYMOND', and finally '? ? as THE WASP'. Each of these is filmed in front of a curtain, and the theatricality is highlighted further when Kikume/Lothar bows to the audience (Fig. 4). In part this fits the particular serial, based as it is around the performances of a stage magician, but introducing key players is a more general feature. The serial announces its own performance.

Other serials introduce the character but not the actor, while using this also as a plot recap. Thus, following the cast list, Mascot's 'One for All and All for One!' (*The Three Musketeers* [1933]) provides successive title cards accompanied by pictures of the characters: 'The Three Musketeers are soldiers of the Foreign Legion', 'Their pal Tom Wayne is a fugitive

4. Mandrake the Magician (1939)

from justice—falsely accused of having murdered his friend Armand Corday, an officer of the Legion', 'The real murderer is El Shaitan, the mysterious and powerful chief of the Devil's Circle, who is plotting an Arab rebellion against the Foreign Legion', 'Wayne's former sweetheart, Elaine Corday, believing him guilty of her brother's death, is riding to capture Tom with the aid of a band of Arabs', 'Meanwhile Tom and his airplane mechanic, Stubbs, flying over an abandoned prison where El Shaitan has stored a large shipment of arms, are attacked by El Shaitan in a sensational air battle'.

Republic initially continued this approach. 'Birth of the Vigilantes' (*The Vigilantes are Coming*) introduces the hero—'Don Loring, disguised as "The Eagle", sets out to prevent Jason Burr's conquest of California'; villains—'Jason Burr—first discoverer of western gold wants to become dictator of California', 'Count Raspinoff—emmissary [sic] of the Tzar, negotiates with Burr to bring California under the Russian flag'; sympathetic support—'Father Jose—beloved leader of a peaceful flock, helps Don meet the menace of Russian tyrany [sic]'; heroine—'Doris Colton—who is held prisoner by Burr, along with her father, a mining engineer', and comic sidekicks—'Salvation & Whipsaw—hardy pioneers who blazed trail with Fremont, find Don a worthy leader'. As Kristin Thompson notes of Hollywood more generally, 'In most films, as soon as the characters appear, or even before we see them, they are assigned a set of clear traits'.[4] In the serial, titles served to assign traits and position the characters as sympathetic or unsympathetic.

An on-screen narrator directly addressed the audience in the first sound serials. 'Folks, before presenting chapter two . . .' he announces in 'A Call to Arms' (*The Indians are Coming*), while 'Circling Death' (*Battling with Buffalo Bill*) begins 'Howdy folks'. At the beginning of Mascot's 'The Fugitive' (*The Lone Defender*) the on-screen narrator tells the audience:

> Last week at this theatre you saw the star, Rin-Tin-Tin, risk his life to save his friend, Valdez. Valdez possesses a watch which gives the description of his secret gold mine, and before dying instructs Bud, the boy who tried in vain to save him, to take the watch to his daughter Dolores. Knowing that Rinty can lead him to the mine, Amos tries to capture Rinty. Raymond, a mysterious figure who is suspected of being the Cactus Kid, interferes and escapes with Buzz and Rinty. They are pursued and set upon by Harkey's men. Rinty, escaping, comes upon a wolf attacking a colt. As he is fighting for his life, and Raymond is being overpowered by Harkey's agents, Dolores suddenly finds herself in the path of the stampeding herd of wild horses. And now, for Chapter Two, 'The Fugitive'.

These introductions assert their identity as talking pictures, while also, particularly in the Universal serials, adopting a folksy, conversational tone. This was not maintained. Universal and Mascot initially shifted to the use of off-screen voice-over but then used printed text. Voice-over narration did not return until Columbia began to use this approach with *Mandrake the Magician*.

A concern to summarize the entirety of the previous chapter is also particularly evident in serials of the early 1930s. The voice-over at the beginning of Mascot's 'Man Eaters' (*King of the Wild* [1931]) reminds the audience that:

> A tiger which he was hunting slew the Rajah of Rampoor and the stroke of its paw has changed the destiny of Robert Grant, a young American. To save the Rajah's kingdom from a pretender,

Grant assumed the dying ruler's identity and was accused of having murdered the Rajah. Proof of Grant's innocence exists in the form of a letter written by the Rajah before his death. A hunter named Harris has the letter in his possession. Grant has escaped from prison and is trailing Harris disguised as an Arab. His real identity is known only to Muriel Armitrage, a girl who has befriended him. Muriel's brother Tom has been accidentally wounded by a woman named Mrs LaSalle who had plotted with Harris and an Arab named Mustapha to make Tom reveal the location of a rich diamond deposit. Suddenly, Harris's ferocious ape-man, Bimi, seizes Tom in his terrible clutch.

Such convoluted plotting looks back to silent serials such as *The Woman in Grey* (1920), discussed by Ben Singer for 'the rabid intensity and omni-directional ubiquity' of their malevolence but also for their confusion of identities.[5] A tiger kills the Rajah and Grant (having assumed the Rajah's identity before disguising himself as an Arab) is pursued for the killing; he pursues Harris, who is plotting with Mustapha against Tom . . .

The practice of summarizing the entirety of the previous chapter was also common in Universal serials of the first half of the 1930s. The studio retained printed recaps to 1936, for instance for 'The Death Plunge' (*Pirate Treasure* [1934]), a title used again two years later by Universal for the second chapter of *The Adventures of Frank Merriwell* (1936), which has:

Dick Moreland made a daring solo flight around the world to win money to finance an expedition to search for treasure buried by a pirate ancestor on an island in the Spanish main.

Stanley Brassett, learning of the treasure sent henchmen to get Dick's chart. Dick battled them for its possession. The henchmen fled, pursued by Dick who in a spectacular leap landed in the bandits' car but, hurled out, narrowly escaped being run down by Dorothy Craig.

Getting in Dorothy's car, Dick pursuing the bandits, leaps into their car, recovers his chart and tosses it to Dorothy.

This provides an extraordinary level of detail, setting out how Dick battled Brassett's henchmen, leapt into their car, was hurled out of their car, narrowly escaped being run-over, got into Dorothy's car, leapt into the henchmen's car again . . . It was one of devices that Republic was to pare down. Relatively extended credits, introductions and summaries could help keep costs down. However, one of the challenges of the serial format was how to find an economic way of providing plot summaries, and this was made particularly acute with relatively brief instalments and where an audience was likely to expect action and pace.

The Sign of the Wolf (1931) starts each chapter with an elaborate scenario involving a veiled woman, a fortune teller, a blow dart and a handwritten note, before providing a summary through the handwriting on the note. It was more common for independent serials to use printed recaps. Sometimes these were of considerable length: 152 words are used in the introduction to 'Thundering Hooves' (*Custer's Last Stand* [1936]), which also serves to introduce eleven characters.

Universal serial-making policy shifted at different times, and this was reflected in their chapter introductions. Serials such as *Pirate Treasure* used densely printed white text on a black background. The effect was to dull the pace. In 'Torrent of Terror!' (*The Roaring West* [1935]): the credits are shown over a montage of racing wagons and stampeding cattle, to the accompaniment of uptempo stock music, but everything then slows

5. *Ace Drummond* (1936)

6. *The Green Hornet* (1939)

and quietens for the recap of the previous chapter, beginning 'Montana Larkin and Jinglebob Morgan joined a land rush to file on a gold claim of which they alone knew'. *Ace Drummond* (1936), one of a number of Universal serials derived from comic strips, initiated the approach of introducing chapters in the form of a comic strip that provided a recap of the previous chapter (as well as highlighting cross-media links) (Fig. 5). *The Green Hornet* (1939) introduced the scrolling text that George Lucas was to adopt for *Star Wars* (1977) (Fig. 6). By the time of *Gang Busters* (1942) Universal had abandoned printed recaps for new footage in which the dialogue served as a recap. This policy was retained for the studio's remaining serials, with some variations. *The Scarlet Horseman's* 'Dry Grass Danger' (1945) is one of the Universal serials in which the chapter title is absent from the chapter itself. It begins with a voice-over announcing (over a brief montage of shots): 'In eighteen hundred and seventy-five the Great Plains country of Western Texas was mistakenly thought to be nothing but desert. But a secret group in the town of Forty-Four know of its hidden wealth: conspirators who incite a Comanche uprising to discourage exploration as a first step in their plan to control the region.'

Universal's final serial, *The Mysterious Mr M*, uses new dialogue to establish the story so far: when insurance investigator Shirley Clinton says 'But don't you think it was time I was told', Captain Dan Blair of the Homicide Bureau obliges, explaining to her, and the audience, that 'Kittridge invented the submarine engine that will revolutionise ocean travel. M is after it, and we think he is using Jim Farrell to get him'.

The effect of Universal's attempt to move away from what had become the standard summary and recap pattern was to accentuate their serials' reliance on explanatory dialogue. Republic adopted a different approach, over time cutting back on the length of chapter introductions. 'The Prisoner Vanishes' (*Dick Tracy vs. Crime Inc.* [1941]) uses two cards, 'THE GHOST—Threatens to destroy New York when the Council of Eight refuses to pay him one hundred million dollars' and 'DICK TRACY—races thru the sky, trying to stop Lucifer from starting a tidal wave'. 'Death's Chariot' (*Perils of Nyoka* [1942]) is introduced with the single, succinct, 'LARRY—Is attacked by a gorilla in Vultura's Temple while trying to rescue Nyoka' (Fig. 7). 'Vengeance' (*Daughter of Don Q* [1946] begins 'Cliff overtakes Donovan who is trying to escape

7. *Perils of Nyoka* (1942)

after attempting to murder another Quantero heir'. Other Republic serials from the first half of the 1940s use similarly brief introductions: 'REX AND CHANG—Arrive at the Pacific Marine Paint Company where Vivian Marsh is being held prisoner by Black Dragon Agents' ('The Japanese Inquisition', *G-Men vs. the Black Dragon* [1943]), 'CAPTAIN AMERICA—Surprises the Scarab's agents, who have started the Dynamic Vibrator after locking Gail and the scientists in a vault' ('Mechanical Executioner', *Captain America* [1944]), 'CRAIG FOSTER—Battles the Purple Monster and Garrett, who are attempting to steal the Jet Ship Launching Rocket' ('The Time Trap', *The Purple Monster Strikes* [1945]). Words were reduced to a minimum, the focus was narrowed from the previous chapter as a whole to the cliffhanger at the end, and the convoluted and omnidirectional plotting of *King of the Wild* gave way to simpler oppositions (Craig Foster against the Purple Monster, Captain America against the Scarab, G-Men vs. the Black Dragon).

Like Universal, Columbia experimented with different styles of chapter introductions. They initially used printed text, then a combination of print and voice-over, then voice-over alone. Their trademark, however, in both print and voice-over, was an exclamatory, breathless and often rapid-fire style of delivery. Thus 'The Murderous Mirror', in common with the other chapters of *The Iron Claw* (1941), opens with a voice-over and printed text announcing:

> A fabulous fortune is at stake! THE IRON CLAW is hot on the trail! He lurks in the dark. He strikes in the back. Murder! Intrigue! Horror! Destruction! Brother against brother! Friend against friend! Who is this man who holds them all at bay? Who is this man who laughs at the law and the underworld alike? WHO IS THE IRON CLAW? Cruel and heartless, he murders Culver Benson. Then, when Bob Lane and Patricia Benson search for him in the Bensonhurst Tunnels, he strikes again!

Only the final two sentences were unique to this particular chapter, the rest being repeated at the beginning of each chapter.

In 'Trap of the Wasp' the introductory voice-over is extended well into the chapter. During an opening fight between Mandrake and one of the Wasp's henchmen, the narrator explains that Mandrake 'is completing the invention of a radium energy machine destined to be of great value to humanity' but also 'sought for destructive purposes by a mysterious criminal known as The Wasp'. The voice-over returns when the henchman starts to use the machine against Mandrake, only at this point recapping the events leading up to the fight. It concludes with: 'in the ensuing struggle the death-dealing device was put into action by a henchman of The Wasp. It ignited a tank of hydrogen dooming Mandrake to certain death!'

The fact that this statement is immediately followed by a sequence showing Mandrake's survival illustrates Columbia's tendency to highlight rather than hide the contradiction of the cliffhanger. The underlying principle in all Hollywood serials was that of escape from an inescapable peril but an effort was generally made to naturalize this. 'But I saw the truck explode, he couldn't have lived through it!' exclaims Zarnoff's henchman in 'The Firebird Strikes' (*The Miracle Rider* [1935]) when he hears that Tom Morgan is still alive, but this remark is made after we have seen Morgan jump from the truck before the explosion and also serves to demonstrate the untrustworthiness of the villain's henchmen. In Columbia serials such as *Mandrake the Magician* this sequence is reversed; the inevitability of death is announced before the escape and the announcement is given the narrator's authority. In 'The Fang Strikes' (*Terry and the Pirates* [1940]), the introduction concludes: 'Terry and Pat, seeking Dr Lee in the jungle, are deserted by their natives and attacked by Fang's renegades. Trapped in a burning hut they are doomed to certain death!' In the sequence that follows they escape through a concealed tunnel. In 'The Shadow Attacks' (*The Shadow* [1940]), the narrator announces that the Shadow, hearing that the Black Tiger's men plan to destroy a television building, 'succeeded in saving the lives of many people, but was himself caught in the explosion and doomed to certain death'. He is then shown surviving the blast, a little dusty from the rubble but unharmed. The miraculous survival was standard for the serial, the narrator's immediately preceding insistence on certain death was specific to Columbia's serials of this time.

Other serials provided a clearer distinction between introduction and recap/take-out. This set pattern is most evident in Republic serials. Thus the introductory titles to 'The Bridge of Terror' (*Dick Tracy* [1937]) end with 'DICK TRACY—G-Man assigned to investigate the Spider Ring, attempts to block the Lame One's efforts to destroy the Bay Bridge'. This is followed by repeat footage from the end of the previous chapter, including shots of Tracy racing to the bridge, and seemingly trapped and about to be hit by a falling girder. Here the take-out is provided by additional shots, one showing Tracy managing to roll aside despite the girder that has already fallen on top of him, another showing the falling girder crashing to the side of him and, after a cut to a shot of the truck driver also on the bridge, a further shot shows Tracy getting up, unharmed.

Raphael Vela labels this 'the cartoon cliffhanger', which, like Warners' Road Runner and Coyote cartoon series (1949–), shows characters surviving impossible situations without regard to realism.[6] A more common variant is the 'disingenuous cliffhanger', which withholds important story information, as in 'The Fang Strikes', where Terry and his companions are revealed to have escaped from the burning hut by a previously unseen tunnel. The most common form of this was the addition of footage showing the jump from stagecoach, car, truck, chariot . . . before it crashed and/or exploded. Thus the beginning of 'The Firebird Strikes' repeats footage from the previous chapter showing Tom Morgan at the wheel of an oil tanker which explodes when Zarnoff's men hit it with a bullet composed of X-94, the explosive Zarnoff has been manufacturing. It adds a shot of Morgan jumping from the truck before the explosion and before the gunman's 'That's the end of Morgan'. Here the take-out is located within rather than after recap. A further variant was provided by

8. *Undersea Kingdom* (1935) Chapter Two

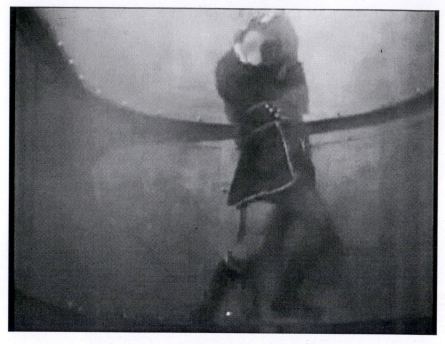

9. *Undersea Kingdom* (1935) Chapter Three

those cliffhangers which took this further by providing false information which is then 'corrected' at the beginning of the next chapter. Thus the first chapter of *Law of the Wild* (1934) ends when John Sheldon, having reclaimed his horse, Rex, escapes along a railway bridge, is forced to turn back by the approaching train, and appears to fall on the tracks. The footage is repeated in 'The Battle of the Strong' take-out but here the final shot is replaced with another showing Sheldon and Rex jump off the bridge and into the lake.

In effect, the corrected cliffhanger provided a cheat ending. The second chapter endings of two early Republic serials provide even clearer instances of this. At the end of 'Undersea City' (*Undersea Kingdom* [1936]) Crash Corrigan rescues Professor Norton from the Transforming Machine but is then shot by one of Unga Khan's men and seen falling down the elevator shaft (Fig. 8). In the next chapter two shots showing Corrigan falling into and down the shaft are replaced by shots showing him jump and then clinging to the side of the shaft (Fig. 9). 'Flaming Danger' (*Robinson Crusoe of Clipper Island* [1936]) ends with Mala forced to stand on a plank on the edge of an active volcano. The plank is upended and Mala falls into the pit of the volcano. The shot of Mala falling is omitted from the next chapter's repeat footage, which includes additional footage showing Mala surreptitiously untying his hands, while his friends Hank MacGuirie, Anthony Tupper, Rex the horse and Buck the dog make their way up the volcano. While Tupper provides a distraction by spraying flashlight powder amongst the crowd, MacGuirie drops a rope down to Mala, the other end of which is attacked to Rex. With the help of the horse Mala is lifted to safety.

The availability of serials on playback formats such as DVD has made it easier to compare cliffhanger chapter endings with the take-out from the following chapter. However, even at the time of its original release, *Robinson Crusoe of Clipper Island* was singled out for its deception. As the *Variety* reviewer put it, in this serial, 'fakery is present in unusual quantities'.[7] Perhaps more significant were the number of 'What the Picture Did For Me' correspondents who complained about its cliffhangers. One went as far as writing at length not just on what was wrong with the serial but also how this could be improved. For this exhibitor, the current practice was

so unnecessary and it holds serials up to ridicule as a whole. For example, at the end of Chapter Seven, Mala and the Princess jump onto a tilting rock and are hurled down a rocky cliff into the water below. At the beginning of Chapter Eight the rock tilts but they clutch at a trailing vine and they are saved. I heard a couple of youngsters remark 'They didn't show this last week'. It is easy enough to criticise but how would I do it, as they must have their suspense at the end of the chapter. Well, here is how I would do it. Mala and the Princess are pursued by the natives. In front of them is a chasm: behind them are the natives in hot pursuit. End the chapter here. The suspense is complete—if they go forward there is the danger of falling into the chasm; if they go backward they fall into the natives' clutches. At the start of Chapter Eight, I would have Mala and the Princess leap across, land on the tilting rock. You can have the thrill of the tilting rock, they grasp the vine and are saved and elude the pursuing natives. All the possible thrills would be extracted from these sequences, without holding up the serial to ridicule. I hope serial producers can learn that there is no need of killing the hero at the end of each chapter and bringing him to life at the start of the next chapter.[8]

Discussing the same serial, another exhibitor had written earlier:

> I wish serial producers had to sit down every day and look at their
> serials over and over and figure how any intelligent person could
> pay their good money to see the hero killed one week and the en-
> tire thing changed the next week. But, what's the use of exhibitors
> complaining about that angle. Producers have clearly shown us that
> they will continue to produce serials the way that they want to and
> make us like it.[9]

Producers of serials generally avoided the direct contradiction evident
in *Robinson Crusoe of Clipper Island* but continued the practice of 'killing'
the hero one week and reviving him the next. The reason seems clear: it
was not just suspense that the cliffhanger provided, but the death of the
hero, week after week, so that he (occasionally she) could be revived in
the next episode.

Producers of serials also generally avoided the approach taken in 'The
Slave Traders', the eighth chapter of Columbia's *The Desert Hawk* (1944).
At the chapter's end, Hawk and his companion Omar are slain by archers
and buried in a pit which is then covered with boulders. 'What will
become of Azala now that the Hawk and Omar have perished?' asks the
narrator. However, chapter nine reminds the audience of the wizard in
the previous chapter who revealed in his crystal ball the fate that *would*
befall them if they continued on their journey, as was depicted in the
second half of the previous chapter. As these events did not actually
take place the hero survives.[10] The hero dies in a different way in 'From
Death to Life', the seventh chapter of *The Phantom Empire* (1935). In
this chapter's recap, Gene Autry is knocked unconscious in the Murania
Armament Tower which is then hit by a radium bomb.[11] Arriving on
the scene, one of Queen Tika's soldiers then announces: 'The Armament
Tower is destroyed! The surface man is dead!' However, speaking by
television phone to Queen Tika, the soldiers later report that Autry still
shows a spark of life, at which the Queen orders them to take him to
the Radium Reviving Chamber. 'We must revive the surface man at
once,' she goes on, 'so that he may tell us who helped him escape from
the Death Chamber. Tell us the name of this infamous traitor. His fate
will be instant death.' At the Reviving Chamber, she is told that Autry is
dead, to which she replies, 'No one is dead in Murania, unless we do not
wish to revive him'. Autry is duly revived, though initially he only speaks
the (incomprehensible) language of the dead and thus is unable to tell

the Queen who helped him escape from the Death Chamber to which she had sent him before she ordered that he be taken to the Reviving Chamber. Distinct in the particular form it takes, this sequence indicates a broader truth. The hero lives on till the end but must appear to die, repeatedly.

'Death Turns the Wheel' (*The Master Key* [1945]) provides a less convoluted example. The efforts of Nazi agents to get hold of Professor Henderson's Oroton machine lead them to trap FBI agent Tom Brant in a burning and collapsing building. 'Brant has evidence that connects me with you Nazis through Brown', Stark tells Donohue. 'Can he identify anybody except Brown?' ask Donohue. Stark replies: 'He can't now, he's in that fire.' However, while Brown was killed in the opening episode, Stark and Donohue are at this stage unaware of what the audience has just seen, Detective Jack Ryan entering the burning building and saving Brant from the fire.

The cliffhanger was designed to create suspense but was also part of a process of death and revival. Rather than being without regard to realism it would be more accurate to say that the demands of realism were less important than the demands of the take-out. This is not unique to the serial. David Bordwell and Kristin Thompson have made the case for realism deferring to narrative in classical Hollywood, and the post-classical Hollywood live-action film is no stranger to cartoon violence.[12] However the use of the cliffhanger and (more generally) of narratives of repeated revival after apparent death made the transcendence of everyday reality an integral part of the film serial. At Mascot this process could approach the sublime. In 'Port of Peril' (*The Galloping Ghost* [1931]) Barbara Courtney is flying to the bedside of her brother, disgraced football player Buddy Courtland, unaware that her plane is defective. Red Grainge has boarded her plane in an attempt to save her, while her suitor, Elton, is flying to her aid in his plane. Barbara and Red bail out using the plane's single parachute but Red becomes aware that it is not strong enough to hold them both. He lets go and falls, in a sequence Jon Tuska links to the dream sequences in *Murder, My Sweet* (1944) and *Spellbound* (1945) for its vertiginous camerawork.[13] Fortunately, rather than hit the ground, he manages to land on the wing of Elton's plane. This in turns crashes on landing, but when Elton asks Red if he is all right the answer is 'I think so'. A more definitive reply comes a moment later when he is able not only to rush to the aid of Barbara when she lands her parachute but also to save the life of Harlow, the football coach, when his car is about to crash due to an attack by agents of the gambling ring.

The take-out here and elsewhere provides not only escape from death but also from any injury and anything but superficial clothing damage. Dick Tracy survives the partial collapse of the San Francisco Bridge unharmed, with his hat still on his head and his suit unruffled. The bridge itself survives. This lack of long-term damage is even more evident in a later Dick Tracy serial chapter, 'The Prisoner Vanishes' (*Dick Tracy vs. Crime Inc.* [1941]). At the start of this Lucifer, working for The Ghost, is dropping bombs in order to create a tidal wave that will engulf New York. The repeat footage from the end of the opening chapter used here includes shots of the waves reaching up the Statue of Liberty, a sequence taken from an early example from the cinema of the apocalypse, *Deluge* (1933). That film features the destruction not only of New York buildings but also of the existing social structure. There are no such consequences in 'The Prisoner Vanishes', which reveals that Tracy stopped the attack by ramming his plane into Lucifer's, bailing out just in time. This sequence is followed by two shots of a newspaper headline: 'TRACY MISSING!! FEARED LOST AT SEA!' then below this, in smaller print: 'His Courageous Action Prevents Destruction of Entire City. DAMAGE CONFINED TO WATERFRONT'. However the key concern is immediately resolved: Tracy and Lucifer have landed their respective parachutes on the same beach, allowing Tracy to return to headquarters with Lucifer as his prisoner.

The absence of consequences is revealed in a different way in the opening section of 'Menaced by Murders' (*Adventures of the Flying Cadets* [1943]). In this Universal serial, Danny and Scrapper crash-land their plane on the railroad, in front of a speeding train. They get out of the plane just before a major explosion, the flames of which engulf the train's engine and front carriages. 'Maybe if we could pretend that we were hurt they'd give us a lift the rest of the way into town', says one of the Flying Cadets. 'Naw, they'd ask us a lot of questions', replies his companion. You would think they might, but the guard urges, 'Let's get going. Number 10 is right on our heels'. Danny and Scrapper take a ride on the train anyway, and their adventures continue. This is a world where planes crash and trains burn but without interrupting the regular timetable. With this combination of excitement and reassurance is it surprising that the serial was popular?

There are occasional signs of injury. Jack Manning sports a head bandage in 'A Call to Arms' (*The Indians are Coming* [1930]), and this sign of injury is worn by secondary characters in two chapters starring Johnny Mack Browne: 'Redskins' Revenge' (*Wild West Days* [1937]) and 'Flaming Arrow' (*Rustlers of Red Dog* [1935]). In both serials the characters played by the films' star remains unscathed. A little after the take-out of 'The Man Nobody Knows' (*Mystery Mountain* [1934]) Jane Corwin is shot by one of the Rattler's henchmen; unusually for a serial we see a trickle of blood, and Jane is taken to the emergency hospital. However, by the next chapter she is back on her horse and shrugging off her injuries; the function of the visit to the hospital is less to tend to her injuries than to introduce Dr Matthews, one of the men suspected of being the Rattler.

While characters rarely show signs of injury, death is not entirely reserved for villains. Tom Wayne's mechanic Stubbs dies at the beginning of 'One for All and All for One!' (*The Three Musketeers*), and Colonel Grayson (father of the heroic Tom Grayson) is killed at the beginning of 'The Mill of Disaster' (*The Fighting Devil Dogs* [1938]). The death of the father (sometimes another relative) is a standard feature of the serial. It provides a motivation for the action and for the son who takes on the father's role (though not the role of fatherhood). However, it is not particularly linked to the cliffhanger. It more often forms part of the opening chapter's set-up of the action, as it does, for instance, in *King of the Texas Rangers* (1941), and when it comes later is as likely to be part of the serial's middle part. This is the case, for instance, in 'The Thunder Riders', the second chapter of *The Phantom Empire*, in the middle of which Betsy and Frankie's father is killed, which in this instance strengthens Autry's paternal role.

In general, then, the opening section of the serial chapter provides a clearly delineated sequence, reintroducing the story and, in particular, key characters, providing a recap of either the entirety of the previous chapter or the immediate, and regularly life-threatening, peril that occurred at the end of that chapter, as well as showing the escape from that peril (the take-out). The take-out can follow the recap or can be dovetailed into it, as is the case with the shot of Tom Morgan jumping from the truck inserted before the shot of the truck exploding. It can bring the action to a halt but in some instances leads directly into further action and threat. At the beginning of 'Red Peril' (*Heroes of the West*), Ann Blaine, escaping from a party of 'hostile redskins', falls in the path of the advancing horses, but is saved by Tom Crosby. However, immediately after this the attackers regroup and circle round the remains of the wagon train. The danger only goes with the arrival of the cavalry. A similar pattern is repeated in other western serial chapters, for instance 'White Treachery' (*The Oregon Trail* [1939]). Aside from just under five minutes

115

10. *G-men versus the Black Dragon* (1943)

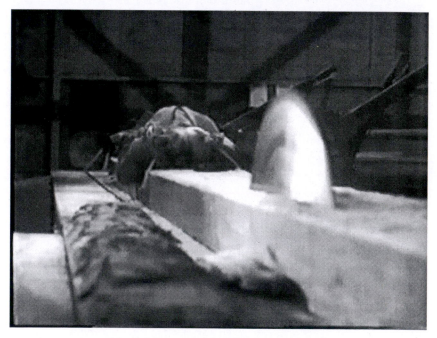

11. *G-Men versus the Black Dragon* (1943)

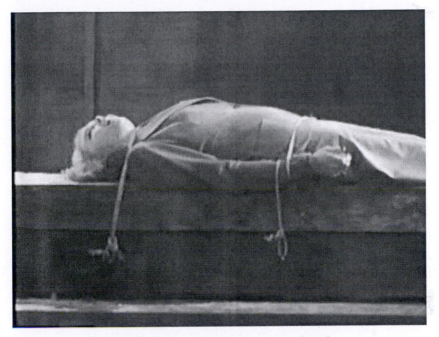

12. *G-Men versus the Black Dragon* (1943)

13. *G-Men versus the Black Dragon* (1943)

in the middle, *Rustlers of Red Dog*'s 'Flaming Arrow' consists entirely of a series of shoot-outs between the wagon trail and the 'redskins'.

The opening section tends to the dominated by the cliffhanger introduced at the end of the previous chapter. Similarly, the closing minutes of the chapter generally introduce a new cliffhanger, which will be resolved in the following chapter. In *The Practical Manual of Screenplay Writing*, aspiring writers of serials were advised that their creativity would be limited to inventing 'a new weenie' or devising 'new methods of torture, new manhole situations, and new take-out devices'.[14] Yet in the main the serial relied on the old situations and take-outs.

The ending of 'The Thundering Herd' adheres to one of the most common forms of cliffhanger: the animal stampede. This features in 'The Queen of the Night Riders' (*The Vanishing Legion* [1931]), 'The Stampede' (*Gordon of Ghost City* [1933]), 'The Battle of the Strong' (*Law of the Wild*), 'Thundering Hooves' (*Custer's Last Stand*), 'The Redskins' Revenge' (*Wild West Days*), 'The Stampede' (*The Great Adventures of Wild Bill Hickok* [1938]), 'The Menacing Herd' (*Riders of Death Valley* [1941]), and 'The Mystery of Ghost Town' (*The Valley of Vanishing Men* [1942]). Different second chapter stock situations were used in non-western serials. The car that careers off the road is used at the end of 'The House in the Hills' (*The Return of Chandhu* [1933]), 'The Death Plunge' (*The Adventures of Frank Merriwell*), 'Shadows' (*The Clutching Hand* [1936]), 'Death Stalks the Highways' (*The Phantom Creeps* [1939]), 'The Prisoner Vanishes' (*Dick Tracy vs. Crime Inc.*), 'The Face at the Window' (*The Green Archer* [1940]), 'The Plunge of Peril' (*The Green Hornet Strikes Again* [1940]), 'The Murderous Mirror' (*The Iron Claw*), 'Flaming Death' (*Don Winslow of the Navy* [1942]), 'Flight to Danger' (*Haunted Harbor* [1944]), 'The Edge of Doom' (*The Monster and the Ape* [1945]). Variations include cars falling down car park shafts ('The Death Plunge', *Gang Busters*, 'Danger Downward', *The Mysterious Mr M*) and motorcycles coming off the road ('The News Reel Murder', *Burn 'em Up Barnes* [1934], 'The Case of the Stolen Ransom', *Federal Operator 99* [1945]).

What varied was how the cliffhanger was recycled. Mascot's 'Nature in the Raw' (*The Lost Jungle* [1934]) ends with Clyde Beatty confronting a tiger in a tiger pit. Two years later, Beatty appeared in the newly formed Republic's *Darkest Africa* [1936], and at the end of 'The Tiger Men's God' he again found himself confronting a tiger in a tiger pit. The two serials appear to use different parts of a single film segment.

As already noted, Republic also recycled the buzz-saw scene introduced in *Blue Jeans*, the sensation stage melodrama of 1890, and familiar enough to be the subject of parody relatively early in the twentieth century. Republic used the situation both at the end of the third chapter of *King of the Royal Mounted* (1940) and at the end of the second chapter of *G–Men vs. the Black Dragon* (1943), 'The Japanese Inquisition'. Yet the 'The Japanese Inquisition' ending reveals how the studio used repetition to refine and develop the art of the cliffhanger. The scene features six characters: three Black Dragon agents, British secret service agent Vivian Marsh (tied to a plank), Chinese secret service agent Chang Sing (tied to a chair), and G-Man Rex Bennett, who arrives on the scene to rescue his fellow agents, just after the buzz-saw machine is turned on (Fig. 10). The fight that ensues between Bennett and the Black Dragon agents is intercut with shots of the buzz saw, Marsh moving towards it, and Chang as struggling but helpless onlooker. Between shots of the other characters, Marsh is filmed from slightly above, with the buzz-saw in the background, from the level of her prostrate body, with the buzz-saw in the foreground (Fig. 11), and from the side, with the buzz-saw to her left (Fig. 12). At the very end of the chapter the camera moves down so that Marsh goes out of shot as she approaches the buzz-saw, the shot resting on the moving wheels taking her towards the blades. The sequence as a whole lasts almost a minute and a half, stretching time and distance in order to extend suspense: shots showing Marsh being carried some distance towards the saw are followed by a shot, almost a minute into the sequence, which shows her feet only a short distance from her starting point (Fig. 13). Spatial and temporal reality is subordinated to suspense and film style.

The sequence is an exercise in editing, camera-work and character movement. It also reinstates the tortured heroine within the serial cliffhanger. Joseph Arthur's *Blue Jeans* features a male would-be buzz-saw victim, as does Republic's *King of the Royal Mounted* at the end of chapter three. Sound serial cliffhangers generally feature a threat to the male hero, but in particular instances Republic placed the heroine in cliffhanging jeopardy, in the films and in their publicity. In 'Satan's Web' (*Manhunt of Mystery Island* [1945]) Captain Mephisto traps Claire Forrest in a fishing net which he lowers into the water in order to get her to reveal the whereabouts of the power control unit for her father's Radiatomic Power Transmitter. Dolores Quantero is also trapped in a fishing net, in 'Vendetta' (*Daughter of Don Q*), this one in the line of fire of a harpoon gun attached to the door handle. Cliff Roberts is wise to this trick, and manages to enter the room without the harpoon killing Dolores, but the fight that follows only ends when Cliff shoots one of the henchmen, whose fall causes the harpoon gun to fire.

Prior to the establishment of Republic, Mascot's emphasis on omni-directional action often led them to combine different strands of narra-tive and action in the cliffhanger. At the end of 'The Fugitive' (*The Lone Defender*) Dolores loses the watch which contains the clue to the whereabouts of the gold mine discovered by her murdered father and then finds herself trapped with Rinty (who has been rendered unconscious) in a burning building. Her friends are also in trouble: Buzz has fallen down a well, and Raymond, suspected of being the Cactus Kid, has seemingly been shot by his pursuers. The collapsing scaffolding in 'Pinholes' (*Shadow of the Eagle* [1932]) combines two lines of action; the pursuit of Craig McCoy and Little Billy, whose car causes the scaffolding to collapse, and Jean Gregory's search for her father, which leads her and the circus strong man onto the scaffolding the moment before it is brought down. Other Poverty Row serials used combined-cliffhangers: Wonder Pictures' 'Paths of Peril' (*The Mystery Trooper* [1931]) ends with Jack, Billy and Red Eagle attacked by Mack and his henchmen, while elsewhere a bear enters the hut where Billy's sister Helen is sleeping. Victory's 'Death in the Laboratory' (*Blake of Scotland Yard* [1937]) ends with Sir James Blake about to be clubbed by the Scorpion and Jerry Sheehan falling down a well, followed by the title 'Who is the Scorpion?'

Republic serials generally involved a careful build-up to the cliffhanger. There are contrasting instances where the cliffhanger lacks any particular emphasis. Metropolitan's 'The Dog of Destiny' (*The Sign of the Wolf*) ends with a fist fight. Mascot's 'Sport of Kings' (*The Adventures of Rex and Rinty* [1935]) ends with Crawford knocking Frank Bradley off his horse in a polo game. At the end of Columbia's 'The Blazing Trap' (*Brenda Starr, Reporter* [1945]), in keeping with that serial's lighter tone, the threat that confronts Brenda Starr essentially consists of a pile of packing cases sent down a ramp. Towards the end of Commonwealth Pictures 'The Thundering Herd' (*The Last Frontier* [1932]) Betty Halliday falls from the wagon she has been driving, pursued by 'Indians', onto the horses in front, then underneath the carriage, before she is rescued by Tom Kirby. The drama of this Yakima Canutt-directed stunt over-shadows the cliffhanger that follows when the wagon overturns, leaving Betty and Tom in the path of a herd of stock footage buffalo. 'House in the Hills' (*The Return of Chandhu*) ends with a fairly standard cliffhanger (Chandhu's car goes off the road) but is unusual for providing no lead-up to this: the car is not being chased and there is no obvious reason why it goes off the road beyond the need for a cliffhanger.

Universal's 'A Call to Arms' (*The Indians are Coming*) provides a different example. Rather than a cliffhanger, it ends with Jack, arrested after being falsely accused of theft, saying goodbye to his beloved Mary as she journeys west to her father. Jack is in trouble, but at this particular moment his problems are not life-threatening. Towards the end of 'Deadly Enemies' (*Jungle Menace* [1937]) Marshall is shot but rather than end here the serial continues for long enough to show Robert Fanning take him away. A title appears, asking 'What will Robert Fanning do with Marshall?' While this leaves an element of doubt, it is not a conventional, film serial cliffhanger. 'The Ghost Talks' (*The Secret of Treasure Island* [1938]), ends with Larry and Toni encountering the ghost of the Black Pirate. Larry fires his gun at the ghost, who laughs. 'Is Captain Cuttle the long lost father of Toni?' asks the voice-over narrator. 'Will Larry Kemp discover the real secret of Treasure Island? Who is the ghost of Treasure Island?' The question asked in the voice-over to 'The Web Tangles' (*The Mysterious Pilot* [1937])—'What became of Jim Dorn after he entered suicide pass?'—indicates the aftermath of a cliffhanger rather than the cliffhanger itself (indeed we have just seen Jim fly through the pass).

Jungle Menace, The Secret of Treasure Island and *The Mysterious Pilot* were the first three Columbia serials (in fact they were made for Columbia by Louis Weiss's Adventure Serials). Cliffhangers are used in the later Columbia serials, though in some instances the studio relied on mystery rather than the clear physical threat of the buzz-saw or the stampeding herd. 'The Unknown Strikes' (*Who's Guilty?* [1945]) ends when the bed Ruth Allen is lying on slides back into the wall, a situation that is given no immediate resolution in the following chapter: Ruth only reappears at a later stage in the following chapter.

The cliffhanger then was not an essential element of the film serial. However, the fact that it was avoided in *Jungle Menace, The Secret of Treasure Island* and *The Mysterious Pilot* but used in later Columbia serials in line with the practice elsewhere suggests that it had come to be expected. In this most formulaic mode of filmmaking change tended to consist of modification rather than overhaul and there was a tendency to return to established practices. With *The Mysterious Pilot* the pattern was varied further: each chapter concluded with a lesson in flying from Frank Hawks (who played the leading role of Jim Dorn), though these are not included in versions of the serial I have seen.[15] This combination of narrative and non-narrative seriality was continued only in the case of the studio's *The Secret Code* (1942). In that serial's 'The Shadow of the Swastika', Dan Barton, disguised as the Black Commando, is forced to escape from the police when they mistake him for one of the villains. The rope that he is using to escape snaps and he falls. The narrator does not ask whether he will survive but 'Has Barton routed the spy ring?' Yet this, for Columbia, relatively succinct question is then followed by a sequence in the offices of Major Henry Burton, Military Intelligence, who proceeds to conduct a lesson in writing and reading secret codes. Each of the fifteen chapters of *The Secret Code* followed a similar format, with the action followed by a lesson in code breaking.

Other Columbia serials include a post-cliffhanger sequence that looks forward to the next chapter. Providing a preview of next week's instalment has become a fairly standard practice in the television serial but was less common in the cinema. From Universal's '*See* CRASHING TIMBERS, CHAPTER THREE OF THE PHANTOM CREEPS at This Theatre *Next Week*' to 'Next Week, CHAPTER THREE, HANDCUFFED TO DOOM, A Republic Serial' (*Dick Tracy Returns* [1938]), most makers of film serials provided only limited text at the end of episodes.

In Columbia's 'Ramparts of Revenge' (*Holt of the Secret Service* [1941]), the cliff-top fall that closes the chapter's action is followed by a series of flash forwards to what will be seen next week, accompanied by a voice-over asking: 'Will the secret service be able to destroy this wicked den? . . . Why have the counterfeiters imprisoned Kay? . . . Will that message they struggle for disclose her secret identity?' In the 'Trap of The Wasp' (*Mandrake the Magician*) the ending has a similar effect to the chapter's beginning, emphasizing life-threatening peril but indicating survival. The chapter action ends with Betty and one of the Wasp's henchmen in a lift hurtling to the ground while Mandrake and Lothar exchange blows with the other henchmen in a room that starts to fill with steam from a burst pipe. This is then followed by scenes from the episode to come, accompanied by the narrator's comments: 'The Wasp seals the lips of those who betray him! Mandrake, hypnotised, is kidnapped and placed in a flaming car! The Wasp traps Betty and Mandrake, with the energy machine he brings the walls of a radio station crashing down on them! Will they escape?' 'Will they escape?' is asked not of the chapter that has just ended but of the end of the *next* chapter. Betty and Mandrake must have escaped from the out-of-control lift and the steam-filled room just shown, if only to face a further peril. Similarly, at the end of Columbia's 'The Fatal Time-Bomb' (*The Spider Returns* [1941]), a montage of shots from the following chapter is accompanied by the narrator's voice-over, which ends: 'Trapped in a burning hut they are doomed to certain death!'

signifying that they have at least lived through the certain death of 'The Fatal Time-Bomb'. Having been doomed to certain death at the beginning of 'The Shadow Attacks' (*The Shadow* [1940]), at the end of that chapter the Shadow is on a truck containing burning gasoline hurtling towards the telephone company building. However the voice-over at the very end of the chapter, and the accompanying images, look forward only to subsequent perils, and ends: 'Deadly gas is ignited! Flames rise up to consume the building! Are all within it doomed? These are only a few of the many thrilling episodes seen next week in "The Shadow's Peril."' Audiences with any familiarity with the film serial or even with Hollywood more generally would presumably have anyway discounted the possibility that Mandrake, the Spider or the Shadow would die, but only Columbia serials of this period combine an insistence on the certainty of their death with evidence of their survival.

Columbia serials could be no less insistent on action than those made at Republic, but they were less focused on placing the chapter end cliffhanger within a clearly delineated pattern of recap/take-out/middle-action/cliffhanger, recap/take-out/middle-action/cliffhanger . . . The approach at Mascot was closer to Republic's (unsurprisingly, since Republic was continuing Mascot's serial production) though Mascot paid less attention to refining cliffhanger mechanics: where they aimed to accentuate the effect of the cliffhanger it was often through a combination of situations rather than through the careful construction of suspense evident in Republic chapters such as 'Japanese Inquisition'. Other minor studios were generally consistent in their deference to the need for a cliffhanger, if less consistent in how this was delivered. Even Universal, known for its emphasis on plot rather than action, almost always ended chapters other than the last with a life-threatening cliffhanger. This did not necessarily mean it was the main focus of the chapter. Chapter titles often pointed to the cliffhanger that came at the end: Republic's 'Flaming Prison' (*Daredevils of the West* [1943]) ends with Duke Cameron trapped inside the burning jail; at the end of Columbia's 'Primitive Sacrifice' (*Jungle Raiders* [1945]) the witch doctor is condemned to die, but manages to swop places with Dr Morse; while Universal's 'The Destroying Ray' (*The Vanishing Shadow* [1934]) ends with Gloria and Stanfield in the line of fire of Stanfield's Death Ray. However, in Universal's 'The Mail Gets Through' (*Tailspin Tommy* [1934]) the mail gets through in the first half of the chapter. It is only towards the end of the chapter that Paul Smith, owner of the mail company, announces an air show to celebrate his retention of the mail contract. It is at the show that Tailspin Tommy's friend Skeeter Mulligan loses control of a plane on the ground, endangering the crowd of spectators and forcing Tommy to imperil his own life by crashing his own plane into the one that is running wild.

Middle Action

As noted earlier, Ben Singer identified an omnidirectional antagonism underlying the plotting of silent serials such as *The Woman in Grey* (1920), depicting as they do a world in which everyone is in competition with everyone else.[16] Developed in relation to the silent serial, this notion can also be applied to an early sound serial chapter such as 'Man Eaters' (*King of the Wild*) which uses convoluted plots featuring a range of characters connected to each other through antagonistic relationships, disputed ownership and concealed identities.

Singer went on to identify a serial pattern based around a steady build-up of tension culminating in the cliffhanger placed at the end of one chapter and the beginning of the next: an episodic structure across the serial as a whole but continuity and linearity within individual chapters from the cliffhanger resolution.[17] While the Columbia narrator refers to 'the many thrilling episodes seen next week in "The Shadow's Peril"', accounts such as Singer's place the serial's episodic nature across rather than within individual chapters. A slightly different pattern is indicated in those accounts which identify the middle action as a mid-chapter minor climax, suggesting at least a rise-and-fall pattern within the chapter.[18] Lance Reardon's pursuit of Captain Mephisto and Claire Forrest in 'Satan's Web' (*Manhunt of Mystery Island*) is halted mid-chapter when his car goes into the water due to a rope that Mephisto has had placed across the road. This is a classic cliffhanger situation except that it is placed in the middle rather than at the end of the chapter and that the shot of Reardon leaping from his car before it went off the cliff is at no point withheld from the audience. More commonly, climaxes within a chapter take the form of some other kind of spectacle, often a fight. There were differences in the organization of individual serial chapters. Singer's notion of a steady intra-chapter build-up to the cliffhanger may have been a reflection on distinctions between the serial and the feature film rather than on plotting and pacing within the individual serial chapter. However, it is worth investigating the contrast between the idea that all roads lead to the end-chapter cliffhanger and the notion of the omnidirectional serial.

Mascot's 'Man Eaters' can again serve to illustrate the latter. From the chapter beginning voice-over that ends, 'Suddenly, Harris's ferocious ape-man, Bimi, seizes Tom in his terrible clutch', the recap continues through shots of Grant attempting to rescue Tom and Bimi attacking Grant. The take-out comes when the ape-man becomes aware of the snake that Harris also keeps in his room, allowing Harris to carry Tom out of the room, only to be immediately set upon by Mustapha and his men, while Muriel, searching for Tom, confronts Mrs LaSalle, and Mustapha tells Harris that Mrs LaSalle has double-crossed them and has run away with Tom.

This piling of one situation on top of another is extended for the remainder of the chapter, during which:

- Muriel receives a letter confirming that Mrs LaSalle has run away with Tom.
- Grant follows Harris, and Muriel follows Mrs LaSalle, to the boat.
- Mrs LaSalle recognises the writing on the letter.
- Finding that the boat has left shore, Muriel is befriended, and has her fare paid, by 'Mrs Colby'.
- Peterson recognises Mrs LaSalle as Mrs Anthony.
- Mrs LaSalle/Anthony reveals that she is in terror of her life. She is shot.
- Grant, appearing at the cabin window shortly after the shooting, discovers Muriel's revolver. He is pursued for the shooting.
- 'Mrs Colby' is discovered in the cabin where the shooting took place. She identifies herself as Mrs Moore, a secret service agent.
- Grant, escaping from his pursuers, gets into the hold where Harris's animals are kept. The animals escape from their cages and make their way into the passenger area.
- Escaping from one of the animals, Muriel runs into Bimi, then enters Mrs LaSalle's cabin, as does Grant shortly after her.
- At the boat's helm, the crew begin to steer the boat so that it avoids hitting a wreck in the water, but they abandon the bridge when an escaped lion appears. Crew and passengers rush to abandon ship.
- Someone turns the cabin door key, locking in Muriel and Grant as the boat starts to sink.

Thus the chapter end provides a climax, combining as it does different threats and mysteries: wild animals on the loose, a sinking ship, characters locked in their room, and the mystery as to who has turned the key. However this belongs to a succession of incidents: the chapter ends with Muriel and Grant locked in the room but might equally have ended with the mid-chapter shooting, the pursuit of Grant for the shooting, the release of the animals, the sinking ship . . .

An extension of the one-thing-after-another approach to plotting is evident in the opening section of 'Shadows' (*The Clutching Hand* [1936]). The opening titles of this chapter explain that super-detective Craig Kennedy is investigating the disappearance of leading scientist Dr Paul Gironda (just as he was about to pass on his formula for making gold). In the recap and take-out Kennedy is almost electrocuted but saved when Mrs Gironda opens a trapdoor sending him into the room below. The new action begins with the arrival of a delivery man just as Kennedy is picking himself up from the floor. 'What are you doing here?' asks the detective to which the man replies that he just came to deliver a package, a point reinforced by shots of the package addressed to Dr Gironda and labelled 'Handle with Care'. An off-screen knocking is heard. Kennedy pulls out his gun and opens the door behind which the sounds are coming. He discovers one of the workmen from Dr Gironda's laboratory clutching his head, who, questioned by Kennedy, says he was working at his bench when someone hit him. A hand appears through an opening in the wall and, unnoticed by those in the room, removes the package addressed to Dr Gironda. At the sound of a car Kennedy rushes outside. He is met by Jameson, his assistant. 'That car, Jameson', says Kennedy, followed by a shot of a car speeding along a deserted country road, 'we've got to catch it'. Kennedy, Jameson and the delivery man race to a car parked in a suburban road and chase after the other car. They are eventually brought to a halt when a truck pulls out in front of them. Two men leap out from the truck. A mid-chapter fight ensues.

While this is centred on one main character (Craig Kennedy) as a form of narrative construction it approaches *Un Chien Andalou* (1929) and the logic of the dream. It is not that unusual for characters in serials to fall down trapdoors but *The Clutching Hand* is distinctive in having that room as the venue for parcel deliveries, adjourning another room containing an essentially unexplained man clutching his head, with the assistant of the man sent down the trapdoor standing just outside. The background contrast between the speeding and stationary car adds to the confused sense of place. The imperatives for *The Clutching Hand* are clear: mystery, peril, the chase and the fight. Logic and coherence were secondary considerations. The end chapter cliffhanger is another car chase that ends with a taxi that crashes off the road and which functions as one in a list of incidents rather any sort of culmination.

Very different approaches are evident in *Tailspin Tommy*'s 'The Mail Gets Through' and 'Captured' (*Dick Tracy's G-Men* [1939]). In the former, once the mail is sent on its way, Tommy and Skeeter are given jobs by a grateful Paul Smith, and then meet up again with Betty Lou Barnes. Bruce Hoyt has a telephone conversation with Wade "Tiger" Taggart, the man attempting to deprive Paul Smith of the mail contract, and Betty goes flying with Bruce, then surprises him by parachuting out of the plane. Aside from not leading up to the cliffhanger, these events only marginally develop the serial's over-arching narrative, instead having the function of establishing the set-up and providing a degree of character development.

'Captured' is orientated towards the end chapter cliffhanger to a much greater extent. Following the resolution of the opening chapter cliff-hanger revealing Dick Tracy clinging to the bottom of a plane and thus escaping from the dynamite-filled boat just before the explosion, the pace (and sound volume) of the chapter drops for a scene showing the G-Men visiting Zarnoff's now abandoned headquarters. A *Star Dispatch* head-line—'TRACY RETURNS TO HEADQUARTERS: Five Thousand Dollars Reward Offered For Zarnoff Capture'—is followed by shots of the disused cannery, Zarnoff's new headquarters. The return to base was a relatively regular way of starting a new line of action: here both hero and villain return. At Zarnoff's new headquarters the tempo is briefly raised again when Lennie Slade, suspected of being an informer, pulls a gun on Zarnoff, but then is sent through a trap-door and shot. For Tracy return to base means both return to the Federal Building but also a new starting point. 'We're no better off than we were before', he says. 'If we could only get some idea . . .' This is the cue for a knock on the door: Duffy bringing news of an unidentified body just washed ashore, allow-ing the process of investigation to re-start.

In what follows Republic's reputation for producing action-packed serials is complicated rather than confirmed. Action makes way for methodical forensic work that locates this serial within the police pro-cedural sub-genre and develops the new line of investigation: as well as the body being identified, Lennie Slade's shoes reveal traces of fish scales that lead to the investigation of three abandoned canneries. Characters at this stage are sedentary rather than active, and the staging is that of the utilitarian office. The opening shot of Zarnoff behind his desk, to the right of the frame, is balanced by a shot of Tracy behind his desk, to the frame's left. These shots are followed by shots of Tracy's secretary Gwen at her desk and (at the other end of the telephone) the man from the Fish and Game Commission at his. Gwen is the sole female in the chapter and her role is strictly that of office worker rather than romantic or sexual interest (in stark contrast to the later roles of the actress credited here as Phyllis Isley but better known as Jennifer Jones).

The sound volume increases again when the G-Men leave the office to investigate the canneries, up to the point when Tracy arrives at the cannery already identified as Zarnoff's new base. A quieter tone is used for a sequence showing Tracy investigating the building (having sent his companion back to fetch the other G-Men) and surprising Zarnoff and his gang. The volume is briefly raised again when Zarnoff repeats his earlier action in the presence of Slade, pushing the button that causes Tracy to fall down the trapdoor. It is briefly raised again when Tracy fires his gun from the under the trapdoor and one of Zarnoff's henchmen pours anaesthetic down onto him, up to the point when Zarnoff says 'Quiet now'. In what follows the music volume rises and falls. A quiet steady beat accompanies sequences showing Zarnoff's set-up of the cliffhanger situation (a gun due to go off at the turn of the door handle, with the variation that the gun will be fired at those on the other side of the door in the expectation that they will return fire, thus killing Dick Tracy). Louder, more strident music accompanies shots of the approaching cars of the G-Men. The more extended shoot-out that might have been expected at an earlier stage only comes in the latter part of the chapter, in the exchange of fire that occurs when the G-Men arrive at the cannery as Zarnoff's men are leaving. The G-Men's entrance to the building echoes and builds on the earlier shots of Tracy entering the building, and leads in to the chapter-end cliffhanger, as music and narrative reach a climax. The whole chapter bar the opening recap and take-out looks towards this climax, with smaller-scale increases in tension along the way followed by a quietening of pace. Images and sequences are repeated, from the shot of the cannery that identifies Zarnoff's new base first to the audience (near the chapter beginning) then to Tracy (mid-chapter), to the trap-door sequence leading to Slade's death that serves to forewarn the audience of Tracy's fate when he surprises Zarnoff, and the G-Men in the corridor shots (first Tracy alone, then the larger group).

Not all Republic serial chapters were organized in this way. In 'The Tigermen's God' (*Darkest Africa*), fighting is limited to wildlife stock footage and the closing sequence in which Clyde Beatty is attacked by a tiger. But it was the studio's first serial, and the chapter was in many ways atypical. 'The Case of the Stolen Ransom' (*Federal Operator 99*) gives a better idea of the direction Republic was to take. The Federal Operator of the title is Jerry Blake, pursuer of Jim Belmont, who has stolen the Princess Cornelia's Crown Jewels. After a take-out in which Blake jumps from his car just before it goes into the gas station, there is again a return to base for both hero and villain, as the new line of action is established; Belmont demands a ransom for the jewels, with a view to getting the money but keeping the jewels. Blake follows the motorcyclist sent by Jim Belmont to collect the ransom, parachuting from his plane so as to land near Belmont's hide-out. Surprising the crooks, he gets away on the motorcycle, though in the ensuing chase his motorcycle goes over a cliff. The chapter illustrates how Republic moved towards reducing narrative to the bare bones: a valuable object that is stolen and then reclaimed. Chase is followed by a new line of action which is followed by pursuit, followed by fight, followed by chase and cliffhanger (in this instance, going over the cliff). In effect, the serial becomes the series, as indicated in the chapter titles: 'The Case of the Crown Jewels', 'The Case of the Stolen Ransom', 'The Case of the Lawful Counterfeit' . . .

Economy of narrative is evident in a different way in Republic's 'Vendetta' (*Daughter of Don Q*). In this chapter the recap and take-out end with the explosion from which Cliff had narrowly escaped. This is followed by a shot of Dolores Quantero driving her car, a shot of Dolores stopping her car to pick up Cliff, then a shot of Dolores, Cliff and the Quantero heir almost killed by Donovan. Asked about other relatives, Cliff and Dolores are directed to a distant cousin, Carlos Manning, who has an antique shop on 3rd Street. 'Good, let's get over there right away, maybe his shop is still open', says Dolores. The next shot is of the antique shop of Carlos Manning. Approximately forty seconds is needed to take hero and heroine from the cliffhanger take-out through the new line of investigation to (unknown to them at this stage) the base of the film's principle villain. A further two minutes and two scenes at the antique shop (the first featuring Dolores, Cliff and Manning, the second in the back room featuring Manning and Donovan) are needed to establish Manning's plan to become Don Quantero's only living heir and the wealthiest landowner in the city, and to take us to the middle action fight. There are none of the narrative complications found in a serial such as *King of the Wild*, and rather than that serial's multitude of characters and motives we are left with a hero and heroine against villain and henchman, with additional characters introduced only to support this central conflict.

Again, a Universal serial chapter offers a useful comparison. 'The Death Flood' (*Lost City of the Jungle*) features the arrival of Rod Stanton, United Peace Foundation investigator, in Zalabar, capital of Pendrang, to check on reports that Sir Eric Hazarias is still alive and co-ordinating a defence against the atomic bomb. He is accompanied by Marjorie Elmore, who introduces Stanton to her father (who is searching for the lost city of the jungle) and to Tai Shan, who is helping Stanton in his search, and who explains that he already knows Dr Elmore. Tai Shan introduces Stanton to his wife and then to the Chief of Police, who arranges an interview with Indra, owner of the Light of Asia Casino, and the woman who controls Pendrang. Indra indicates to Stanton that in order to meet Geoffrey London (the man who Stanton believes is Hazarias) he must first see London's secretary, Malborn. Malborn indicates to Stanton that meeting London will be difficult, and sends Stanton back to the Chief of Police. It is only after all these meetings that Stanton and Tai Shan find a note directing them to the sacred Pool of Light, in fact a plant by the Chief of Police, and to the cliffhanger. The extended nature of Stanton's attempt to meet London/Hazarias may have had something to do with the fact that Lionel Atwill, who played the villain, died during the production, but the resulting weight given to dialogue rather than action (though no one says 'Let's get over there right away') is broadly representative of Universal serials of this time. This is omnidirectional but without the mad intensity of a serial such as *King of the Wild*.

Republic generally emphasized action, but in a more structured way than Mascot or other minor studios. In particular, the studio retained and refined the fist fight. Much of a chapter such as 'Charred Witness' (*Secret Service in Darkest Africa* [1943]) is devoted to fighting but this is organized into set-piece fights along the lines outlined by Roberts, Herman and Mathis. A new line of action is seemingly established when Rex Bennett returns to the French Diplomatic Headquarters in Casablanca and tells his colleagues that locating their radio station will enable them to locate the Casablanca axis agency. This line of inquiry is interrupted by a phone call from the German agent, Baron von Rommler, impersonating Sultan Abou Ben Ali (who he has chained in the cellar). The false Sultan tells Rex that an attempt has been made on his life and asks him to go to an abandoned fisherman's shack to investigate. Reaching the shack, Rex is met by Wolfe and two other German agents. The ensuing fight lasts just under two minutes and consists of over forty shots: long shots of the stuntmen and medium shots and one close-up of the actors. The sequence has some narrative significance; when Wolfe demands that Rex tell him the whereabouts of the United Nations underground headquarters in Berlin the false address that Rex gives allows him and his allies to locate the radio station, thus returning the narrative to the line of action indicated earlier. However, this in effect means that the narrative leads from one fight to another. The fight is at the centre of the chapter, while the middle action fight is one of three fights in the chapter, the others being at the beginning (including the machine gun attack on Rex at the end, this lasts just over a minute) and end (about one minute forty seconds). From the end of the opening credits to the start of the closing credits the chapter lasts thirteen minutes forty-five seconds, just over a third of which is devoted to fighting.

Secret Service in Darkest Africa was directed for Republic by serial veteran Spencer Gordon Bennet, who also worked for Universal and Columbia. The Republic serials most famous for their fight scenes are those directed by William Witney and John English. As *Dick Tracy's G-Men* has already demonstrated, Witney–English serials did not necessarily revolve around a middle-action fight, though this is evident in another Dick Tracy serial chapter: 'The Prisoner Vanishes' (*Dick Tracy vs. Crime Inc.*). Going to the house of Dr Metzicoff, Tracy is met at the door by a man claiming to be the psychiatrist's butler. He is actually a henchman of The Ghost who has bound and gagged the real Dr Metzicoff and locked him in a cupboard. Tracy's discovery of the deception leads to a fight consisting of thirty-seven shots over a period of a minute and fourteen seconds. It uses the full space of the Metzicoff entrance hall, stairs and the landing, and culminates with the false butler crashing through the first floor balustrade, making for the door, but stopped by Tracy when he leaps from the first floor to the chandelier onto the ground floor and grabs his opponent before he can escape. Acrobatic stunt work includes leaps, rolls and cartwheels. This is the 'kinesthetic artistry' that Scott Higgins has linked to the Hong Kong Kung Fu films of the 1960s and after.[19] Witney's account of how he took inspiration from watching Busby Berkeley filming dance numbers is an oft-repeated story but does point to how the fight has an equivalent function to the dance.[20] Its only real narrative significance in this context is to delay Tracy's return to jail until just after The Ghost has helped Lucifer escape, thus leading into the chase and cliffhanger that make up the final section of the chapter. The fight exists as spectacle; the appeal of serials such as these rested both in their back-and-forth narrative and the spectacle of the fist fight.

Prior to its more dialogue-based final serials, individual Universal serials had varied the emphasis placed on the fight outside chapter beginnings and endings. 'Flaming Arrows' (*Rustlers of Red Dog*) is as action-based as any serial. An 'Indian' attack takes up most of the first half of 'The Flaming Forrest' (*The Oregon Trail*); the second half includes a brief gunfire exchange but no further fighting. A fifteen-second gunfight between Buck Gordon and Radigan's men in 'Stampede' (*Gordon of Ghost City* [1933]) follows a significantly longer sequence in which Mary Gray attempts to ride away on Gordon's horse which repeatedly rides back on Gordon's whistle: here Gordon's relationship with Gray takes precedence over action. Buck Gordon was played by Buck Jones, and the serial is constructed around Jones's persona and his tendency to emphasize heterosexual relationships and romance to a degree absent in other serials.

The situation was a little different at Columbia, where frenetic fights could be more comic than tense. Director James Horne, who made twelve serials for the studio between *The Spider's Web* (1938) and *Perils of the Royal Mounted* (1942), was quoted in one article as saying that in the serial 'No more than sixty feet of dialogue are possible at any time or the chant "When do we fight?" will start'.[21] However, while this gives a good idea of the pace of the serial he directed, Horne is best known for slapstick Laurel and Hardy comedies and aspects of these were retained in his Columbia serials. In the middle action of 'The Stolen Range Finder' (*Captain Midnight* [1942]) Captain Midnight rescues John Edwards from Ivan Shark's henchmen. The comedic tone is set when the henchmen (whose incompetence is repeatedly emphasized) burst through the door and fall on the floor, and the fight's frenetic pace is accentuated by the fast-motion of under-cranking and the hysterically blaring music. Punches and reactions are performed in an exaggerated style, and the fact that the fight ends in a burning building only adds to this effect.

The approach adopted at other studios varied. Stunt specialist and fight coordinator Yakima Canutt worked on *The Clutching Hand* and numerous other minor studio serials. Fighting in these could be brief (as in Mascot's 'The Fatal Warning', *The Mystery Squadron* [1933]), restricted to chapter beginnings and endings (Metropolitan's 'The Dog of Destiny' [*The Sign of the Wolf*]) or interspersed across the chapter. Stage and Screen's 'The Mystery Ship' (*The Black Coin* [1936]) features a brief exchange of gunfire during a car chase, a scene in which hero Terry Navarro fights one henchman while James Hackett pretends to fight another so that he will not be suspected of engineering Navarro's capture, a fight between two further henchmen when Navarro escapes, leading into a larger scale fight when Navarro's escape through the window lands him in Hop Sing's room. Sol Lesser's 'The House in the Hills' (*The Return of Chandhu*) resolutely downplays action. Chandhu has arranged for the local Museum to collect the Egyptian Mummy he has in his house, but the men from the museum are attacked and their attackers make off with Princess Nadji in the casket. However, the attack lasts only seconds, while the kidnapping of Princess Nadji is achieved through drugging her with the scent of a flower, and more time is devoted to the slowly soporific effect of the flower.

Both Universal and Columbia could play up elements other than the fight. The 1946 Columbia serial chapter, 'Jump to Eternity' (*Chick Carter, Detective*), includes shooting, but only at the chapter end. In Universal's 'A Call to Arms' (*The Indians are Coming*) Jack Manning tells Mary Woods that the moonlight is very beautiful tonight. They go outside and talk about the picture of Mary that Jack kept with him. Romantic music plays in the background. They almost kiss. The serial existed as a distinct form of cinema but particularly at the Hollywood Majors it could take on something of the appearance of other Hollywood films. *Chick Carter, Detective*, with its story of the search for the missing Blue Diamond, essentially belongs to a B-crime film world of nightclubs, apartments and taxis. *The Indians are Coming*, for all its reputation as the serial that brought the kids back to the cinema, is essentially a traditional romantic western melodrama.

In all these examples the chapter middle action has two primary functions: moving from one cliffhanger to the next, and providing spectacle of some kind. Spectacle regularly consisted of the fight, usually given some narrative significance but often extended beyond that. Yet it could take other forms. In 'The Thunder Riders' it was provided through the robots, television and gleaming architecture of *The Phantom Empire*'s underground kingdom of Murania. That futuristic image is also found or at least suggested in *The Lost City* (1935), which relied particularly on Ken Strictfaden's electrical effects, *Undersea Kingdom* (1935) and the *Flash Gordon* (1936–40) and *Buck Rogers* (1939) films. In 'Freezing Torture!' (*Flash Gordon Conquers the Universe*) this is combined with mountaineering and avalanche footage taken from *The White Hell of Pitz Palu* (1929). The spectacle of 'Thundering Doom' (*The Great Alaskan Mystery* [1944]) is mainly provided by *S.O.S. Iceberg* (1933), Hollywood's re-edited version of *S.O.S. Eisberg* (1931), another German film featuring Leni Riefenstahl. Scenes of Inuit life and polar bear hunting fill up the time between cliffhangers. Aerial footage or photography of airplanes (flying, tail-spinning, crashing) was used for spectacle in serials from *The*

Mystery Squadron (1933) to *Junior G-Men of the Air* (1942). 'The Typhoon of Terror' (*The Perils of Pauline* [1933]) combines this with scenes of revolution in China and storm at sea. The spectacle of place wasn't always provided by stock footage. Republic made effective use of industrial locations in chapters such as 'The Mysterious Friend' (*Daredevils of the Red Circle* [1939]), and Mascot of Los Angeles locations in, for instance, 'Pinholes'. 'Crossed Trails' (*The New Adventures of Tarzan* [1935]) uses not only stock wildlife footage but some extraordinary location shooting including scenes shot at the Mayan remains at Tical, Guatemala. It was unique in taking a serial shoot so far.

Where stock footage was used it was regularly identified as spectacle. 'Hey Pat, look' is the cue for wildlife stock footage in 'The Fang Strikes' (*Terry and the Pirates*). 'Something interesting Captain Tyler?' asks Mercedes Colby in 'Battling a U-Boat' (*Don Winslow of the Coast Guard* [1943]), followed by, 'My, I never thought there were so many seals in the world', when the Captain has passed her the binoculars and she (and we) have had a chance to see the seals. Essentially spectacle for its own sake, in this sequence a gesture is made towards a narrative link when Captain Tyler suggests that the number of seals is likely to mean some disturbance in the water. This is followed by a cut to a shot of the Japanese submarine preparing to attack the hospital ship. Airplane footage was repeatedly signalled as spectacle. Not only is 'The Secret of the Desert!' (*The Phantom of the Air* [1933]) dominated by airplane footage and aerial photography: the opening section uses an air show for the setting, as do parts of other Universal serials such as 'The Mail Goes Through' (*Tailspin Tommy*) and 'Plunge of Peril' (*Junior G-Men of the Air*). Serials also incorporated musical, comic and other performance acts. Over six minutes of the middle of 'The Phantom Killer' (*The Mystery of the River Boat* [1944]) is taken up with a series of performance acts aboard the 'Morning Glory' riverboat that functions as the serial's main setting, from knife-throwing to tap-dancing. There is only minimal deference to the serial's narrative concerning the ownership of bayou land containing nitrolene deposits. More generally, aside from Columbia's tendency to transform villains into clowns, the comedian sidekick was a relative regular character in Mascot serials.

Universal's 'The Road to Opar!' (*Tarzan the Tiger* [1929]) features La, Priestess of the Sun Worshippers, 'who has sworn that she will have no other mate than Tarzan', and spends the time in erotic dance with her group of female Sun Worshippers. Made in 1929 and released in silent and sound but not talking versions, this serial falls outside this chapter's territory: it is mentioned here because it provides a form of spectacle almost absent in later serials. The first *Flash Gordon* film approaches it, with its scenes in which Dale Arden is almost forced into marriage with the Emperor Ming (as Tarzan's wife is almost forced to become one of the wives of Achmet Zek in *Tarzan the Tiger*), whose daughter wants Flash Gordon and who surrounds himself with female servants. Tuska has referred to 'the increasingly awareness of the female body in Mascot productions', as revealed through tight-fitting jodhpurs and Verna Hillie's appearance in *Mystery Mountain* without the aid of a support garment, adding: 'And, even so, the feeling persists that the Mascot chapter plays, as serials and "B" Westerns in general, were intended only for the very young!'[22] It was an awareness that Republic was to pick up on, though in some serial chapters women are either absent or close to being so. There are no women at all in 'Human Target' (*Spy Smasher* [1942]) and only a stationary female figure is seen (and never heard) in the court scene in 'Masked Victory' (*The Lone Ranger Rides Again* [1939]). Nita van Sloan's one line in Columbia's 'Death Below' (*The Spider's Web* [1938]) is 'But Dick, I . . .': the only other woman featured in the chapter is an unnamed secretary. In contrast, the very low-budget *Queen of the Jungle*'s 'Radium Rays' (1935) almost slips into exploitation film territory in a bathing scene showing the naked back of Joan Lawrence, but it is the clothed female body that is emphasized in shots of the satin-clad Sonya Rokoff in 'The Crushing Walls' (*Shadow of Chinatown* [1936]) and Nyoka's wet jungle outfit in 'Queen of the Beasts' (*Jungle Girl* [1941]). In 'Tunnel of Terror' (*Flash Gordon*) the hero's half-clothed torso is the visual spectacle to a greater extent than the more dressed Princess Aura (Fig. 14).

Middle action could have a function other than spectacle: to move the serial's overall narrative forward. In 'Ringed by Fire' (*Secret Agent X-9* [1945]), as in *Lost City of the Jungle*'s 'Death Flood', it serves to mark the central characters arrival at the serial's main location (Shadow Island in the case of *Secret Agent X-9*). 'The Typhoon of Terror' (*The Perils of Pauline*) starts the action on its round the world journey. Second chapters could continue the work of the opening chapter, setting up the situation that would be played out in the remaining chapters. *Tailspin Tommy*'s 'The Mail Gets Through' establishes Tommy as an official pilot. *King of the Wild*'s 'Man-Eaters' provides complications to an already complicated narrative. However, the cliffhanger invariably draws the narrative back to where it was before, so that once again Tommy and Grant, along with other serial heroes, are faced with a life-threatening situation.

14. *Flash Gordon* (1935)

This links the serial to more general understandings of narrative: characters have a goal, but en route to that goal they encounter obstacles and delays. The wagon trail that is trying to get to Oregon in *The Oregon Trail* is repeatedly hindered by the schemes of Sam Morgan and Bull Bragg; in 'Flaming Forests' this takes them to a metaphorical and spatial dead end. The Boy Scouts in *Young Eagles* (1934) whose plane crashes in the South American jungle spend the rest of the serial attempting first to survive and second to get out of the jungle; in 'Drums of Hate' the obstacle they meet consists of a tribe who fatten them up so that they will make a better sacrifice. Like other Hollywood protagonists, they survive such difficulties and eventually get to go home. The difference with the film serial lies in the relative importance given to the obstacle rather than the goal. At the very end of *S.O.S. Coast Guard* (1937) Terry Kent marries Jean Norman. The marriage plot is at the heart of innumerable narratives, functioning as it does to provide a goal and closure, and in that sense, at odds with the 'open' serial.[23] As a 'closed' serial *S.O.S. Coast Guard* concludes with the closure of marriage, though it lacks any lead-up to the wedding. Kent and Norman are shown together (they start off

136

'Barrage of Death' trapped together in the hold of a ship at the bottom of the sea), but they don't even demonstrate the sort of relationship that Buck Gordon and Mary Gray have in *Gordon of Ghost City*. In *S.O.S. Coast Guard* Kent has another, more overt goal: to thwart Boroff's plan to sell his mass disintegrating gas to the government of Marovania. It is this that provides the drive that within 'Barrage of Death' takes Kent from one apparent watery grave to another.

Conclusion: The Meaning of the Serial

Fugitives from justice, men, women and dogs trapped in burning buildings, stampeding horses, cars that crash off the road, planes out of control, attacks by tigers, trap-doors, chases, fights, buzz-saws, death rays, explosions . . . Or, as *The Iron Claw* had it: 'Murder! Intrigue! Horror! Destruction! Brother against brother! Friend against friend!' In the light of these and other threats, sensations and consolations we might draw on the case made by Singer for a symptomatic reading of the silent serial queen melodrama. For Singer, melodrama was 'both dystopian, portraying worst-case scenarios of the victimization of innocents and competitive individualism run rampant, and utopian, offering a comforting affirmation of moral oversight and inevitable poetic justice'.[24] The serial queen melodrama, with its narratives of cultural discontinuity and social atomization, and of imperilled and empowered women, was a more specific response to urban modernity and the emerging image of the New Woman.[25] Many of the characteristics that he identified in such films were explicitly evoked in the sound serial (which had its own *The Perils of Pauline* as well as *Perils of Nyoka*) or perpetuated in stories that, in their own way, oscillated between empowerment and imperilment, and gave expression to the intimate relationship between excitement and anxiety.[26]

Singer introduced this argument with some caution, acknowledging that stories about hostile and sexualized competition were not unique to the era he was examining. It is worth retaining that caution. My own purpose is, first, to examine the nature and structure of the Hollywood sound serial, rather than to use them for social or cultural diagnosis. In a different context, Chris Baldrick and Robert Mighall have argued that, despite the growing body of criticism using Gothic horror literature as an index of contemporary anxieties, such material is particularly unreliable in this respect given its '*generic obligation* to evoke or produce fear. One might with equal misplaced confidence cite *Punch* magazine or the comic operas of Gilbert and Sullivan to establish the widespread cheerfulness and levity of Victorian culture'.[27] Similarly, the cliffhanger is obliged to produce tension. There is some justification for Singer's appeal to Martha Vicinus's suggestion that 'Melodrama is best understood as a combination of archetypal, mythic [elements] and time-specific responses to particular cultural and historical conditions'.[28] Yet that very emphasis on the time-specific response raises questions for any attempt to extend Singer's argument to a different context. His stress on the serial as a response to metropolitan modernity cannot simply be transferred to a later date when the base of the serial's appeal was outside the major American cities and when the gendered and generational characterization of the film serial audience had shifted at least to some extent.

Given that the film serial was devoted to the heightening and amelioration of tension, what we can do is examine the manner in which this was achieved and how it was inflected. The examination of serials made between 1930 and 1946 reveals consistency and variations. There are links between an early sound serial such as *King of the Wild* and the omnidirectional antagonism that Singer identified in *The Woman in Grey*, made just over a decade before. Later Republic serials from *Dick Tracy's G-Men* to *Daughter of Don Q* move away from a battle in which everyone is in competition with everyone else, syphoning tension into a conflict between two clearly defined forces. However this shift cannot be understood only in terms of different periods. Columbia serials such as *The Iron Claw* recycle, but also parody, an older serial model.

The study of the sound serial teaches us that new and past practices co-exist. This is evident on the aesthetic as well as the industrial level. Yet past practices that endure or are recovered take on new meanings. The image of the 'serial queen' was still invoked in the sound serial but she was no longer the central figure she had been in the 1910s. Dolores Quantero is introduced in the opening chapter of *Daughter of Don Q* as an active heroine, returning from the golf course to chase away the villain's henchman with her ju-jitsu skills. The take-out at the beginning of 'Doorway to Death' (*The Tiger Woman* [1944]) sees the Tiger Woman of the title racing to save Allen Saunders, condemned to die in the flaming lava pit by a false drum message. Yet subsequent action in both serials is largely reserved for the male heroes. Though publicity regularly suggested the return of the serial queen and Republic serials in particular regularly dwelt on women in jeopardy, most female characters in the serials of the 1930s and 1940s lacked even the imperilled but central role of the earlier serial-queens.

In the silent serials, noted Singer, there was 'no such social or biological entity as a mother'.[29] Similarly, mothers rarely appear in the sound serial, located as it is outside the domestic sphere. If they are not entirely absent, occasions when they are present serve to emphasize their marginal status within the world of the serial. The opening chapter of *Clancy of the Mounted* (1933) begins with a horseback chase accompanied by the same stirring music used in other Universal serials such as *The Roaring West*, but the expectation that this will lead Royal Mountie Tom Clancy to a fight or an arrest is overturned when he enters his brother's house and tells him to roll up his sleeves. A shot of Tom pouring water into a bowl, followed by the sound of a baby, reveals the situation: as Tom says, 'In the service of the mounted you must know a bit of everything', and evidently everything includes delivering babies. There is a mother here, but what is most remarkable about the scene is the way in which she is almost totally excluded even from the scene in which she gives birth. We see Tom and his brother Steve, but it is only towards the end of the scene that we get a glimpse of Maureen, Steve's wife. Initially she appears at the very edge of the frame (Fig. 15); this is followed by two shots in which her face is shown, the second of which has her smiling, looking up, but never speaking. Steve is shown crouching over his son's crib, while Maureen remains separated from the baby, gazing at the ceiling.

Alongside the absence of the mother, Singer noted that in the serials of the 1910s 'the frenzy of hostile competition was triggered, without fail, by the murder or incapacitation of a father figure . . . In serial-film melodrama, as in modern society as a whole, the rise of rampant individualism and antisocial will coincided with the downfall of benign paternalism'.[30] Again, this is not quite the unfailing narrative of the serials I have examined, and during the 1930s there was some tendency to move away from the family entirely. In the first Dick Tracy film, Dick's brother Gordon comes under the spell of The Spider. The second, *Dick Tracy Returns*, finds the G-Man fighting against the Stark gang, headed by the malevolent Pa Stark. However, family relations play no part in *Dick Tracy's G-Men* or *Dick Tracy vs. Crime Inc.* In the sound serial more generally there was a move towards emphasizing professional rather than personal motivation. Yet the death (*Black Arrow* [1944]), absence (*Perils of Nyoka*) or other incapacitation (*Scouts to the Rescue* [1939]) of a father or father figure continued to be used as a key narrative feature. However, rather than rampant individualism and the downfall of the patriarch, the narrative repeated in such films tends to be one in which the son steps into his father's shoes (or the Scouts come to the rescue). This is most

15. *Clancy of the Mounted* (1933)

apparent in Republic serials such as *King of the Texas Rangers* (1941) in which the death of Tom King Sr in the opening chapter leads to Tom King Jr stepping up to carry on his father's good work.

This is less a symptomatic reading than a statement of what is implicit or explicit in the serial. Even the racial attitudes underpinning these films could be overtly expressed, most starkly in the final title to 'Radium Rays' (*Queen of the Jungle*): 'Will David Worth meet his death at the hands of Joan Lawrence? Or will her white blood overcome her savage instinct in time to stop the sacrifice?' *The Lost City* infamously features a scientist whose 'magic' includes the ability to turn black people white, and a cast of black characters whose speech is reduced to a grunt. These are extreme examples but a racial hierarchy is implicit in other serials, accounting for, but not restricted to, the number of 'jungle' or 'oriental' settings. Digging a little further down, Jon Tuska linked the figure of Bimi the ape-man in *King of the Wild* to a broader, Depression-era American fascination 'with the notion of the brutish and the bestial seeking sympathy and human understanding' evident also in films such as *Frankenstein* (1931), *Island of Lost Souls* (1933) and *King Kong* (1933).[31] This association between

140

human and beast was evident also in, on the one hand, the presence of animals with human characteristics (Mascot's major star of the sound era was Rin-Tin-Tin), on the other hand the treatment of Africans and Native Americans as akin to the animal world.[32] Such attitudes are not, of course, unique to this period, but took on a particular form and significance in the United States between the First and Second World Wars. A further study would need to examine the relationship between the 'Red Peril' of serials such as *Heroes of the West*, the 'renegade Indians' who are invoked in innumerable serials, and the white men disguised as Indians who appear in chapters such as *White Eagle*'s 'The Jail Delivery'. It would need to assess the significance of characters such as Mala, both the lead character of *Robinson Crusoe of Clipper Island*, and Ray Wise, Hollywood's 'Jewish-Eskimo star' who appeared under the name 'Mala'.[33] It would also need to address the significance of the serial's different audiences, within and beyond the United States. One aspect to this is the way in which the serial, for all its emphasis on defying the impossible, down to a repeated triumph over death, could be the form of cinema closest to the experiences of its audience. This is most evident in the minor studios' serials from the first half of the 1930s. Filmed on location rather than on the sound stage, serials such as *The Vanishing Legion* (1931), with their stories of disputed land ownership, the threat of death and the promise of wealth, were in their own way rooted in a world familiar to those who watched them.

As this suggests, there are complexities within even those serials that avoid complexity, though to explore them properly it is necessary to move from examining the individual chapter of a wide range of serials to the analysis of patterns across chapters in a small number of serials.

5

Four Serials and a Feature, 1932–38

'I was never able to discover a coherent plot in these serials', wrote J.P. Mayer in his investigation into British cinema audience. 'A considerable amount of shooting goes on, with nerve-racking persecutions of the bad men who have kidnapped the beautiful, innocent blonde secretary. There is no lack of submarines (they are usually Japanese, and only 'recently' Nazi) being hunted down by aeroplanes, ships, etc., etc.'[1]

Mayer's suggestion that the serial offered submarines rather than story distinguishes this variety of film from what has become known as classical narrative. Hollywood films, Kristin Thompson argues, tend to be organized around four, roughly equal parts, divided by turning points: the set-up, the complicating action, the development and the climax.[2] The set-up establishes the initial action, the complicating action initiates a new direction, the development witnesses the struggle towards his or her goals, and involves action, suspense and delay, while the climax begins once all premises and lines of action have been introduced and consists of a straightforward progress towards the final resolution. Dividing the narrative into large scale parts allowed the spectator room to breathe between the action and space for other staples of classical storytelling, 'exposition, motivation, romance, and redundancy, but also humour, motifs, subplots, and the like'. It also allowed for gradual character change: without this structure *Jaws* (1975) might just be a string of shark attacks.[3]

Thompson's approach to classical Hollywood and New Hollywood is based on the examination of films but also guides to writing film scenarios such as William Lord Wright's *Photoplay Writing* (1920). 'There must be the opening of the story, the building and the plot development; the big situations and the climax; comedy relief and a happy ending', advised Wright, in a passage quoted by Thompson.[4] In fact, Wright prescribed this structure as appropriate for the two as well as the five-reel

142

film. His experience was as much with the short film and the serial as with the feature. In the 1920s Wright was in charge of serial production at Universal. His final credits include story contributions to *The Indians are Coming* and *Tarzan the Fearless* (released in 1933 in serial and feature versions).

In the section of *Photoplay Writing* devoted to the serial Wright advised that future serials would lack masked men, criminal conspirators, detective stories, chases, cheap sensationalism and the end-chapter hazard or thrill endangering the lead: 'clean stories of adventure, full of romance and devoid of crime are what are wanted for the present day serial picture'.[5] He cited the first chapter of *Winners of the West* (1922) as an example of this change, depending as it did 'a great deal on heart interest, with just a suggestion of what may follow'.[6] Wright was wrong. Future serials did not lack cheap sensationalism. In the sound era romance was abandoned or pushed to the margins. Serials such as *The Vanishing Legion* (1931) made an appeal to sentiment and even tears but this disappeared over time. There is little evidence of character change in the Hollywood serial. Motivation was reduced to a minimum. In general cliffhangers, which continued to be based around a hazard or thrill faced by the lead, were not turning points but points where the action returned to where it was at the previous cliffhanger. Wright's blueprint for the 'improved' serial was written at a time when Universal was responding to the threat of censorship and needs to be understood in that context.

In moving on to the 1930s, this chapter examines the cross-chapter structure in four serials: *The Lost Special* (1932), *The Whispering Shadow* (1933), *Jungle Jim* (1937) and *Daredevils of the Red Circle* (1939). In *Breaking the Glass Armor* Thompson used a neo-formalist analysis of the films in Universal's Sherlock Holmes series, *Terror by Night* (1946), to demonstrate how the complexity of the classical Hollywood system is evident even in the ordinary film.[7] I have a similar concern with looking beyond the established classics. Like *Terror by Night*, *The Lost Special* is a train-based serial based on the writing of Arthur Conan Doyle. *Jungle Jim* is a later Universal serial. *The Whispering Shadow* was made for Mascot, *Daredevils of the Red Circle* (the closest of the four to classic status) for Republic. This will not provide a comprehensive overview of variations in the 1930s sound serial. For a start it does not include a Columbia serial, nor a western, a genre which constituted a high proportion of serials made from the 1920s onwards. It will however allow for a relatively detailed examination of the serial structure across chapters, and will indicate ways in which the serial provided its own distinct form of storytelling. It provides an opportunity to examine serials made by both Major and Poverty Row studios and to examine those made at different stages in Universal's history. The fact that one of the above films, *The Whispering Shadow*, is also available in a feature version, will also allow me to compare serial and feature versions of the same story.

The Lost Special

The Lost Special was the final film directed by Henry MacRae, subsequently production supervisor for Universal serials. Credits of each chapter announce the story as 'by Sir Arthur Conan Doyle' and the serial takes as its starting point the situation that forms the basis for the story of the same name, originally included in Conan Doyle's 1898 collection, *Tales of Terror and Mystery*. In the Conan Doyle story a man charters a special train to take him from Liverpool to London; the dead body of the driver is later found, but no trace of the train or its passengers. It is not explicitly identified as a Sherlock Holmes story, but it is a puzzle narrative in which speculations as to the solution include one from 'an amateur reasoner of some celebrity at that date' whose letter to *The Times* on the subject includes the Holmesian statement that 'when the impossible has been eliminated the residuum, *however improbable*, must contain the truth'.[8] The actual solution is only revealed in the final part of the story, in the form of a confession from the criminal. This reveals that he had been employed by a syndicate with unlimited resources to prevent either the victim or his documents reaching a trial at which he was due to give evidence. With this end in mind, a temporary track had been used to take the train off the Liverpool to London route onto a disused colliery line, enabling the perpetuators of this scheme to do away with their victim, his documents, his companion and the train. The latter is disposed of in a disused colliery pit and all traces of the crime removed, including the temporary track.

In the Universal serial the train is carrying a cargo of gold bullion. In addition, while the full explanation of how the train disappeared comes at the end of the short story, the film depicts the trick at the very beginning of the first chapter (repeating this in the final chapter). Revelation of the identity of the man behind the plot is only minimally delayed. The film centres on two families, one headed by Horace Moore, who runs the States-Pacific Railroad Company, the other by Potter Hood, President of the Galconda Mining Company. The first scene in which Potter Hood appears also features his business partner, Sam Slater, who, it is revealed, had suggested that the entire shipment of gold be sent on the stolen train. The following scene reveals Slater and his gang at his headquarters (the Red Spot Club) plotting the next move, the theft of the train that will carry the remainder of the gold. The main focus, however, is on Potter Hood's son Tom (accompanied by his friend Bob) and Horace Moore's niece, Betty (accompanied by her friend Kate Bland) and their efforts to identify the thieves and reclaim the gold.

In her analysis of *Terror by Night*, Kristin Thompson illustrates how 'a film that started as an apparent murder mystery gradually drains the puzzle elements away, and in its second half it becomes more orientated towards suspense'.[9] Universal's serial is based on a mystery story but does not even start as a mystery. Though the characters' lack of knowledge may leave an audience wondering when Potter Hood will realize that his secretary is out to defraud him, at the end of first chapter they are more immediately directed towards the question of whether Betty and Kate will get out of their car in time, Betty having driven it across the railroad track just in front of the train taken over by Tom and Bob in order to prevent a second gold bullion theft.

Universal's *The Lost Special* thus conforms to the cliffhanger principle. It needs an overarching narrative, and while it does not present the audience with any questions about how trains can disappear or even about who makes them do this, gaps in the characters' knowledge gives them a motivation that carries through from chapter to chapter and provides an overarching structure. It lacks the 'stairstep construction' that Thompson identifies in *Terror by Night* (and classical Hollywood more generally).[10] At the end of the first chapter Tom and Bob are driving the train so fast that it smashes Betty's car. At the end of the second chapter Tom, Bob, Betty and Kate are in the train engine as it speeds ahead, but this time Bob (who has worked on trains before) has been shot and Bob doesn't know how to stop the train. At the end of the third chapter Tom, Bob and Betty are being chased in a motorboat. These are variations rather than developments; a consequence of the film serial's demand for action and spectacle. This demand is also met through regular fight scenes. The first three chapters feature two scenes of fist-fighting on the train roof, one accompanied by a fight in the train engine, a series of gun attacks on the train, and an extended brawl at the Red Lantern Club.

The fight with Slater's men towards the end of the second chapter leads to the discovery of a notebook on one of Slater's men. The entries are in code but in the next chapter Tom and Bob are able to get hold of the code-book, which in the fourth chapter leads to a laboratory for breaking down gold bars though this only leads to the fourth cliffhanger (a fire at the laboratory). The initial train-plus-gold-bullion-plus-criminals scenario is effectively repeated across the first two chapters but then gives way to a series of situations arising from Tom, Bob, Betty and Kate's attempt to track down the perpetrators. Attempts by Slater's gang to kidnap Potter Hood are followed by similar attempts on Betty Moore and Tom Hood. The back and forth pattern is given different motivations and locations but these attempts do little to progress the narrative. The kidnapping of Potter Hood is ostentatiously in order to get him to sign a document stating that he has reclaimed the stolen gold. It seems more likely to have been driven by the availability of the set for *The Old Dark House* (1932), here given a basement containing a water sluice room, put there, one of Potter's captors explains, 'for what purpose nobody knows, but what we do know is that this room is waterproof and soundproof'. The sluice room lacks any obvious realist explanation but it has a clear function in a narrative based around repeated imperilment, realized when Potter, Tom and Betty are trapped in the room as it fills with water. Only the final chapters witness some of the 'progress towards closure' that Thompson identifies in *Terror by Night*, as evidence of Slater's villainy becomes clear to Tom, Bob, Betty and Kate, and eventually to Potter.[11]

The train robbery establishes the characters' primary motivation: on Bob's part, preventing a further robbery and bringing the criminals to justice, on Slater's part, getting hold of the rest of the gold and avoiding detection. Betty is given further motivation: she introduces herself at the beginning as a reporter for the *Clarion*, and her aim is to get the story for the paper. In chapter three, when Potter Hood tells her that chasing after a band of criminals is not a woman's job she replies: 'But it's my job to get the story for the *Clarion*. And to prove to you that the tragedy of the lost special was no fault of the General Manager of the State Pacific, Mr Horace Moore, my uncle'. Here Betty highlights a further narrative drive: towards the reconciliation of the Hood and Moore families, introduced at the beginning as blaming each other for the robbery, but ultimately linked through Betty and Tom's relationship.

Betty's reporter role gives the film an explicit concern with story, though this is initially understood as little different from spectacle. Towards the end of the first chapter her search for the lost special fortuitously takes her and Kate to the very spot where Slater's gang plan their second train robbery. When Kate points out the lost train isn't around here, Betty replies, 'I've got to have it for my story'. 'There isn't a story around here', Kate tells her, 'You have to have people in a story . . .'

Kate would have realized her mistake if she knew her Aristotle better, and in particular Aristotle's dictum that there could not be a tragedy without action, but there could be a tragedy without character.[12] Betty is better informed, knowing that she and Kate wouldn't be there if there wasn't action, and thus a story, if one that belongs to melodrama rather than tragedy. Soon she is pointing out her friend's error. 'Look, a fight, I knew I'd get my story', she exclaims, driving her car fast enough to keep pace with the train: Tom and Bob having also fortuitously arrived on the scene, Tom is fighting a couple of Slater's men on the roof of the train.

The serial continues in a similar manner, with repeated attention drawn to Betty's story. At beginning of chapter three Bob outlines his plan for capturing Slater's men so that they can find out who stole the gold. 'Great, and I'll get my story for the *Clarion*' interjects Betty. 'Boy, what a story, let's go' says Betty when Tom and Bob are about to pursue a new line of investigation, and when Tom suggests that it would be too dangerous she insists that 'my paper is not going to be cheated out of that story'. 'We can get Betty's story, Tom' says Bob, and Kate adds that he is 'putting a creep on Betty's story'. Tom and Bob leave without her nonetheless, Bob with a parting, 'Now don't you worry, we'll bring you back a good story'.

This search for a story continues until the final chapter, when Gavin, one of Slater's men, agrees to talk. By now Betty, notebook in hand, has a more developed notion of story, drawing on the Aristotelian understanding of tragedy as an imitation of wholeness, and a whole as 'that which has a beginning, a middle and an end'.[13] 'Begin at the beginning, of course, I've got to have this right for my story', she tells Gavin (Fig. 16). This is the cue for a rare thing in a Universal (as opposed to Mascot or Republic) serial, repeat footage from the opening chapter. The deadline is also introduced for the first time: 'Don't stop him please, I've got to make the afternoon deadline for this story', she interjects at one point; 'I've got to make the afternoon editions for this story', she adds later. Gavin only reaches the point of the story where he would name the man behind the plot, Slater, when Slater himself arrives: his identification as the villain is left to Tom. Dialogue, which had earlier given way to the dramatization of the repeated footage, makes way for action when Slater is shot attempting to escape. Finally, Porter Hood tells Betty that he would rather the news of Slater's criminality wasn't published. 'But Mr Hood, I'm a reporter, and as a reporter I've got to turn my story in to the paper', she answers. 'That's right, Betty, as a reporter, but as Mrs Thomas Hood . . .' replies Tom. 'Don't you think you could kill the story for the

16. *The Lost Special* (1932)

honour of the family.' 'But it was such a wonderful finish to my story', she insists, weakly. 'Yes, it is a wonderful finish to *our* story', says Tom, and leads her out of the frame, followed by the departure of Kate and Bob. Only Porter Hood is left in the final shot, tearing up the pages of Betty's notebook.

The message is clear: the story Betty has been composing is negated in the interest of family honour and her transformation from female reporter to wife. Betty Moore will become Mrs Thomas Hood. The narrative ends with the most familiar of Hollywood goals, the formation of the heterosexual couple, and in this instance with the promise of marital closure (and a form of Aristotelian unity). However romance is given no greater weight here than it is in the marriage of Terry Kent and Jean Norman (another reporter) at the very end of *S.O.S. Coast Guard*. There is no romantic embrace at the end of *The Lost Special*; the union is as much that of two families as two individuals. Betty's own career ambitions are subjugated, though at no point given much substance. There is a long line of female reporters in the series and serial film, from *The Active Life of Dolly of the Dailies* (1914) to *Brenda Starr, Reporter* (1945). Such roles provide 'story' and deadlines precisely because they can lead the woman into danger, but also serve to introduce scenes of newspaper life and camaraderie. The latter are absent from *The Lost Special* making even the deadline introduced in the final chapter an artificial one.

The other narrative strand, the investigation into disappearance of the gold bullion special, gives a structure for the serial as a whole. It is introduced at the very beginning and helps provide motivation across the chapters. The final chapter returns to the beginning and provides a resolution in the form of the capture of the villain's henchmen and the death of the villain, after he has confessed his crimes and revealed the whereabouts of the stolen gold. The weight given to Gavin's confession make this a relatively extended resolution for a serial, but between the initial set-up and the final chapter *The Lost Special* does not so much build up to a climax as provide a rise and fall pattern structured around a series of cliffhangers.

The Whispering Shadow

The different chapters of *The Lost Special* are bound together by the search for the missing train and its cargo. In that sense the lost special is *The Lost Special*'s 'weenie', as Lewis Herman put it, 'the thing, the object, the papers, the will, the secret formula, the treasure map, the pearl of great value which sets the suave bad guy off on his trail of mayhem and arson against the good guy and his gal'.[14] However, neither train nor gold function quite in the same way as, for instance, the ring in *The Adventures of Frank Merriwell*, which is physically possessed by heroes and villains, and which bears an inscription that leads to the discovery of gold. The coded notebook discovered at the end of the second chapter serves as a sought after object but is not given narrative weight.

The Whispering Shadow provides a clearer example of how a physical object could be used to link the different chapters, if also of how the pursuit of that object leads to a dead end when it proves not to be the desired object after all or when, along the treasure hunt principle, it is simply one clue that leads on to another. In *The Whispering Shadow*, in addition, the search narrative is combined with a mystery plot. *The Lost Special* establishes the identity of the primary villain in the opening chapter, and a similar strategy is adopted in *Jungle Jim* and *Daredevils of the Red Circle*. The identity of the Whispering Shadow is only revealed in the final chapter of the serial of that name. Other Mascot serials such as *The Hurricane Express* and *The Wolf Dog* work on similar principles. The concealment of the villain's identity until the end was also used in serials from *The Fighting Devil Dogs* to *Mandrake the Magician*.

The Whispering Shadow also contains elements of the detective story. It features 'renowned' investigator Raymond, and, in the manner of the traditional detective story, a series of suspects who are repeatedly made to appear suspicious. This operates at a textual and extra-textual level. Professor Strang, one of the suspects, is played by Bela Lugosi, given top billing despite his secondary role. Jim Harmon and Donald F. Glut describe the film as mimicking Karl Freund's photography in *Dracula* (1931).[15] While most serials avoid a distinctive visual style, here the play of light and shadow is emphasized, though in the context of Los Angeles locations (notably the Belkins Storage Company warehouse) rather than the old world Gothic settings of *Dracula*. Mascot serials were often generic hybrids, most obviously in the case of *The Phantom Empire*, cinema's lone science fiction singing western serial. *The Whispering Shadow* is a hybrid in its own way: an action serial that is also a mystery-detection narrative, and perhaps a comedy. At one point *Variety* announced that Harry Langdon was to appear in the serial.[16] While this never happened, the film features Karl Dane in his final role before his suicide. Dane had won fame for his performance in *The Big Parade* (1925) but subsequently appeared in comic parts.

The film's principal hero is Jack Foster. He is the active hero, and his role is thus equivalent to characters such as Jerry Sheehan in *Blake of Scotland Yard* or Allan Parker in *Drums of Fu Manchu* (1940), men of action who assume a more significant role than their nominal superiors, Sir James Blake (in the case of *Blake of Scotland Yard*) and Sir Dennis Nayland Smith (in *Drums of Fu Manchu*). In *The Whispering Shadow* Foster usurps Raymond's role to the extent that he is responsible for the final deduction that unmasks the Shadow.

The first chapter of *The Whispering Shadow* establishes Jack's motivation: one of a series of mysterious attacks by the Whispering Shadow leads to the death of Jack Foster's brother, Bud. It also establishes that two criminals have hidden the imperial jewels of the Czar in the Empire Transport Company Warehouse. The criminals learn of the mysterious attacks through a newspaper headline: while *The Lost Special* features a reporter whose work remains unpublished, here the newspaper headline is used as means of communication. Concluding that the Shadow must be after the jewels, one of the criminals, Slade, escapes from jail and sets out to reclaim the jewels. News of their escape in turn reaches local Wax Museum owner, Professor Strang. The final part of the first chapter sees a succession of characters at the Empire Transport Company Warehouse, either because they are after the stolen jewels or because they are after those who are after the jewels. These include Professor Strang and his daughter Vera, Slade, the Shadow's gang (who arrive on roof of the building by autogiro), Raymond, Jack Foster, Bradley (President of the Empire Transport Company), Jerome (Vice-President), and company employees Sparks, Steinbeck and Jarvis. When Slade gets hold of the parcel he has been looking for, Strang attempts to get it off him, but the Shadow's gang get hold of it. Pursued by Jack, they return to their autogiro and attempt to escape.

The struggle for the weenie continues in the following chapters. These can be broken down as follows:

2. The parcel falls onto the roof, where it is picked up by Slade. He loses it to Vera, but then gets it back off her, and escapes by commandeering the car driven by Jerome. Jack follows on his motorbike, and succeeds in overpowering Slade, but discovers that the parcel is empty. He concludes that its contents must have been taken by Vera.

3. Vera tells her father that she doesn't have the jewels; in fact they have been obtained by Jerome, who has hidden them in a briefcase concealed under the seat of a chair in the Warehouse radio room. Jerome takes the briefcase home, only to find Slade already there, disguised as a gardener. Strang and Vera also arrive on the scene, and Jerome escapes from Slade when Strang starts to fill the room with gas. Jerome opens his concealed safe and takes out a box, but this is taken off him by Strang, who is in turn robbed by Slade, who is then pursued by Vera, Jack and the Shadow's men.

4. The Shadow's men get the parcel off Slade, but discover that it contains papers rather than the jewels. When they report back to the Shadow he tells them that the papers are also of great value to him. Vera tells Jack that her father has a right to the jewels. Jerome returns to the warehouse, where he hears the Shadow threatening to tell the world who he is if he doesn't give up the jewels, having learnt this information from the papers discovered by his men. The Shadow sends a man, Dupont, to get the jewels off Jerome, but when Jerome goes to collect them, he is intercepted by Jack, who in turn loses the jewels to Jarvis.

5. Jarvis pretends to his colleague Steinbeck that he didn't get the jewels. He goes to his room at the Palace Hotel. The receptionist

at the hotel, known as the Countess, is in league with the Shadow's men. She tells them of Jarvis's arrival. Dupont kills Jarvis, and the Countess and Young (another Shadow henchman) attempt to frame Jack.

6. Dupont and the Countess search Jarvis's room for the jewels. Vera tricks a policeman into allowing her into the room, and discovers a receipt from the hotel safe, which she gives to her father. Strang goes to the hotel with the aim of using the note to obtain the jewels, but he is preceded by Slade, now disguised as a cleaner. However Slade finds only the safe door (with two hotel employees tied up behind it); the Shadow's men have taken the safe itself. Jack follows Steinbeck to the hotel and then gets into a struggle with the Shadow's men, allowing Strang to get away with the parcel.

7. While attempting to escape with the parcel from the Palace Hotel, Strang is knocked out by Steinbeck. Steinbeck takes the parcel back to the radio room, where, after a fight, it is taken off him by Jack, but after a shoot-out the Shadow's men get it off him.

8. It is revealed that Jack hid the jewels before the Shadow's men took the parcel off him. In order to turn over the jewels to the police, he goes to the truck where he has hidden them in a belt. He is attacked again by the Shadow's men.

9. The Shadow's men are frightened away when Bradley arrives on the scene along with others working for the company. While Jack is still unconscious, Bradley gets the jewels off him. He later tells Jack that he has to leave for a while.

10. Young, who has been persuaded to join forces with Slade, gets the key to the safe deposit box in which Bradley has hidden the jewels, and forces him to write and sign an authorization to open the box. Jack and the Shadow's men arrive on the scene, and in the commotion Vera gets hold of the authorization but not the key.

11. Young is shot and Jerome discovers the safe deposit key. Slade thinks Vera has both the key and the authorization, but is killed attempting to get them. Vera gives the authorization to her father, who goes to the warehouse in an attempt to get the key. Jerome attempts to get the authorization off Strang, but is knocked out by Vera. The Shadow arrives, gets the key and the authorization, but is attacked by Jack.

12. The Shadow escapes, but Jack gets the key. In a series of final revelations, Strang is identified as the Foreign Minister of the Federated Baltic States, the jewels having been entrusted to him as security for a loan. Steinbeck is a special agent of a neighbouring state sent to stop the loan. Jerome is the only survivor of the House of (I think this is what he says) Balcanov, attempting to reclaim the jewels which he considers to be rightfully his. Sparks is revealed as the Whispering Shadow. He dies attempting to escape. Before his death he reveals that he been after the jewels for the wealth they will bring, enabling him to protect his 'Death Ray' invention.

The diamond in *Terror by Night*, notes Thompson, has no significance in itself: its return serves only to prevent a blot on Holmes's reputation.[17] However it is given a definite visual presence. A preamble to the main story, telling of the discovery of the Star of Rhodesia and how its owners have all met with a violent death, opens with a shot of a magazine feature on it that becomes a close-up of the diamond. On the train Holmes is shown the diamond by Lady Carstairs. After he reveals that he swapped a fake jewel for the real one he gives the latter to Lestrade, who is seen studying it carefully, just before he is attacked by Moran's henchman, allowing Colonel Moron (identified as a master jewel thief) to pocket the Star. The man pretending to be Inspector MacDonald then takes the Star off Moran, but Holmes gets it off him, and the film ends with a shot of Holmes showing the Star to Watson and Moran.

In contrast, the jewels in *The Whispering Shadow* are something of a chimera. Jerome takes a brief look at them in chapter three, and Jack is seen hiding them in a belt at the end of chapter eight, footage that is repeated at the beginning of chapter nine. Otherwise, the different characters chase after a parcel supposedly containing the jewels but that proves to be empty or to contain something else: papers, a hotel safe receipt which proves useless when the safe itself is stolen, another package, a belt, a key to a safety deposit box, and a note giving authorization to open the box. These do not serve to bring the jewels closer. On the contrary, the jewels seem to recede in the course of the film, and this emptiness is only reinforced in the chapter six scene in which Jack discovers a safe door without a safe.

Names add a further sense of surface grandeur concealing an inner emptiness. The central location is the *Empire* Transport Company. When the location shifts in chapter five it is to the *Palace* Hotel, where the receptionist is called the *Countess*. *The Whispering Shadow* gives a peculiar imperial identity to its often dingy Los Angeles locations.

The failure to grasp the jewels has a narrative function, allowing as it does for the story to be extended across chapters. However, this makes the 'development' circular rather than linear. The serial here deals with the narrative extension of its format through playing out repeated frustration, as characters again and again are deceived into thinking they have got hold of what they are seeking, and through a convoluted narrative structure of multiple characters with different motivations. This is in contrast to *The Lost Special* in which the opposing sides are clearly established, with the potential complication of the Potter Hood/Horace Moore rivalry progressively receding into the background. In both serials the conflict involves repeated physical battles and on occasions similar cliffhanging situations. While one of the locations in *The Lost Special* is fitted with a sluice room, Dr Strang's Wax Museum comes complete with a room with collapsing walls. Where the serials diverge is that in the Mascot film no one even gets as far as the 'for what purpose nobody knows' justification given in *The Lost Special*. We simply have to accept that places like Dr Strang's Wax Museum are likely to be equipped with this sort of facility.

The peril of the collapsing room is evaded in the take-out of the following chapter. Possession of the jewels is never achieved. In the final chapter the key to the safe deposit box is recovered but not the jewels themselves. Resolution comes with the unmasking and death of the Shadow, who is revealed not to have been interested in the jewels themselves, but only in the wealth they would bring him that would enable him to protect his Death Ray invention.[18] As in *The Lost Special*, the male and female lead are together at the close but otherwise there is no particular emphasis on romance and again the final fade-out is on another figure: on this occasion, Strang, in apparent deference to Lugosi's stardom. It was with some justification that a later *Variety* feature on Mascot boss Nat Levine announced: 'Loved Brawls, Not Sex Mush'.[19]

In the route to this point *The Whispering Shadow* does not merely repeat the basic pattern of overlap-takeout-pursuit-fight-cliffhanger. It makes greater than usual use of the economy chapter. Revisiting past events fits the conventions of the detective story. As Thompson notes, narration within this genre typically 'first presents us with either the murder, the discovery of the body, or the moment at which the protagonist-detective is called in'; the lack of reordering of events beyond the local level indicates how *Terror by Night* diverges from such conventions.[20] The chronology of events is re-ordered in Conan Doyle's 'The Lost Special': the Herbert de Lernac confession that takes up the latter part of the Doyle story returns to the events recounted at the beginning, providing the story's explanation by filling in the details missing in the original account. Universal's *The Lost Special* repeats but undercuts this by also providing this information at the beginning. Repetition is more extensive in *The Whispering Shadow*. It includes chapter five, when Jack's narrow escape from death by electric disc is the cue for repeat footage from chapter one showing the death of the Shadow henchman at the point of confession was by the same radio death ray. The same chapter later repeats footage from chapter two, including the collapsing room cliffhanger. Chapter six then repeats material from chapter five. Chapter eight includes repeat footage from chapter one, when Jack tells Vera of how the death of his brother has led him to suspect Professor Strang. Chapter ten includes repeat footage from chapter three and from chapter one, while chapter twelve repeats footage from chapters four and five, intercut with brief additional footage to confirm the identity of the Shadow. These sequences are in addition to the recap footage used at the beginning of each chapter but the first. The repeat footage used in the middle of chapter twelve has a function in the identification of the villain though not for any deduction in which the audience can share since it depends, like many cliffhanger take-outs, on a shot previously withheld from the audience. In the serial as a whole, the repetition is more significant in allowing a second view of set-pieces such as the collapsing room and the abortive flight of the autogiro.

The Whispering Shadow diverges further from detective and classical conventions in its use of space. Rather than the mapped out locations used in the traditional detective story (literally in those novels that come complete with an accompanying room plan), the film features a villain able to kill at a distance by means of an electric disc, and able to project his voice and shadow across space.[21] Thus in the opening chapter, Jack races to the deserted country road where Bud is driving his truck only to be confronted by the villain's projected whisper and shadow. In this it is similar to other serials of the time, which regularly arm villains with an omniscient form of television (used in the etymologically correct sense of distant vision), here varied through the early-talkie emphasis on radio.[22] What *The Whispering Shadow* lacks is any real attempt at explanation. At the end the Shadow says he might as well demonstrate how he was able to project his voice and image, but he does nothing of the sort, merely using this in his attempt to escape. His henchmen are repeatedly shown sitting around a table in a darkened room, listening to his instructions

17. *The Whispering Shadow* (1933)

18. *The Whispering Shadow* (1933)

and warnings. The room's location is never established. Adding to the sense of disorientation is the way in which editing is repeatedly used to make false spatial connections. Serials regularly use eye-line matches to link shots filmed at different places and times, as when stock wildlife footage is juxtaposed next to new film of an onlooker in order to indicate that they are looking at the wildlife. Setting out as it does to suggest that different characters might be the Shadow, *The Whispering Shadow* uses editing to match shots which the narrative goes on to indicate have no connection. In chapter four a shot of the Shadow's henchmen listening to the Shadow is followed by a shot of Professor Strang, crouching over the equipment in his Wax Museum as if he had just been speaking. In chapter six a similar shot is followed by a shot of Steinbeck, a sinister gleam in his eye as he looks up from his radio equipment (Figs 17 and 18). Such juxtapositions follow the serial's perennial concern to deceive the audience.

The Whispering Shadow cannot be called 'classical' in any meaningful sense of the word. It has better claim to be an incoherent text in that its efforts to build up suspicion and intrigue overstep the resolution it finally provides. This leaves it as something of a low-rent, speeded-up *Fantomas* (1913) without the purpose of that film's titular villain. Nor can it properly be seen as having the stair-step structure that Thompson identifies in *Terror by Night*. While the jewels recede from view the Shadow himself is finally identified, but in the final chapter, hurriedly. This is in line with other serials, and with Bertram Millhauser's notion that after the initial reels the serial story is practically dropped until the final reel, when the mystery is solved.[23]

The feature version, which has a running time of just over an hour, highlights the narrative redundancy of the serial's middle chapters. I have seen no evidence of a 1930s release for such a version. Gary Rhodes reports that in France, *The Whispering Shadow* was released as a two-part feature, *The Shadow That Kills*, part one being *The Master of Mystery*, part two *The Lair of the Shadow*, though posters for different chapters indicate that *L'ombre qui tue* was released in France as a twelve-chapter serial.[24] It is possible that the feature version (available through Sinister Cinema) was a re-edit for television. The titles at the beginning are the same as for the serial, down to the words 'a 12-part serial', and the end title also has 'A Mascot Serial'. It nonetheless provides a way of examining how the chapters of a serial could be compacted into feature length.

The first half hour of the feature version is simply the serial's opening chapter. What follows consists of the opening few minutes of the second chapter, a sequence from the fourth chapter, followed by material from the tenth, eleventh and final chapters. The cliffhangers are lost, both in the sense that sequences such as the walls closing in on Jack and Vera are no longer there and in the fact that while at the end of chapter ten in the serial Jack appears to shoot Vera but it is revealed at the beginning of chapter eleven that it is Young who he shoots: in the feature we simply see Jack shoot Young. The recaps have also gone, though the feature version still has to make time for the repeat footage in chapter twelve as this is necessary for the identification of the Shadow. The majority of chapters two to nine are missing also. Some characters, such as the Countess, no longer appear, while others, such as Young, appear without introduction. This adds a little to the confusion, yet overall *The Whispering Shadow* is no more confusing as a feature than as a serial.

Jungle Jim

Jungle Jim was based on a comic strip drawn by Alex Raymond, illustrator also of the *Flash Gordon* strip. Both strips were launched on 7 January 1934. Written by Don Moore, weekly editions of *Jungle Jim* continued to appear until 1954. It was the first significant strip with a jungle setting to appear after *Tarzan*, though differed from it both in its Asian rather than African setting and in having a central character who was a western hunter-explorer. A radio series, *The Adventures of Jungle Jim*, was broadcast between 1935 and 1954. Johnny Weissmuller played the title character in a series of *Jungle Jim* films made for Columbia between 1948 and 1956 (though for the final films he used his own name), and a *Jungle Jim* television series ran in 1955 and 1956. The Universal serial differs from its source in using an African setting. It followed on from earlier comic strip adaptations that had begun with *Tailspin Tommy*. It was co-directed by Ford Beebe, whose career in serials ran from a contribution to the screenplay of *The Girl and the Game* (1915) to co-directing *Overland Mail* (1942), and Cliff Smith, who shared directing credits on six Universal serials released in 1936–37. Henry MacRae shared producer credit with Ben Koenig, who had previously worked for Mascot.

The serial's chapter introductions allude to their source through the comic book style that Universal adopted at this time, and acknowledge Alex Raymond as author, but indicate the difference between film and print versions. Thus the second chapter begins:

Jungle Jim, famous African explorer, and his pal, Mallay Mike, are trailing a murderer through the jungle.

LaBat, the murderer, and his partner, Slade, are searching for the lost heiress to a fortune.

Joan Redmond, the missing heiress, has grown up among lions in the jungle.

A war party of natives who regard Joan as their goddess are sighted by Jim and Mike who head for a rocky elevation to avoid them.

In the sound era the 'jungle goddess/queen/princess' theme was used also in *Queen of the Jungle* (1935) (essentially, the 1922 *Jungle Goddess* recycled with some new footage), Universal's *Call of the Savage* (1933), *Jungle Queen* (1945) and Columbia's *Congo Bill* (1948). The later has the same premise as *Jungle Jim*: a search for a missing heiress by both the eponymous hero and a relative after her money that leads to a white woman who rules over the indigenous population. This was itself a variation on the narrative of *Tarzan the Fearless*, where Tarzan is the heir in the jungle. In *Jungle Jim* LaBat's murder of Jim's friend Red provides the hero's initial motive (he fights for justice first), but like LaBat, Slade (no direct relation to the other villainous Slades who appear in *The Whispering Shadow* and *Dick Tracy's G-Men*) and their employer, Bruce Redmond, Jim and Mike are also searching for Joan/the Lion Goddess.

The notion of the serial narrative as a conflict between the heroine–hero team and the villain expressed through a back-and-forth struggle for the physical possession of the heroine and of some highly prized object seems particularly appropriate here, though in this case the heroine is the 'weenie'. This is not a retrospective reading. The *Jungle Jim* press-book included an item titled 'What is A Weenie?' which suggest that the secret of the serial's appeal lay 'in what Hollywood writers call 'the weenie':

A 'weenie' is anything—a girl, a treasure, a fortune—over which two men or a group of men can fight or contend. The contest for the 'weenie' forms the foundation for the plot of the story.

Sometimes a story has two 'weenies' or even three. A good example of this is contained in Universal's exciting new serial, 'Jungle Jim' . . .

In it the prizes over which the opposing forces fight are a girl and a fortune she has inherited. 'Jungle Jim', played by Grant Withers, and his pal 'Malay Mike', played by Raymond Hatton, are on the girl's side. Pitted against them are a sinister escaped convict, known as the 'Cobra', and a group of men who would kill the girl so that they can inherit the money.[25]

This points to the serial's multiplication of villains and motives. Jim and Mike are pitted against the Cobra and his sister Shanghai Lil as well as Bruce Redmond, LaBat and Slade. The back-and-forth struggle is primarily a struggle between those attempting to get Joan out of the jungle and those who don't want her to get out. Leaving the jungle and going to New York will allow Joan to claim her inheritance, and for that reason Bruce wants her to stay there so that he can be the one who makes that claim. The Cobra and Shanghai Lil are identified as fugitives from justice who have persuaded Joan that the Cobra is her father. They need her to remain in the jungle as it is through her that they hold sway over the local people. They also need to prevent knowledge of their whereabouts reaching the outside world. The situation shifts to some extent at different stages. Joan's role changes. Initially she is the Lion Goddess, hostile to Jungle Jim's party. As her hostility turns to sympathy and even love for Jim, in the fourth chapter she also learns of her true lineage and comes to disassociate herself from the Cobra. In the same chapter, believing Joan to have been killed, the Cobra and Shanghai Lil devise a plan to leave the jungle for New York, pretending to be the heir to the Redmond fortune. LaBat, through his murder of Red Hallihan, provides Jungle Jim's initial motivation, but is killed himself by a leopard in chapter six, allowing Jim's motivation to switch to that of helping Joan.

In all this the Cobra's castle serves as the central location (the castle in the jungle not being unique to this serial: see also *Call of the Savage* and *The Phantom* [1943]). It is identified as a destination in the first chapter, while from the second chapter it features through repeated arrivals and departures. Thus:

2. Movement to and from the castle. Jim and Mike are captured and taken to the Cobra's castle. They are allowed to leave after Jim has fought and killed a tiger on condition that they leave the jungle. When Joan discovers that their guns have been returned to them without ammunition she follows them with a supply of bullets.
3. Movement from the castle. Fearing that Joan is making for the coast with Jim and Mike, the Cobra sends a message to the neigh-

bouring chief, telling him to capture the white men and put them to death.

4. Movement to the castle. Jim and Mike survive, and the Cobra's warriors capture Slade, LaBat and Bruce and take them to the castle. The Cobra proposes to his sister that they get Slade to take them to the coast so that they can claim the Redmond fortune. Slade and his party do not trust them, and shut Shanghai Lil in the castle dungeon. Needing more ammunition, Jim and Mike return to the castle arsenal just as Slade's party are about to explode the ammunition they are not taking themselves.

5. Movement from the castle. The Cobra frees Shanghai Lil from the dungeon. Jim and Mike hide in the castle, managing to evade the Cobra and his warriors. They escape from the castle and go in search of Joan.

6. Movement to the castle. The Cobra's warriors capture Jim and Mike and bring them back to the castle. In order to get Joan to return, the Cobra has the drums announce that they are to be executed at dusk.

7. Movement to and from the castle. Joan and her faithful servant Kolu return in time to save her friends. She tells the Cobra that she is going away with Jim but agrees to stay when Shanghai Lil promises that Jim and Mike will receive safe conduct to the coast if she stays. Slade and Bruce are brought back to the castle. The Cobra agrees to let them go if they get rid of Jim and Mike. Joan leaves to find Jim when she hears of their plot.

8. Movement from the castle. When Slade tells Joan that Jim and Mike have been killed she agrees to leave the castle, going with them to the coast.

9. Movement to the castle. Slade and Bruce ask Hawks (a pilot forced to land his plane close to the castle) to help them rescue Joan from the Cobra. They arrive back at the castle shortly after Joan, Jim and Mike have been escorted there by the Cobra's warriors.

10. Movement from and to the castle. Jim escapes from the castle but returns to rescue Mike. Slade, Bruce and Hawks force Joan to leave with them. Slade plans to get Hawks to fly him and Joan out of the jungle (the plane will only carry three people, so he plans to leave Bruce behind).

11. Movement to the castle. Having discovered that Hawks is a Secret Agent looking for the Cobra and Shanghai Lil, Slade returns to

the castle, and proposes that the Cobra (an ex-flier) fly the three of them to safety. Jim and Mike return to the castle.

12. Movement to and from the castle. Attempting to escape, Slade and the Cobra are captured by Mike and the warriors. They are taken back to the castle and put in the dungeon until the planes that Hawks has wired for takes them away. Joan tells the warriors she is going away but promises to return.

Interspersed with this is a repeated process through which Joan, in her role as weenie, is captured and rescued. Thus in chapter three her search for Jim leads to her capture by Slade from whom she is subsequently rescued. A romantic relationship between Joan (played by the 16 year-old Betty Jane Rhodes) and Jim (played by the 33 year-old Grant Withers) is indicated, notably in the final shot of the two on a boat leaving the jungle, but again remains undeveloped.

The back-and-forth struggle is also combined with extensive shots of wildlife, animal fights and other stock footage. A significant proportion of this was taken from the location filming done for Universal's *East*

19. *Jungle Jim* (1936)

of Borneo (1931), footage that can also be found in serials such as *Call of the Savage* and *The Perils of Pauline*. Some effort is made to integrate this into the narrative. Thus the volcano featured in *East of Borneo*, and in *Call of the Savage* (for the chapter nine cliffhanger) as well as Joseph Cornell's *Rose Hobart* (1935), is reactivated in chapter seven of *Jungle Jim* (Fig. 19), providing a means by which the Cobra maintains his hold over the superstitious warriors by pretending to be able to control the elements.[26] Elsewhere such material halts the narrative. In chapter eight, Slade, Bruce, Joan and a party of warriors arrive in a village where they are told a lion has killed a child. As the village's own warriors are away on a hunt, Joan agrees that their party of warriors will kill the lion. 'You mean we must wait while our safari hunts the lion?' asks Slade. They must, as must the narrative. The ensuing sequence uses the same animal hunt shots as an equivalent sequence in chapter ten of *Call of the Savage*. The narrative then resumes as Joan and the others return to the village where they encounter Jim and Mike but also hear the Cobra's drums now ordering death to all white men.

Other, briefer sequences include moments such the first chapter sequence when a shot of one of the guides saying 'Look bwana' to Jim is followed by successive shots of giraffes, elephants and birds all supposedly moving away from Jim and his party though across quite different landscapes, and the chapter ten sequence where a montage of vegetation silhouetted against the rising sun, zebras, lions and other animals, is used simply to signify jungle/the wild. In part this is padding, a cost saving device like the use of the castle from Universal horror films. Original filming (including some animal sequences) thus could be limited to the vicinity of Los Angeles, helping to extend the narrative across twelve chapters. Yet while this material was often inessential to the narrative it was essential to what this genre provided: scenes of wildlife, scenes of animals fighting animals, animals attacking people, people shooting animals, animals and people, as well as of people who the titles repeatedly identify as 'savages'. Space and place become subordinate not just to narrative but also to the demand for sensation and spectacle. This operates both through the use of eye-line match editing to join different locations and through the construction of a jungle setting that is identified as African but is in fact (like Mascot's *The Lost Jungle*) inter-continental. The presence of tigers in Africa is given a nominal explanation through an opening sequence in which the shipwrecked ship which landed Joan in Africa was carrying a cargo of caged animals, tigers included. There is also an acknowledgement of sorts of the mismatch in Mike's 'Confound tigers. Always getting in my way. Ain't no business in this country nohow' (spoken just after he has shot one of those tigers). In effect, the film offers a menagerie or circus rather than a geographical location in the way in which it mixes lions, tigers and other animals from elephants to rabbits, and combines footage from *East of Borneo* with travelogues and scenes shot on the studio backlot.

Throughout all this there is an insistent and explicit concern with 'whiteness'. In his influential article on 'whiteness as an ethnic category', Richard Dyer refers to how difficult it is to 'see' whiteness:

> It is the way that black people are marked as black (are not just people) in representation that has made it relatively easy to analyse their representation, whereas white people—not there as a category and everywhere everything as a fact—are difficult, if not impossible, to analyse *qua* white.[27]

In contrast, in *Jungle Jim* 'white' does exist as a category, and is articulated to a greater degree than 'black'. In the first chapter Slade is introduced telling Bruce Redmond 'I tell you there is no mysterious white woman living in the jungle'. LaBat counters, 'My number one black boy has seen her with his own eyes . . . He tell me she's white . . .' The exchange is echoed in the comments of Tyler (the friend of Joan Redmond's father who initiates the search for her): 'The skipper of the little boat that brought me here said something about a white girl, a sort of a goddess among the blacks'. In the chapter there are no further references to 'black' but repeated references to 'white': 'Then we come to this stone castle I've been telling you about. It's where we find this white girl, this Lion Goddess' (LaBat), 'WHITE MEN COMING' (message sent by the drums and printed as a subtitle), 'White man's safari's coming to this country' (the Cobra, translating for his sister the message given to him by one of his warriors), 'White men! Well what are you going to do?' (his sister's response), 'My dear sister, as long as I am the White Cobra of the Busambos you have nothing to fear' (the Cobra's reply), 'WHITE MEN COMING, DRIVE THEM BACK' (drum message) (Fig. 20). 'White men, they'll never get my lions' (Joan, hearing the drums—the first words she speaks), 'Bwana Jim, war drums, [inaudible] by white men very bad' (guide to Jim).

Jungle Jim does not quite echo *Queen of the Jungle*'s contrast between 'white blood' and 'savage instinct'. The opening titles to chapter six of *Jungle Jim* identify the Cobra as the 'white ruler of a savage African tribe'

20. *Jungle Jim* (1936)

but as this highlights, the film's villains are white, including the white-suited man who identifies himself as the 'White Cobra'. Joan associates white men with hunters/killers. However, this is in accordance with the film's narrative of white superiority. In essence the warriors and villagers seen in the film are of the jungle and presented in a similar way to the lions, tigers and other animals, as faithful or hostile but superstitious and savage while capable of being tamed. Dyer ends his discussion of the British-made, Africa-set *Simba* (1955) by saying that the film endorses 'the moral superiority of white values of reason, order and boundedness, yet suggests a loss of belief in their efficacy'.[28] If *Jungle Jim* indicates any such loss of belief it keeps this under wraps. Unlike *Simba* it is not a film that addresses questions of inter-racial relationships. It uses images of 'black' and 'white' for sensation, but it is underpinned by an ideology of the benevolence of white imperial rule, illustrated in Joan's farewell message to return, 'before many moons, bringing with us the things I promised to make you happy'.

There are elements of classical Hollywood narrative within *Jungle Jim*. It provides the clarity also at the heart of *The Lost Special* rather than the confusion of *The Whispering Shadow*. Motivation is spelt out to a greater degree than the Mascot film, while the triangular structure engineered through two sets of villains allow for a development absent from *The Lost Special*. Time and space are mapped out even if the details are not filled in. Like the Universal's B-series film, *Terror by Night*, the serial's story has a prologue. In this instance it demonstrats how Joan Redmond (and assorted non-indigenous animals) came to Africa, and while the serial's locations can be divided into the basic categories of coast/jungle/castle, this does map the narrative to a greater degree than *The Whispering Shadow* or even *The Lost Special* (which takes its inspiration from a phantom railway line). 'Primarily tuned to the juvenile appetite for action and still more action', commented one reviewer, 'the story continuity, nevertheless, has decided appeal for the adult who inclines towards screen-fare of the action-thrill genre'.[29] In no way does this take the serial away from a back-and-forth serial structure; indeed, the 'What is a Weenie?' feature in the film's pressbook suggests that this was precisely the principle on which it was constructed. *The Lost City* is a far cruder serial in comparison, and unlike that serial *Jungle Jim* allows selected black characters to speak. The latter remained firmly within a genre of white criminals, goddesses and hunters whose rule may be despotic or benevolent.

Daredevils of the Red Circle

Of the four serials considered in this chapter, *Daredevils of the Red Circle* is the one with the most substantial reputation. Favourable reception dates from the initial release of the serial's first chapter. 'Oh boy, does this start off swell' began the *Showman's Trade Review*, continuing, 'Your audiences won't have to be kids again to enjoy this, for although it's highly fantastic, it is performed and acted with such skill that even the most sceptical theatregoer will find himself almost overcome with suspense'.[30] The serial was one of Republic's twelve-chapter 'stream-line' releases rather than one of the studio's more heavily promoted fifteen-chapter serials. Directed by John English and William Witney, its cast included (as the three daredevil heroes), Herman Brix, Charles Quigley and regular stuntman David Sharpe, as well as Charles Middleton and Miles Mander as the villain and the industrialist he impersonates. Female lead Carole Landis plays a more limited role than Cecilia Parker as Betty Moore in *The Lost Special*, Viva Tattersall as Vera Strang in *The Whispering Shadow* and Betty Jane Rhodes as Joan Redmond in *Jungle Jim*. Its reputation rests on its cliffhangers (particularly the one

21. *Daredevils of the Red Circle* (1939)

that closes the first chapter), the acrobatic performance of its three leads, Middleton's portrayal of the malevolent escaped convict Harry Crowel/39013 (the prison number, pronounced as 'thirty-nine Oh thirteen', by which he is generally referred) and its unadorned emphasis on action and suspense.

Daredevils of the Red Circle announces its commitment to action from the start with a short montage of newspaper headlines and explosions. The initial set-up is established in the first two minutes. Having established that 39013 is waging war against Horace Granville for helping send him to prison, Dr Malcolm (one of his assistants), tells the escaped convict that five of the major Granville enterprises have already been wiped out. A shot shows a list with both the San Mateo Hydro-Electric Dam (12,000,000—presumably valued at $12 million) and the Los Gatos Mining Co. (8,000,000) crossed out and ticked. Four further enterprises are listed: the Granville Amusement Center (2,000,000), the Channel Tunnel (10,000,000), the Tri-City Gas Company (20,000,000) and Commerce Steamship Lines (14,000,000) (Fig. 21). This provides a basic narrative framework. In chapter one 39013 succeeds in sabotaging both the Amusement Center and the Channel Tunnel. He attempts to destroy the Tri-City Gas Plant in chapter four and again in chapter nine. He never actually gets as far as the Commerce Steamship Lines. How then does the serial sustain its narrative over twelve chapters?

Perhaps Dr Malcolm's list is incomplete. It includes only two of five enterprises that have already been destroyed, and might therefore be supposed to list only some of the remaining enterprises. The Gas company does not seem to be a single entity: in chapter two the threat is against the Granville Chemical Co., in chapter seven it is the Granville Radium Mine, in chapter eight the Verdugo Pass Pipeline and the wells of Kettle Drum Valley. In chapter five the intended victim is the District Attorney who, along with Horace Granville was responsible for sending 39013 to prison.

An alternative is that the audience pays no attention to the detail of a list shown on the screen for about two seconds, being more concerned with the forthcoming action.[31] The narrative is anyway sustained by the attempt to hunt down 39013 and 39013's attempt to eliminate those who are working against him. The attack on the Granville Amusement Center provides the middle-action of chapter one but also introduces the heroes of the title and their motivation: the attack leads to the death of Sammy, the brother of Daredevil Gene, the motivation for the Daredevil's offer of help to Granville in bringing 39013 to justice. This in turn leads in to the other element of the set-up: when the Daredevils go to Granville they are actually offering their services to 39013, who, with the aid of an exact facial mask that also modifies his voice, is impersonating Granville. The real Granville is kept locked in the jail that 39013 has built for him. This is revealed in the chapter one sequence following the Daredevils introduction to 'Granville'. 39013 maintains his power through his impersonation ('When I wear this mask I am yourself' he tells Granville) and through a device in the room where he keeps Granville prisoner, which needs to be filled with liquid at regular intervals: if it isn't, lethal gas capsules will drop onto the floor, killing Granville after a short interval. The lethal gas capsules provide and promise regular suspense: in a variation of the set-up for *The Phantom Empire*, in which Gene Autry has to get back in time for his radio broadcast so that Radio Ranch can keep the broadcasting contrast, 39013 has to return to the jail in time to replenish the liquid or Granville will die.

Daredevils of the Red Circle's framework is thus numerical and mechanical. The list of Granville enterprises is significant in fitting the serial's concern with numbers which lasts to what is almost the final line, following the death of the villain: '39013 has added up to zero', announces Daredevil Gene. Numbers define the villain's status as a convict and Horace Granville's wealth. Chapter six is titled 'Thirty Seconds to Live', a reference to a bomb that will go off in thirty seconds, a more immediate version of the gas capsules that will fall to the ground if 39013 does not return in time. This connects the film to Republic's larger strategy. There were other Republic serials that used an explicitly numerical approach to plotting. The serial is inherently numerical, while *The Lone Ranger*, for instance, features five individuals who each could be the Lone Ranger, but who are killed off over the course of the fifteen chapters, leaving the one, genuine Lone Ranger. Republic developed the machinery of suspense though devices such as the bomb due to go off after a set time and through pacing and build-up. This is in marked contrast to the belated and unfulfilled newspaper deadline introduced in the final chapter of *The Lost Special*.

While villains in the other serials discussed in this chapter are motivated by the desire for wealth and power, *Daredevils of the Red Circle* is distinct in being driven by revenge and malevolence. The villain as an agent of destruction was certainly not unique to *Daredevils of the Red Circle*. In the late 1930s and early 1940s it was a common premise in Columbia serials such as *The Spider Returns*, the opening chapter titles of which announced that '. . . factories blow up, ships burn at sea, a bomber crashes, powder plants explode . . .' However, such destruction was commonly undertaken out of a desire for wealth or power; in *The Spider Returns* the Gargoyle is working for a foreign power. By impersonating Granville, 39013 has achieved power, but in attacking the different Granville enterprises he is effectively undermining his own position. This plot contradiction is highlighted in the penultimate chapter, when Granville, finally released from his prison, explains that by promising Dr Malcolm and Stanley (who also works for him) large portions of his fortune, 39013 had bribed them to join him in his plan for revenge. This implies that Dr Malcolm and Stanley are acting against their own interests, since in assisting in acts of sabotage against different Granville enterprises they are diminishing their reward. The campaign of destruction has more logic in the case of 39013, since what he is interested in is Granville's suffering. Alternatively, he is Hyde to Granville's Jekyll, the variation being that this Hyde assumes the appearance of his better self in order to carry out his destructive acts.

Daredevils of the Red Circle thus takes the serial a step further in its central, sadistic premise. It does this also with Sammy's death in the first chapter. In narrative terms this has a similar function to the death of Bud in *The Whispering Shadow* and Red Hallihan in *Jungle Jim*, providing as it does the heroes' motivation to track down 39013. The difference is that Sammy is a child. In line with the notion that children were introduced into the serial with a young audience in mind, as a hero-worshipping character with whom they could identify, Sammy looks up, literally and metaphorically, to the three Daredevils. But once this is established, he is killed off, undercutting any function he may have served as an identification figure.

All this adds to the serial's intensity but creates narrative problems. According to the list of Granville enterprises seen at the beginning, the villain's campaign of destruction are all but completed by the end of the first chapter, and there seems to be limited scope in other narrative paths. It is not essentially a mystery story: as in *The Lost Special*, what might be a mystery (through the existence of a disguised villain) is revealed at the beginning, leaving the heroes but not the audience in the dark. The one mystery it retains, the identity of the individual who periodically sends 'Red Circle' messages to the daredevils, is dressed up to the extent that the sender is shown cloaked and hooded, and some attempt is made to mislead the audience as to the sender's identity. Thus shots in chapter nine of Stanley listening through the wall shortly before the appearance of a further message (similarly to the shots of Strang and others in *The Whispering Shadow*) suggest that he may be the messenger. On two occasions the messages direct the Daredevils to the action: 'Investigate the Tri-City Gas Plant' they are told in chapter four, and in the following chapter the message reads: 'Plans Wanted Black Clinic 11 PM Sharp. Password 39013'. Otherwise, they warn the Daredevils of danger ('Don't Go It's a Trap', Chapter 2), and thus function to build up suspense (the Daredevils ignore the warning), or taunt 39013 ('You Guessed Wrong. The Red Circle is still operating', Chapter 7). Here they are inessential embellishments, while their function in initiating action highlights the point that action periodically grinds to a halt to the extent that a mystery message is necessary to get it moving again.

The identity of the Red Circle messenger becomes a more significant plot element in chapter seven, when 39013 arranges a plot to get rid of Blanche (Horace Granville's granddaughter) because she might be responsible for sending the messages. His plot involves sending her down the flooded Granville radium mine, stopping the pumps and the mine shaft lift by sabotaging the power supply, cutting the phone lines, then causing a landslide to prevent the power being reconnected. In addition to this, his henchmen take over the power house to electrify the main line so that the power line can't be repaired, and when they are overpowered a second group of henchmen arrive to do the same. That is, 39013 is the classic example of the villain who over-elaborates. The end result of his machinations is that Blanche's trousers get a little wet: she is otherwise unhurt.

Daredevils of the Red Circle is both the most dynamic of serials and a serial with nowhere to go. Heroes and villains occupy the same house. Following the repeat footage of the chapter eleven economy chapter, a flashback is used to illustrate Blanche's story of how she had become aware of 39013's deception, and how she had been blindfolded and taken in a car on an hour's journey to see her grandfather, that is, how she had been deceived into thinking that her grandfather was being held elsewhere when in fact he was under the same roof. Blanche's car journey is echoed throughout the serial, as the Daredevils are sent on expeditions that are in fact being orchestrated from the Granville mansion, and which repeatedly lead back to where they started.

Near the beginning of chapter ten, Dixon (a Granville employee not in league with the villain) tells the Daredevils that 'we're still no closer to capturing 39013'. 'I think we are', replies Gene, but Dixon has a point: chapters two to nine have not moved the narrative forward. Things do progress in chapter ten, which sees the revelation of 39013's impersonation of Granville, and the long awaited fall to the floor of the toxic gas capsules. However chapter eleven (the economy chapter) goes back to the beginning, while chapter twelve provides the final chase and the death of 39013. 'And so we close the lid on this grim memento of Crowle's power,' pronounces Granville, closing the box that contains the mask of his face, but also closing the case in a more general sense (Fig. 22). Like the other serials discussed here, *Daredevils of the Red Circle* is a closed narrative, ending with resolution: the defeat and death of the criminal, the restoration of the imprisoned industrialist to his rightful status and (less significantly) the solution to the mystery of Red Circle messages. In this instance there is not even the romance highlighted at the very end of *The Lost Special*, *The Whispering Shadow* and *Jungle Jim*, only the Daredevils' male group. The very end is reserved for a shot of the serial's one African-American character. The manservant 'Snowflake' has a role in the serial as the Daredevils' helper, along with Tuftie the dog, but also as a figure to be laughed at, and this is his role at the film's end, when he catches his head in the concealed door used by 39013, to the amusement of Blanche and the Daredevils. Race is not the

171

22. *Daredevils of the Red Circle* (1939)

issue that it is in a serial such as *Jungle Jim*, but a clear racial hierarchy remains.

Daredevils of the Red Circle thus displays many of the features common to the serial, not just racism but a narrative pattern involving an initial set-up, a closing resolution, and in between a lack of development. There may be holes in that narrative but not the incoherence evident in *The Whispering Shadow*. It shows even less development than the other serials discussed here, but this should be taken less as a shortcoming than as a particular form of filmmaking. Sharing with certain other serials an interest in industrial infrastructure (mines, factories, lines of communication . . .) it is based on an opposition between capitalist power and malevolent destruction. It imagines a scenario in which they become one and the same. Its repetitive nature allows it to accentuate and perfect those elements in which the serial, and particularly Republic serials, specialized: the fight, the chase, the stunt, the cliffhanger.

Where are you now, Batman?
Aftermath and Conclusion

Universal abandoned the serial in 1946, but production continued at Republic and Columbia, at a reduced level. Most accounts have the quality of Republic serials declining from the mid-1940s: for Hurst, 'From the end of the Second World War, the old magic was missing more and more often. Rising production costs, the problem of a loss of market, and the failure of the studio to adapt to changing times and tastes all contributed to the decline'.[1] The policy of releasing four serials a year was scaled back, initially to three plus one re-release, then to two and two re-releases. Fewer writers were employed, shorter running times were introduced, the amount of stock footage used was increased. These measures were a consequence of Republic's budget consciousness, and they kept serial production alive if not necessarily vital. Republic released their final serial, *King of the Carnival*, in 1955, and abandoned all film production in 1958. Sam Katzman, not known for his lavish spending, had taken over serial production at Columbia in 1945.[2] The studio stuck to the fifteen-chapter serial format but in the 1950s reduced production to two serials a year. In 1956 Spencer Gordon Bennet, director of serials since *Sunken Silver* (1925), completed Columbia's final serial, *Blazing the Overland Trail*.

Television is the obvious culprit for the death of the film serial but is best seen as part of a broader demographic and cultural shift. In the 1920s the film serial had survived (just) in the face of another rival, radio. Serials had been dependent on the regular audience provided by the neighbourhood theatre with a generally loyal audience; after the Second World War audiences tended to be more mobile and less inclined to limit themselves to a particular cinema or (with an increasing range of leisure pursuits) to the particular medium of cinema. Cinemas that screened serials relied on their regular production: the reduced production after

Universal left the business may have helped Columbia and Republic in the short-term as it left them a bigger proportion of the market but in the longer-term it made the serial less attractive to exhibitors. The spread of television contributed to this, as characters such as Dick Tracy and the Lone Ranger became better known, and easier and cheaper to see, in versions made for the small screen. More generally, the regular programme became associated with television rather than the cinema.

Television's screening of film serials contributed to the decline of cinema serial audience.[3] *The Lost Jungle* had been shown on television as early as 1939 but it was after the Second World War that television began to broadcast film serials on a regular basis.[4] Flamingo Films, formed in March 1949, began supplying serials to local television stations, and then to DuMont TV's Serial Theatre, which started on September 1950. *Billboard* identified it as 'A daily *Serial Theatre* for children' shown at 5.30.[5] KTLA (TV) Los Angeles broadcast *The Comics* in 1950, made up of Universal serials such as the *Flash Gordon* and *Don Winslow* films. WATV began showing serials on weeknight evenings in 1950, and in 1951 Republic sold 175 films (including serials) to the Los Angeles station KPTZ, bringing the studio short-term profit. Columbia was still re-releasing its serials in cinemas and so initially held back from television sales, but in 1956 Universal sold its thirty-one remaining serials made since 1934 to Jerry Hyams' Serials Inc., a subsidiary of Hygo TV Films.[6] *Billboard* identified the sale as 'the first big group of motion picture serials to be brought into TV in, at least, four years. Unity Television has 22 serials' including *The Phantom Empire* and *The Three Musketeers*, 'Motion Pictures for Television (thru Guild Films) has eight Universal serials, including *Flash Gordon* . . . Hollywood TV service has eight or more serials. Associated Artists Productions has a couple more serials, including "Rin Tin". Many of these were produced by Mascot Productions in the 1930s'.[7] WBKB, Chicago, was running two chapters per day in its noontime 'Happy Pirates' show. KRON-TV San Francisco would be running the serials in a 6.00–6.30 'Adventure Time' show. More than feature films, serials were seen as well suited to the time slots available on television. WNBT ran serials on Sunday morning. Screen Gems advertised series as 'ideal strip programming for the juvenile audience!'[8]

The serial was always a malleable format and the move from cinema to television brought further changes to the serials themselves. In 1956 it was noted that the trend was 'to strip the cliff hangers in a half-hour slot anytime between noon and 7.00 p.m. In most cases the stations are assigning a local personality to emcee the show in a live wrap-around'.[9] A more fundamental revision came when Republic sold twenty-six serials for television broadcast in retitled versions that had also been re-edited into single one hundred minute features.[10]

American public service broadcasting subsequently latched onto the serial as a means of low-cost broadcasting. Between 1980 and 1988 PBS's *Matinee at the Bijou* was shown mainly weekend mornings and afternoons though in the evenings in some parts of the U.S. It included public domain features, cartoons and serials (often shown in shortened versions). As the television matinee was not restricted to a single day of the week there was no need to combine matinee and evening screenings (as had happened in cinemas), accentuating the demarcation of the serial as children's entertainment, though in particular instances the serial was used for night-time television entertainment for adults. In Florida, a Saturday 3.00 p.m. show included John Wayne in *Winds of the Wasteland* (1932), a newsreel, a Betty Boop cartoon and chapter five of *Junior G-Men*.[11] In Kentucky a Saturday 10.00 a.m. show included *Submarine Alert* (1943), a 1937 short and a 1944 cartoon and newsreel, and chapter three of *Zorro's Fighting Legion*.[12] In New Hampshire a Saturday 6.00 p.m. show included Crash Corrigan in *Cowboy Commandos* (1944), two shorts, *Pretty Women* and *Tree in a Test Tube*, and chapter four of *Don Winslow of the Navy*.[13] In South Carolina, *Matinee at the Bijou* was given an 11.00 p.m. Saturday slot.[14]

Serials from an earlier time continued to be shown in the cinema in and beyond the 1950s, though the influence they had on a new generation came as much from television programming as cinema screenings. While Joseph McBride has traced Stephen Spielberg's return to the serial in *Raiders of the Lost Ark* (1983) and subsequent Indiana Jones films back to his childhood viewing at the Kiva Theater, Scottsdale, Arizona, Garry Jenkins emphasizes television as the means by which George Lucas was introduced to the serial, quoting the *Star Wars* director as saying 'I used to love the Flash Gordon serials . . . They were a primary influence on me. The way I see things, the way I interpret things, is influenced by television'.[15]

There was an appeal to a different audience following the success of television's cartoonish *Batman* series (1966–68) when Hollywood's Cinema Theater screened a four and half hour marathon of all chapters of Columbia's 1943 serial. According to Bob Thomas 'Crowds broke the house records', with a largely adult audience.[16] The television series but also the film serial and memories of children's matinees were invoked by

175

Brian Patten in his poem, 'Where are you now, Batman?', published in the Penguin Modern Poets 1967 *Mersey Sound* volume. It begins:

Where are you now, Batman? Now that Aunt Heriot has reported Robin missing?

And Superman's fallen asleep in the sixpenny childhood seats?

Where are you now that Captain Marvel's SHAZAM! echoes round the auditorium,

The magicians don't hear it,

Must all be deaf . . . or dead . . .

The Purple Monster who came down from the Purple Planet disguised as a man

Is wandering aimlessly about the streets

With no way of getting back . . .[17]

A variation was published in *The Liverpool Scene*, titled 'Where are you now, Superman?' and after a similar opening, and another reference to Flash Gordon's lonely wandering, 'Weeping over the girl he loved 7 universes ago' went on: 'We killed them all simply because we grew up . . . We think we are too old to cheer and boo now,/But let's not kid ourselves . . .'[18] *The Liverpool Scene* also included Roger McGough's 'Goodbat Nightman' and Adrian Henri's 'Bat Poem', which famously moves from 'All those damsels in distress/Half-undressed or even less/ The Batpill makes 'em all say yes' to 'Help us out in Vietnam/Batman/ Help us drop that Batnapalm/Batman'.[19] Batman lived on, but the hero of the xenophobic wartime propaganda of Columbia's 1943 serial looked different to a 1960s generation.

Alan Moore later recalled the elegiac tone of Patten's poem as an influence on his own work.[20] The lost serial characters and superheroes of Moore's contribution to *The Watchmen* (1986–87) were back on the big screen in the 2009 film of the same name (without Moore's name in the credits). Other heroes and superheroes who had appeared in the film serials (such as Tarzan, the Lone Ranger, Zorro, even Frank Merriwell) continued to be reinvented, reborn or rebooted in the second half of the twentieth century and into the twenty-first, with varying degrees of success.[21] In Republic's 1943 serial, *Captain America*, the title character was in fact District Attorney Grant Gardner, in *Easy Rider* (1969),

Captain America was a Harley Davidson motorcycle, in the cheap and bizarre 1973 Turkish film *Three Giant Men* Captain America and Santo did battle with Spider Man, reimagined as a sadistic villain. The first official feature film adaptation appeared in 1990, but it was with *Captain America: The First Avenger* (2011) that the superhero moved up the box-office charts, reinforcing the point that the appeal of narratives of death and rebirth was not limited to a younger age.

The earlier, serial adventures of such characters often seemed forgotten though there had been some recognition of the serial almost from the beginnings of a serious interest in film and film history. In London the Film Society had shown the first two episodes of *What Happened to Mary* at the New Gallery Kinema in Regent Street on Sunday 16 January 1927, along with extracts from *Sport and Interest in a Fresh Light* (1926), *Emak Bakia* (1926) and *The Joyless Street* (1925). Further episodes followed on 13 February and 8 May.[22] The *Flash Gordon* films were acknowledged on their initial release when the British Film Institute's *Sight and Sound* put the films' hero on the cover.[23] The Museum of Modern Art in New York showed a programme of American serials in 1942, including episodes from *The Exploits of Elaine* (1915) but also *Buck Rogers* (1939) and *The Adventures of Red Ryder* (1940).[24] 'Today, serials seldom gain the critical attention they deserve, though they continue to enthral vast audiences', announced the Film Library curator, Iris Barry, describing serials as 'essentially cinematic', and a continuation of a tradition that went back to the beginnings of narrative cinema.[25] The Theodore Huff Memorial Film Society followed a 16 August 1955 programme of silent serials with a 21 February 1956 programme that included (presumably an extract from) *Ben-Hur* (1925) and a selection of sound serial episodes. On 16 April 1957 it screened *The Indians are Coming* in a programme of early westerns. It screened further sound serials in 1960, 1961 and 1962, after which, aside from a lone screening in 1973 that included an episode of the now missing *Detective Lloyd*, the only serials it showed were silent.[26] *Films in Review* published occasional articles on the serial by William Everson and others, and there were descriptive articles, interviews and reproduced publicity in publications such as *Screen Facts*, *Those Enduring Matinee Idols*, *Views and Reviews*, *Film Fan Monthly* and *Serial Quarterly*.[27] Interviewed in 1966, avant-garde filmmaker Kenneth Anger spoke of his regret for the films Hollywood no longer made, most of all for the serials: 'I have my favorite serials which I have seen over and over. *Flash Gordon*, *Daredevils of the Red Circle*, *Chandu*. Luckily, in Europe they have copies of the American serials, and I get to see them again over here'.[28]

It was largely left to fans and collectors to preserve the memory of the serials, through screenings, publications, websites, rediscoveries and restorations. The survival of the vast majority of Hollywood's serials is a consequence of this work. In 1972, Sherman Krellberg's Goodwill Pictures received a letter from the Rank Organisation telling him that the British government's Factory Inspectorate had ordered them to move all their nitrate film to an open area 'with immediate effect' and that they were therefore in the process of moving his copies of *Don Winslow of the Navy* and *Don Winslow of the Coastguard* to a temporary store in the car park of their Denham laboratories. The British National Film Archive told Krellberg that they had room for one *Don Winslow* serial but not two. They kept *Don Winslow of the Navy* until Krellberg asked for it back: *Don Winslow of the Coastguard* was destroyed.[29] However, other prints were preserved elsewhere, and with the arrival of new methods of viewing (VHS, DVD, streaming video . . .) a new audience has been able to watch the adventures of Don Winslow and his friend Red Pennington and their fight against the Scorpion.

The sound serial sits here alongside 1930s Poverty Row western features, 1940s crime series films, cheap 1950s science fiction movies, and other Hollywood films which were dismissed as worthless on their initial release. A developing interest in the margins of cinema has included some interest in the serial, though often through a focus on those few examples that have already achieved a certain profile.[30] Some attention has been paid to serials that offer a particularly striking generic mix.[31] An interest in what Lawrence Alloway referred to as 'Violent America' has occasionally been extended to filmmakers such as William Witney.[32] However, while a developing interest in cult and paracinema cinema has helped draw attention to films that don't conform to established criteria or even to notions of competence, the serial's regimented structure has not particularly endeared it to this form of reclamation.[33] While notions of authorship can be adapted to a Poverty Row director such as Edgar Ulmer (or even the paracinematic Edward D. Wood Jr), there are grounds for supporting William K. Everson's argument that the regimented production process prevented individual directors imposing their own style on the serials they made.[34] Interest in the silent serial has often focused on the role of women within the films and as film viewers: the sound serial offers limited scope for this sort of approach. The wider, cross-media interest in seriality has often focused on the 'open' as opposed to 'closed' serial, or at least on the serial as a long-form narrative that lends itself better to complexity. Again, this does not easily fit the

Hollywood sound serial, with its finite and regular number of chapters and reliance on stock characters and situations.

This does not mean that the film serial is unknown. Serials feature characters who remain familiar. The very term 'cliffhanger', invented by *Variety* at the beginning of the 1930s largely to denote this form of cinema has passed into general and widespread use. The image of the Saturday children's matinee has endured, with the serial at its heart. In many ways contemporary Hollywood supplies the serial of the 1930s to the 1950s writ large, with sequels instead of episodes and grander effects than the Lydecker brothers could provide. However, while those earlier serials remain familiar at this level, in other ways it can seem that remarkably little is known about a group of films that were seen by so many.

In attempting to address that, I have encountered a number of arguments, assumptions and assertions that are either incomplete, uncertain, incorrect or at least need further clarification. Key among these are the following:

1. *From at least the 1930s the film serial was essentially designed for, and watched by, children attending Saturday matinee screenings.*

This assertion does not do justice to the serial's audience range. The image of the Saturday matinee is a powerful one, and many children initially encountered the serial (and cinema) in this context, but this does not define the limits of the serial. Evening or screenings on other days of the week attracted significant numbers of children, but the tradition of including a chapter episode on the regular bill did not disappear with the introduction of synchronized sound, with the result that in particular location serials were regularly watched by adults as well as children. A tendency to focus on the first-run cinema and what was new in film-making has obscured the persistence of earlier filmmaking and film viewing practices.

The film serial provided a particular form of action and suspense cinema that had an adult as well as a youth appeal. The attention that the serial attracted at specific moments in its history also brought in other adult audiences. The way in which cinema was supervised and regulated (less through the Production Code than through local pressure groups) made it in the interest of studios and exhibitors to promote the serial as suitable for children, and the success of particular films taught both the value of developing this market. The long-term, though not constant, trend was towards the child viewer, and the particular ways in which television programming was stratified along the lines of the age of the prospective viewer helped cement the association between the serial and child. How this worked out in terms of audience breakdown deserves further investigation: that serial audiences continued to contain a mix of ages after 1930 seems clear. The practice of also releasing some serials in a feature version suggests an attempt to appeal to a wider audience, and this provides some confirmation of the association between children and the film serial, though it reinforces the point that the material within the serials was often similar to other forms of action-orientated, low-budget filmmaking less defined as children's viewing. Serials also had an important international market which deserves further scrutiny.

2. *In the 1910s serials were for adults and to a significant degree appealed to women.*

The strongest evidence for the film serial's appeal to adult audiences comes from the initial years of the serial's existence. What is most striking about this period is the extent of the specific appeal to women. Film historians have been correct to note this. However, in paying attention to this the early serial's appeal to men and children has often been neglected. Children were part of America's film serial audience throughout its history.

3. *The film serial was a form of melodrama and developed out of the stage melodramas of the late nineteenth and early twentieth centuries.*

Serials were identified as melodramas at the time of their release. They avoided the domestic entanglements often linked to film melodramas, but they presented a conflict between good and evil, dramatizing stories of victimhood and threat ameliorated by poetic justice, relying on character types rather than psychological depth, and on sensational situations and coincidence rather than classical causality and proportion. These features clearly identify them as melodramas. A significant number of serials were based around the death or incapacitation of a father or father-figure. In this sense they were family melodramas, if family melodramas located outside of the home. They borrowed melodramatic situations from the theatre, and continued to use these into the 1940s. However, the melodramatic tradition on which they drew came from popular literature as well as the theatre, while in terms of performance they looked to other forms of spectacle such as the circus and the sports field. The influence of popular stage melodramas of the late nineteenth and early twentieth century was more directly felt in the feature film than in the serial. The episodic nature of the latter paralleled the print serial rather than the acts of a play.

4. After the initial few years the film serial steadily declined in popularity.

The earliest years of the film serial saw it achieve its greatest popularity. It retained widespread appeal into the 1920s. It became more marginal in that decade but it would be wrong to portray its history as one of steady decline. In the mid- and late-1930s it took on new life and while it continued to be looked down on it was also noted for its remarkable success. After the Second World War it became a diminishing force, but film serials continued to be produced into the second half of the 1950s.

5. During the sound era serials made little money; alternatively, serials were Hollywood's biggest money-makers.

Information on Hollywood's spending and takings can be difficult to come by, particularly in the case of the serial. Budgets are available for some serials, though in some instances the source for reported costs is unclear. Different accounts give figures for *Flash Gordon* that other evidence suggests is inflated. The evidence that does exist confirms that sound serial costs were kept as low as possible. However more money was put into serials in the late 1930s and the first half of the 1940s, at Universal and Republic.

Takings (at least net profits) are generally even more difficult to establish than spending. Here also some quoted figures lack supporting evidence and seem too high. Frederick Othman's suggestion that each serial Henry MacRae made for Universal realized around $500,000 net does not seem plausible, and the more widely quoted figures for *The Indians are Coming* are also questionable. Figures that have been quoted for Republic's *The Lone Ranger* are more reliable and indicate that the serial could make a significant return. Earlier, Mascot had demonstrated that the serial could be a profitable venture if costs were kept down. Given that they were (in most instances) shown as part of a programme, the box-office value of the serial is difficult to gauge. They offered no assurance of audience return and involved a commitment that brought its own risks. The children who did watch them paid below-average ticket prices and in general serials played in cinemas with below-average charges. To some extent they may have been used to cultivate the film-going habit among the young but in general they were shown for a more immediate return. Cinemas continued to include serials on the programme because they were judged to bring in more customers than they drove away, and because they could be fitted into a mixed programme. They lent themselves to a particular approach to film exhibition, one that was successful enough to last several decades for some. The extent to which cinema takings found their way back to the production companies is complicated by the way in which serials were distributed through a variety of exchanges, through the States Rights' system, and through sales to overseas distributors. Serials were a particularly adaptable form, and could bring in some sort of return after their initial run. If particular examples were highly successful the majority would appear to have brought in modest profits. It is difficult to be more precise but more work here should provide a more detailed picture.

6. *The serial is distinct from the series; alternatively, both are forms of seriality.*

For Hollywood there were clear ways in which the serial represented a distinct form of film production. The *Film Daily Yearbook* list of serials made since 1920 was based on an accepted category that was distinct from the series.[35] Publications such as Buck Rainey's *Serials and Series* acknowledge connections between different forms of the sequence but also distinctions.[36] There are distinctions also between different forms of the serial, which took a particular form on film. Its finite nature distinguishes it from 'open' serials but it also differs from the serialized novel. The majority of the film serials itemized in *Film Daily* or by Rainey provide a series of adventures within an overarching framework that was not designed for development across chapters. To an extent this blurs the distinction between serial and series and thus justifies those accounts that alternate between those terms. There are also good reasons for seeing these as part of a broader pattern of sequential narrative, and for moving away from notions of self-contained wholeness. The serials discussed here provided a particular combination of the serial and series. They developed as a form of entertainment designed to fit a regular timeslot over a set period of time with overlaps linking episodes, attracting a regular audience while accommodating the irregular viewer. They point to how film viewers did not restrict themselves to complete films watched at a single sitting.

7. Cinema-going has entailed going to see a film.

At first sight this would appear to be the least controversial of the above statements; after all, it defines cinema-going today. However, the statement highlights a problem within film history. The emphasis on the single feature is misleading for earlier periods, when cinemas offered a programme (a further variety of sequence) that combined different films or films and other forms of entertainment. At a time when cinema in general was at its most popular many exhibitors included a serial on the programme: in some instances it could be the main attraction. We have moved on from the notion that film history is limited to the study of a small number of film classics but could do more examine the totality of what people saw at the cinema.

This study has examined one aspect of that, an aspect often ignored in film histories not written by fans. The serial played a vital role in film history at a time when film narrative was moving beyond the single reel. It is relevant to the contemporary film franchise and the construction of narrative worlds that can run across media as well as different films. It was also important in the years following 1930, for the film industry and for millions of viewers, young and old, within and beyond the United States.

Appendix

Hollywood Serials, 1930–1946,
and the endings of their second chapters

Listed below are Hollywood serials made in the 1930–46 period, their production company, director or directors, number of chapters and the title of their second chapter. Second chapter endings are given for serials I have been able to view (that is, all but four serials made in 1930, four in 1931, three in 1932, and one in 1933). Descriptions are taken from what is shown at the chapter end but also the summary provided at the beginning of the following chapter.

1930:

The Indians are Coming—Universal; Henry MacRae; 12; 'A Call to Arms':
Wrongly arrested for theft, Jack is forced to stay behind when Mary travels west.

The Jade Box—Universal; Ray Taylor; 10; 'Buried Alive!'

The Lightning Express—Universal; Henry MacRae; 10; 'A Scream of Terror'.

The Lone Defender—Mascot; Richard Thorpe; 12; 'The Fugitive': Dolores is trapped in a burning hut, Rinty is knocked out, Buzz falls down a well, Ramon appears to be shot.

Terry of the Times—Universal; Henry MacRae; 10; 'The Fatal': 30.

The Voice from the Sky—G.Y.B. Films; Ben Wilson; 10; 'The Cave of Horror'.

1931:

Battling with Buffalo Bill—Universal; Ray Taylor; 12; 'Circling Death': Bill Cody and his party are attacked by a band of Blackfeet.

Danger Island—Universal; Ray Taylor; 12; 'Death Rides the Storm'.

Finger Prints—Universal; Ray Taylor; 10; 'A Fugitive of Fear'.

The Galloping Ghost—Mascot; B. Reeves Eason; 12; 'Port of Peril': Red Grainge and Buddy's sister Barbara chase after the speedboat carrying Barbara's brother, but find themselves trapped and about to be crushed between a ship and the dock.

Heroes of the Flames—Universal; Robert Hill; 12; 'Flaming Hate'.

King of the Wild—Mascot; Richard Thorpe and B. Reeves Eason; 12; 'Tiger of Destiny': Harris's animals escape from their cages, the ship begins to sink, and Muriel and Grant are locked in a cabin.

The Lightning Warrior—Mascot; Armand Schaefer and Ben Kline; 12; 'The Wolf Man': Hanging to a mining car above a sheer drop, Jimmy falls while Rinty fights the Wolfman.

The Mystery Trooper—Wonder Pictures/Syndicate; Stuart Paton; 10; 'Paths of Peril': Jack, Billy and Red Eagle are attacked in the Chief's tepee by Mack and his henchmen, while an enormous bear enters the cabin where Helen is sleeping.

The Phantom of the West—Mascot; Ross Lederman; 10; 'Stairwell of Doom': Attempting to rescue Mona from the Phantom, Jim falls down the stairwell of the burning hotel.

The Sign of the Wolf—Metropolitan; Forrest Sheldon and Harry S. Webb; 10; 'The Dog of Destiny': Butch and his henchmen invade the Winslow residence where Ruth is demonstrating the secret of the jewels. When Tom and Bud come to her rescue a fight ensues.

The Spell of the Circus—Universal; Robert Hill; 10; 'The Phantom Shadow'.

The Vanishing Legion—Mascot; B. Reeves Eason; 12; 'Queen of the Night Riders': The Vanishing Legion stampedes a herd of horses through Happy Cardigan's camp. Happy falls in their path.

1932:

The Airmail Mystery—Universal; Ray Taylor; 12; 'Hovering Death'.

Detective Lloyd—Universal; Henry MacRae; 12; 'The Panther Strikes'.

The Devil Horse—Mascot; Otto Brower; 12; 'Chasm of Death': Bob Norton and the boy ride El Diablo in an attempt to escape from the men summoned by Lucy Weston, but the horse fails to leap across the ravine.

Heroes of the West—Universal; Ray Taylor; 12; 'Red Peril': Indians ambush Noah Blaine and attack the work train. Butch Gore uses the attack to shoot Tom Crosby.

The Hurricane Express—Mascot; Armand Schaefer and J.P. McGowan; 12; 'Flying Pirates': Larry, Gloria and her father escape in the get-away plane of the Wrecker's gang, but the gang machine-gun the plane. It catches fire and crashes.

Jungle Mystery—Universal; Ray Taylor; 12; 'The Ivory Trail'.

The Last Frontier—RKO; Spencer G. Bennet and Thom L. Story; 12; 'The Thundering Herd': Tom and Betty's wagon overturns in the path of a herd of stampeding buffalo.

The Last of the Mohicans—Mascot; B. Reeves Eason and Ford Beebe; 12; 'Flaming Arrows': Alice has been tied to a stake and Hawkeye is shot as he attempts to rescue her.

The Lost Special—Universal; Henry MacRae; 12; 'Racing Death': Tom, Bob, Betty and Kate are attacked on the train by bandits. Bob is wounded. The train runs wild. A bullet hits the steam gauge, which explodes.

The Shadow of the Eagle—Mascot; Ford Beebe, Colbert Clark, Wyndham Gittens; 12; 'Pinholes': Jean Gregory is attempting to rescue her father from agents of the Eagle while Craig McCoy races to her aid, pursued by the directors of the airplane company. Jean climbs out onto a scaffolding platform, but the scaffolding is knocked down by Craig's car.

1933:

Clancy of the Mounted—Universal; Ray Taylor; 12; 'Brother Against Brother': Tom Clancy trails Bordeau and his brother Steve to a trapper's cabin, but when he orders the fugitives to open the door, Bordeau fires his gun. Tom falls.

Fighting with Kit Carson—Mascot; Armand Schaefer and Colbert Clark; 12; 'The White Chief': Escaping from the Mystery Riders, Joan falls off her horse, while Kit Carson and his friend Nakomas, chased by agents of Cyrus Kraft, fall off their horse and over a cliff.

Gordon of Ghost City—Universal; Ray Taylor; 12; 'The Stampede': Mary falls in the path of stampeding horses.

The Mystery Squadron—Mascot; Colbert Clark and David Howard; 12; 'The Fatal Warning': Fred flies his plane in an attempt to rescue Bill from the Mystery Squadron though Bill manages to escape in one of the Squadron's planes. Fred and Bill's planes collide.

The Phantom of the Air—Universal; Ray Taylor; 12; 'The Secret of the Desert': In the fight that ensues when Mortimer Crome's men invade Thomas Edmonds' laboratory, a beaker is shot, flooding the laboratory with poisonous gas.

The Return of Chandu—Principal; Ray Taylor; 12; 'The House in the Hills': The car Chandu is driving goes off the road.

Tarzan the Fearless—Principal; Robert Hill; 15; 'The Storm God Strikes'.

The Three Musketeers—Mascot; Armand Schaefer and Colbert Clark; 12; 'All For One and One For All': Fleeing from the Devil's Circle, Tom and Renard find themselves on the edge of the abyss, standing on a shrinking floor.

The Whispering Shadow—Mascot; Albert Herman and Colbert Clark; 12; 'The Collapsing Room': Jack and Vera are trapped in Professor Strang's collapsing room as the walls close in on them.

The Wolf Dog—Mascot; Colbert Clark and Harry Fraser; 12; 'The Shadow of a Crime': In order to escape from Bryan's agents, Bob fires his electric ray at a can of gasoline. The building collapses around him.

1934:

Burn 'Em Up Barnes—Mascot; Colbert Clark and Armand Schaefer; 12; 'The News Reel Murder': Barnes's motorcycle is shot at and crashes off the road.

The Law of the Wild—Mascot; Armand Schaefer and B. Reeves Eason; 12; 'The Battle of the Strong': Sheldon falls in the path of stampeding horses.

The Lost Jungle—Mascot; Armand Schaefer and David Howard; 12; 'Nature in the Raw': The tiger that Clyde confronts falls into the animal pit but so does Clyde. The tiger leaps at him.

Mystery Mountain—Mascot; B. Reeves Eason and Otto Brower; 12; 'The Man Nobody Knows': The Rattler lays dynamite under the safe containing the wrench bearing his fingerprints. Railroad detective Ken Williams reaches the building at the point when the dynamite explodes.

The Perils of Pauline—Universal; Ray Taylor; 12; 'The Typhoon of Terror': The Hargrave party fight with Bashir and his men on the deck of the Nantung while the ship sails into a raging storm.

Pirate Treasure—Universal; Ray Taylor; 12; 'The Death Plunge': Dick reclaims his treasure map but the thieves fight him on the roof of a tall building. He falls while trying to cling to the awnings outside the building.

The Red Rider—Universal; Lew Landers; 15; 'A Leap for Life': Chased to the edge of the lake by Portos and his men, Red and his horse Silver jump into the water.

Tailspin Tommy—Universal; Lew Landers; 12; 'The Mail Gets Through': During an air circus, Skeeter attempts to warm up a plane for one of the contestants. When he loses control of the plane, Tommy stops the runaway plane by crashing his own plane into it.

The Vanishing Shadow—Universal; Lew Landers; 12; 'The Destroying Ray': Van Dorn uses his death ray against Dorgan's henchmen but Gloria and Stanfield find themselves in the line of fire.

Young Eagles—First Division; Spencer G. Bennet, Vin Moore and Eduard Laurier; 12; 'Drums of Hate': Boy Scouts Bob and Jim are captured by a tribe of barbaric Indians. Jim is thrown into the temple pit.

1935:

The Adventures of Rex and Rinty—Mascot; B. Reeves Eason and Ford Beebe; 12; 'Sport of Kings': Unscrupulous sportsman, Crawford, has his men steal Rex while he fouls Bradley in a polo game.

The Call of the Savage—Universal; Lew Landers; 12; 'Captured by Cannibals': Seeing Mona and Borno about to be burnt at the stake, Jan leaps to their rescue, but he is surrounded by spear-carrying cannibals.

The Fighting Marines—Mascot; B. Reeves Eason and Joseph Kane; 12; 'Isle of Missing Men': A car full of dynamite is sent down the track and explodes in front of Corporal Lawrence and Sergeant McGowan as they approach the Tiger Shark's cave.

The Lost City—Sherman S. Krellberg; Harry Revier; 12; 'Tunnel of Death': Bruce Gordon is attacked by one of Zolok's giants, who drags him into the Tunnel of Fire.

The Miracle Rider—Mascot; Armand Schaefer and B. Reeves Eason; 15; 'The Firebird Strikes': Tom Morgan is trapped in Zaroff's radio controlled glider. Zaroff crashes the glider.

The New Adventures of Tarzan—Burroughs-Tarzan; Edward Kull and W.F. McGaugh; 12; 'Crossed Trails': Tarzan walks into the trip wire that Raglan has laid in the caves, detonating an explosion.

The Phantom Empire—Mascot; Otto Brower and B. Reeves Eason; 12; 'The Thunder Riders': The plane in which Betsy and Frankie have stowed away is hit by a missile fired from the underground city of Murania.

Queen of the Jungle—Screen Attractions; Robert Hill; 12; 'Radium Rays': Joan Lawrence orders that David Worth be sacrificed to a horrible death by the radium rays of the jungle God Rad.

The Roaring West—Universal; Ray Taylor; 15; 'The Torrent of Terror': The dam bursts, flooding the town and the jail where Montana is held.

Rustlers of Red Dog—Universal; Lew Landers; 12; 'Flaming Arrows': Wood is shot while riding for help during an Indian attack.

Tailspin Tommy in the Great Air Mystery—Universal; Ray Taylor; 12; 'Roaring Fire God': Tommy finds that the controls of his plane are jammed, sending him and Skeeter straight towards the volcano.

1936:

Ace Drummond—Universal; Ford Beebe and Cliff Smith; 15; 'The Invisible Enemy': The Dragon's flyers shoot at Ace Drummond's plane, causing it to crash.

The Adventures of Frank Merriwell—Universal; Cliff Smith; 12; 'The Death Plunge': Chasing after the thieves who have stolen the ring his mother gave him, Frank leaps into their car. The car goes off the road and into the sea.

The Black Coin—Stage and Screen; Albert Herman; 15; 'The Mystery Ship': Captain 'Shark' Malone has Terry Navarro tied up in a sack and thrown into shark infested water.

The Clutching Hand—Stage and Screen; Albert Herman; 15; 'Shadows': Craig Kennedy pursue the criminals in a taxi. The driver jumps out and the taxi goes off the road.

Custer's Last Stand—Stage and Screen; Elmer Clifton; 15; 'Thundering Hooves': Encountering a buffalo stampede, Kit Cardigan and Belle Meade take shelter behind Kit's horse.

Darkest Africa—Republic; B. Reeves Eason and Joseph Kane; 15; 'The Tiger-Men's God': Clyde Beatty is pushed into a tiger pit and attacked by a tiger.

Flash Gordon—Universal; Frederick Stephani; 13; 'The Tunnel of Terror': Flash, attempting to prevent Ming's marriage to Dale, encounters a monster in the Tunnel of Terror.

The Phantom Rider—Universal; Ray Taylor; 15; 'The Maddened Herd': Cattle stampede through the town, entering the jail where Buck is prisoner. The building catches fire and starts to collapse.

Robinson Crusoe of Clipper Island—Republic; Mack V. Wright and Ray Taylor; 14; 'Flaming Danger': Captured by Komatoans, Mala is forced to stand on a plank above the volcano. The plank is up-ended and Mala falls.

Shadow of Chinatown—Victory; Robert Hill; 15; 'The Crushing Walls': Joan is trapped in Victor Poten's hydraulic room. The walls close in on her, and Martin and Wally's attempt to stop the machinery is halted when Grogan arrives and attacks them.

Undersea Kingdom—Republic; B. Reeves Eason and Joseph Kane; 12; 'The Undersea City': Crash Corrigan is shot and falls down the lift shaft.

The Vigilantes are Coming—Republic; Mack V. Wright and Ray Taylor; 12; 'Birth of the Vigilantes': The Eagle stages a raid on Jason Burr's powder magazine but finds himself locked in the building. It explodes.

1937:

Blake of Scotland Yard—Victory; Robert Hill; 15; 'Death in the Laboratory': The discovery that Sir James Blake has been impersonating Count Basil Segaloff leads to a fist-fight which ends with Jerry falling down a well and the Scorpion about to club Blake.

Dick Tracy—Republic; Ray Taylor and Alan James; 15; 'The Bridge of Terror': Dick Tracy and Steve Lockwood escape from the Spider Ring's Lair but their plane is shot and crashes into a bridge.

Jungle Jim—Universal; Ford Beebe and Cliff Smith; 12; 'The Cobra Strikes': Jungle Jim and Labat fight hand-to-hand above a high waterfall. Jim falls.

Jungle Menace—Columbia; George Melford and Harry Fraser; 15; 'Deadly Enemies': Marshall is seriously wounded and taken to the Shields' plantation.

The Mysterious Pilot—Columbia; Spencer G. Bennet and George M. Merrick; 15; 'The Web Tangles': Jim Dorn evades the police by flying his plane through Suicide Pass.

The Painted Stallion—Republic; William Witney, Alan James and Ray Taylor; 12; 'Rider of the Stallion': Driving his wagon across the river during a storm, Clark Stuart is knocked out. The wagon sinks.

Radio Patrol—Universal; Ford Beebe and Cliff Smith; 12; 'The Hypnotic Eyes': Pat O'Hara trails Selkirk to the Egyptian Quarter but then is trapped between a door and a crushing device.

Secret Agent X-9—Universal; Ford Beebe and Cliff Smith; 12; 'The Ray That Blinds': Dexter and Pidge gain on Brenda's gang, but when a member of the gang shines a light in their direction, Pidge loses control of the car and it crashes.

S.O.S. Coast Guard—Republic; William Witney and Alan James; 12; 'Barrage of Death': The Coast Guard fire at a cabin launch, unaware that Boroff's men have tied up Jerry Kent and left him in the launch. The boat is destroyed.

Tim Tyler's Luck—Universal; Ford Beebe and Wyndham Gittings; 12; 'Dead Man's Pass': Tim meets an ivory safari on a narrow trail in Gorilla Canyon. When gorillas start throwing rocks the safari leader falls, and when Tim goes to his rescue he falls as well.

Wild West Days—Universal; Ford Beebe and Cliff Smith; 13; 'Redskins' Revenge': A horse stampede saves Kentucky and Lucy Wade from being burnt at the stake, but when they attempt to ride to safety their horse is tripped and Lucy falls in the path of the still stampeding horses.

Zorro Rides Again—Republic; William Witney and John English; 12; 'The Fatal Minute': Zorro attempts to find the time bomb in the railroad warehouse but is knocked out and left in the building. The bomb explodes.

1938:

Dick Tracy Returns—Republic; William Witney and John English; 15; 'The Runway of Death': Tracy comes to as his car is sent down a ramp and crashes.

The Fighting Devil Dogs—Republic; William Witney and John English; 12; 'The Mill of Disaster': Attempting to rescue his friend Lieut. Corby from being burned by an acetate torch, Lieut. Grayson is knocked down under a steel girder, which falls in his direction.

Flaming Frontiers—Universal; Ray Taylor and Alan James; 15; 'Death Rides the Wind': The Indians abandon their attack on the cabin where Tex Houston, Mary Grant and Buffalo Bill are sheltering but only when a cyclone arrives. The cabin is destroyed.

Flash Gordon's Trip to Mars—Universal; Ford Beebe and Robert Hill; 15; 'The Living Dead': Fleeing from the Claymen, Flash Gordon and his friends find themselves trapped below the cave's descending ceiling.

The Great Adventures of Wild Bill Hickok—Columbia; Mack V. Wright and Sam Nelson; 15; 'The Stampede': Wild Bill and Ruth fall in the path of the stampede caused by the Phantom Raiders.

Hawk of the Wilderness—Republic; William Witney and John English; 12; 'Flaming Death': Yellow Weazel's men are about to burn Kioga at the stake.

The Lone Ranger—Republic; William Witney and John English; 15; 'Thundering Earth': The Lone Ranger races to stop the attack on the wagon train but is caught in the rockfall engineered by Jeffries' men.

Red Barry—Universal; Ford Beebe and Alan James; 13; 'The Curtain Falls':

Red Barry is chasing after Quong Lee's men when they open a trap door. Red falls into a room where he is attacked by a lion.

The Secret of Treasure Island—Columbia; Elmer Clifton; 15; 'The Ghost Talks': In attempting to escape from Carter Collins, Larry and Toni come face-to-face with the ghost of the Black Pirate. Larry fires his gun at the ghost. The ghost laughs.

The Spider's Web—Columbia; Ray Taylor and James W. Horne; 15; 'Death Below': The Spider rescues Neta from the Octopus. They use a hoist to descend the building but the hoist control is released and they hurtle down at speed.

1939:

Buck Rogers—Universal; Ford Beebe and Saul A. Goodkind; 12; 'Tragedy on Saturn': Buck's ship comes under fire when it is mistaken for the enemy.

Daredevils of the Red Circle—Republic; William Witney and John English; 12; 'The Mysterious Friend': The Daredevils are attacked while investigating the Granville Chemical Plant, and Gene falls into a water tank covered with burning oil.

Dick Tracy's G-Men—Republic; William Witney and John English; 15; 'Captured': The gun trap set up by Zarnoff causes a shot to be fired when one of the G-Men touches the door-handle. They return fire with their machine guns, unaware that Tracy is behind the door.

Flying G-Men—Columbia; Ray Taylor and James W. Horne; 15; 'Flight of the Condemned': The Flying G-Men are about to take a captured member of the spy ring north for questioning but become the target for bombs dropped by an enemy plane.

The Lone Ranger Rides Again—Republic; William Witney and John English; 15; 'Masked Victory': Bart and Slade are about to lynch Scott for killing Grover. The Lone Ranger arrives with Grover. Slade shoots the Lone Ranger.

Mandrake the Magician—Columbia; Sam Nelson and Norman Deming; 12; 'Trap of the Wasp': While Betty Houston is in a falling elevator, Mandrake and Lothar are knocked unconscious in a room filled with steam.

The Oregon Trail—Universal; Ford Beebe and Saul A. Goodkind; 15; 'The Flaming Forest': Margaret Mason falls off the burning wagon. Jeff Scott comes to her rescue, but just as the flames reach the explosives.

Overland with Kit Carson—Columbia; Sam Nelson and Norman Deming; 15; 'Condemned to Die': Supporting the trappers against the Black Raiders' attack, Kit Carson is caught in the explosion of an ammunition wagon.

The Phantom Creeps—Universal; Ford Beebe and Saul A. Goodkind; 12; 'Death Stalks the Highways': Bob West is knocked out by the invisible Doctor Zorka and his car sent down the road. It goes over a cliff and explodes.

Scouts to the Rescue—Universal; Ray Taylor and Alan James; 12; 'Avalanche of Doom': On the trail of counterfeiters, G-Man Hal Marvin pursues them into the hills but is halted by a rockfall orchestrated by resentful Indians.

Zorro's Fighting Legion—Republic; William Witney and John English; 12; 'The Flaming "Z"': Zorro goes to rescue Ramon from the mission, which Don Del Oro has had mined. Zorro's escape is blocked and the mission explodes.

1940:

Adventures of Red Ryder—Republic; William Witney and John English; 12; 'Horsemen of Death': Pursuing Shark's killer, Red Ryder falls in front of the horses ridden by the Sheriff's deputies.

Deadwood Dick—Columbia; James W. Horne; 15; 'Who is the Skull?': Deadwood Dick boards the stagecoach that agents of the Skull are attacking. The coach breaks free from the horses and goes over a precipice.

Drums of Fu Manchu—Republic; William Witney and John English; 15; 'The Monster': Allan Parker follows the hypnotized Dr Humphreys to Fu Manchu's base but Fu Manchu sends him through a trap-door into a water tank where he is attacked by an octopus.

Flash Gordon Conquers the Universe—Universal; Ford Beebe and Ray Taylor; 12; 'Freezing Torture': Flash and Zarkov lead an expedition to Frigia, where bombs dropped by one of Ming's space ships cause an avalanche.

The Green Archer— Columbia; James W. Horne; 15; 'The Face at the Window': Spike Holland, ace insurance investigator, chases after Bellamy's crooks, but one of the crooks drives his car off the road.

The Green Hornet—Universal; Ford Beebe and Ray Taylor; 13; 'The Thundering Terror': The Hornet chases Mortensen onto a train heading for a collision.

The Green Hornet Strikes Again—Universal; Ford Beebe and John Rawings; 15; 'The Plunge of Peril': The Hornet jumps into the car of the fleeing Kolten Munitions Plant Superintendent. The car crashes through the barrier to a bascule bridge just as the bridge is being raised. The car goes into the river.

Junior G-Men—Universal; Ford Beebe and John Rawlings; 12; 'The Blast of Doom': Billy Barton and Gyp hide in the Torch Gang's vault house, unaware that it is being used to test the new explosion devised by Billy's kidnapped father.

King of the Royal Mounted—Republic; William Witney and John English; 12; 'Winged Death': King's plane heads for a crash.

Mysterious Doctor Satan—Republic; William Witney and John English; 15; 'Thirteen Steps': While holding Dr Satan and his men at gunpoint, the Copperhead unknowingly walks under the Doctor's electrocution device. Dr Satan pulls the switch.

The Shadow—Columbia; James W. Horne; 15; 'The Shadow Attacks': The Shadow is trapped on a burning truck driven by the Black Tiger's men towards a powder house.

Terry and the Pirates—Columbia; James W. Horne; 15; 'The Fang Strikes': Fang's men throw their spears at the building where Terry and Pat are sheltering.

Winners of the West—Universal; Ford Beebe and Ray Taylor; 13; 'The Wreck at Red River Gorge': Jeff Ramsay leaps aboard the stolen work train. While he fights the thieves the train goes off the track and falls down a ravine.

1941:

Adventures of Captain Marvel—Republic; William Witney and John English; 12; 'The Guillotine': Electrocuted, Captain Marvel is carried unconscious towards the guillotine. The guillotine blade falls.

Dick Tracy vs. Crime Inc—Republic; William Witney and John English; 15; 'The Prisoner Vanishes': Chasing after Lucifer and The Ghost, Tracy's car crashes when the criminals spill oil on the road.

Holt of the Secret Service—Columbia; James W. Horne; 15; 'Ramparts of Revenge': A fist-fight between Holt and Blackie ends when one of them falls over the cliff.

The Iron Claw—Columbia; James W. Horne; 15; 'The Murderous Mirror': Patricia Benson is captured by the Iron Claw, and in the night-time car chase that follows, the Claw has a mirror placed in the road. Bob Lane's car crashes when he attempts to avoid the reflected lights.

Jungle Girl—Republic; William Witney and John English; 15; 'Queen of the Beasts': Found out in her impersonation of the Lion Goddess, Nyoka is condemned by Shamba to death by fire.

King of the Texas Rangers—Republic; William Witney and John English; 12; 'Dead End': Barton's men blow up the tunnel with the train inside and King on the roof.

Riders of Death Valley—Universal; Ray Taylor and Ford Beebe; 15; 'The Menacing Herd': Escaping from outlaws, Jim falls in the path of stampeding horses.

Sea Raiders—Universal; Ford Beebe and John Rawlings; 12; 'Flaming Torture': Billy Adams and Toby Nelson are trapped in a burning warehouse.

Sky Raiders—Universal; Ford Beebe and Ray Taylor; 12; 'Death Rides the Storm': Robert Dayton's plane is struck by lightning, crash lands and catches fire.

The Spider Returns—Columbia; James W. Horne; 15; 'The Fatal Time Bomb': The Gargoyle's men leave the Spider in the building just before the time bomb is about to detonate. The building explodes.

White Eagle—Columbia; James W. Horne; 15; 'Ambush': Warning the soldiers of the wagon full of explosives about to be dropped on them, White Eagle is left behind when the explosion occurs.

1942:

Captain Midnight—Columbia; James W. Horne; 15; 'Stolen Range Finder': One of the Shark's men drives a truck across the runway where Captain Midnight is about to land. The Captain's plane crashes.

Don Winslow of the Navy—Universal; Ford Beebe and Ray Taylor; 12; 'Flaming Death': Don Winslow trails Paul Barsac but Merlin sends a burning car down the road. It crashes into Winslow's car and both cars go over the cliff.

Gang Busters—Universal; Ray Taylor and Noel Smith; 15; 'The Death Plunge': Bill Bannister's car collides with a car driven by members of Dr Mortis's gang. The car falls down the shaft of the multi-storey car park.

Junior G-Men of the Air—Universal; Ray Taylor and Lewis Collins; 12; 'The Plunge of Peril': An agent of the Black Dragonflies plans to drop Ace Holden from his plane. Ace unties himself but the plane crashes in front of an oncoming train.

King of the Mounties—Republic; William Witney; 12; 'Road to Death': Dave King rides to save Carol Brent, who lies unconscious in a driverless car. The car hits a truck carrying explosives.

Overland Mail—Universal; Ford Beebe and John Rawlins; 15; 'Flaming Havoc': When Gilbert is knocked out during an Indian attack on the wagon train, Barbara tries to revive him, while Jim leaps onto the wagon and grabs the reins. Flaming arrows set the wagon on fire, and it overturns.

Perils of Nyoka—Republic; William Witney; 15; 'Death's Chariot': Attempting to escape in a chariot, Nyoka is chased by Cassib's Warriors. One of them knocks her out. The chariot car goes over a cliff.

Perils of the Royal Mounted—Columbia; James W. Horne; 15; 'The Night Raiders': Sergeant MacLaine chases the killer of Little Wolf but is trapped on a wooden bridge between a fire at one end and Black Bear's men at the other. The bridge collapses.

The Secret Code—Columbia; Spencer G. Bennet; 15; 'Shadow of the Swastika': Disguised as the Black Commando, Dan Barton escapes from the police but is left hanging onto a rope, which snaps.

Spy Smasher—Republic; William Witney; 12; 'Human Target': At the end of a fist fight the man in the Spy Smasher outfit is shot.

The Valley of Vanishing Men—Columbia; Spencer G. Bennet; 15; 'The Mystery of Ghost Town': When Consuelo Romeros' wagon overturns, Wild Bill Tolliver comes to her aid, only to find himself in the path of a herd of stampeding horses.

1943:

The Adventures of Smilin' Jack—Universal; Ray Taylor and Lewis Collins; 13; 'The Rising Sun Strikes': Machine gun fire is aimed at Jack. He falls.

Adventures of the Flying Cadets—Universal; Ray Taylor and Lewis Collins; 13; 'Menaced by Murderers': Danny Collins and his friends chase after the Black Hangman's men, who throw grenades at their speedboat. The speedboat hits a buoy.

Batman—Columbia; Lambert Hillyer; 15; 'The Bat's Cave': Batman falls from an electrified high-wire.

Daredevils of the West—Republic; John English; 12; 'Flaming Prison': Duke Cameron is trapped inside a burning jail.

Don Winslow of the Coast Guard—Universal; Ford Beebe and Ray Taylor; 13; 'Battling a U-Boat': Don Winslow leads an attack on the U-Boat, but the exchange of fire leads to an explosion on Winslow's ship.

G-Men vs. the Black Dragon—Republic; William Witney; 15; 'Japanese Inquisition': While Rex fights the Black Dragon agents, Vivian March is tied to a plank moving towards the buzz saw.

The Masked Marvel—Republic; Spencer G. Bennet; 12; 'Death Takes the Helm': The Masked Marvel fights one of Sakima's agent on a launch packed with explosives. The launch collides with a ship and explodes.

The Phantom—Columbia; B. Reeves Eason; 15; 'The Man Who Never Dies': The Phantom is attacked by a lion.

Secret Service in Darkest Africa—Republic; Spencer G. Bennet; 15; 'The Charred Witness': Rex's discovery of the Axis Radio Station leads to a fight, which ends when Rex is pushed in the direction of the generator.

1944:

Black Arrow—Columbia; Lew Landers; 15; 'Signal of Fear': Attempting to thwart a fake Indian raid organized by Jackson, Black Arrow fall into a burning building.

Captain America—Republic; John English and Elmer Clifton; 15; 'Mechanical Executioner': Captain America is knocked out by one of the Scarab's men. His prone body lies in the path of the tractor which the Scarab's henchmen sends in his direction.

The Desert Hawk—Columbia; B. Reeves Eason; 15; 'The Evil Eye': Captured by the Emir of Telef, the Hawk is tied and stretched between two horses.

The Great Alaskan Mystery—Universal; Ray Taylor and Lewis Collins; 13; 'Thundering Doom': Dr Miller, inventor of the petraton, and his party, are marooned on a rapidly melting iceberg.

Haunted Harbor—Republic; Spencer G. Bennet and Wallace Grissell; 15; 'Flight to Danger': Patricia Harding is ambushed while driving Kassim to safety. She loses consciousness and her car somersaults down the hill.

The Mystery of the Riverboat—Universal; Ray Taylor and Lewis Collins; 13; 'The Phantom Killer': Hearing Jenny's screams, Steve goes to her aid. The fight with her mysterious assailant leads to Steve falling into the river.

Raiders of Ghost City—Universal; Ray Taylor and Lewis Collins; 13; 'Flaming Treachery': Secret Service Agent Steve Clark and his companions are in a cabin besieged by outlaws. The cabin catches fire.

The Tiger Woman—Republic; Spencer G. Bennet and Wallace Grissell; 12; 'Doorway to Death': Allen Saunders and the Tiger Woman are besieged in a shack. The shack explodes.

Zorro's Black Whip—Republic; Spencer G. Bennet and Wallace Grissell; 12; 'Tomb of Terror': The Black Whip is shut in the bank safe which has been mined with explosives. The explosives are detonated.

1945:

Brenda Starr, Reporter—Columbia; Wallace W. Fox; 13; 'The Blazing Trap': Brenda is led into a deserted warehouse. A pile of packing cases are sent down a ramp towards her. A staircase collapses.

Federal Operator 99—Republic; Spencer G. Bennet, Yakima Canutt and Wallace Grissell'; 12; 'The Case of the Missing Ransom': Blake's motorbike goes over a cliff into the lake.

Jungle Queen—Universal; Ray Taylor and Lewis Collins; 13; 'Jungle Sacrifice': Pamela is captured and about to be sacrificed to the crocodiles.

Jungle Raiders—Columbia; Lesley Selander; 15; 'Primitive Sacrifice': Condemned to death, the witch doctor swaps places with Dr Moore. Meanwhile Bob and Joe, trying to find the secret entrance to the village, slide down a hill.

Manhunt of Mystery Island—Republic; Spencer G. Bennet and Wallace Grissell; 15; 'Satan's Web': Captured by Captain Mephisto, Claire Forrest is tied up in a fishing net and dunked in water. Lance Reardon comes to her rescue, but during his fight with Mephisto Claire is once again lowered into the water, and this time she doesn't come up.

The Master Key—Universal; Ray Taylor and Lewis Collins; 13; 'Death Turns the Wheel': Flash Faust kidnaps Janet Lowe. Cornered by the police, he drives his car off a bridge.

The Monster and the Ape—Columbia; Howard Bretherton; 15; 'The Edge of Doom': Ken Morgan chases Professor Ernst but his car goes off the road.

The Purple Monster Strikes—Republic; Spencer G. Bennet and Fred Brannon; 15; 'The Time Trap': The Purple Monster and Garrett escape with $100,000, using the ladder they have used as a bridge between two buildings. Craig follows but the thieves push out the ladder and it falls.

The Royal Mounted Rides Again—Universal; Ray Taylor and Lewis Collins; 13; 'The Avalanche Trap': Outlaws organize a series of rockfalls to descend on Corporals Wayne and Frenchy.

Secret Agent X-9—Universal; Ray Taylor and Lewis Collins; 13; 'Ringed by Fire': X-9 attempts to hide from the Nazis in the water, but they pour oil on it and set it alight.

Who's Guilty?—Columbia; Howard Bretherton and Wallace Grissell; 15; 'The Unknown Strikes': When Ruth Allen lies on her bed it slides backwards into the wall.

1946:

Chick Carter, Detective—Columbia; Derwin Abrahams; 15; 'Jump to Eternity': Farrell and Spud pursue Vasky to the roof but Farrell's leg is caught in a rope and he falls.

The Crimson Ghost—Republic; William Witney and Fred Brannon; 12; 'Thunderbolt': Following the course of the Radium Detector, Duncan Richards is led into the path of Professor Chambers' Death Ray.

Daughter of Don Q—Republic; Spencer G. Bennet and Fred Brannon; 12; 'Vendetta': The fight between Cliff and the henchmen of Carlos Manning ends when Cliff shoots one of the henchmen, but his fall causes the harpoon to fire at Dolores, who is tied up in a fishing net.

Hop Harrigan—Columbia; Derwin Abrahams; 15; 'The Secret Ray': Hop, Tank and Dr Tober are attacked by Hunter's men, using Tober's Destroying Ray. Thinking that Hop and Tank have betrayed him, Tober parachutes out of the plane, leaving Hop and Tank plunging towards the earth.

King of the Forest Rangers—Republic; Spencer G. Bennet and Fred Brannon; 12; 'Shattered Evidence': King is knocked out in a fight with Spear, and Spear throws a spiked frame on top of him.

Lost City of the Jungle—Universal; Ray Taylor and Lewis Collins; 13; 'The Death Flood': Rod Stanton and Tai Shan unsuccessfully try to stop Hazarias's men from blowing up the Pool of Light and are engulfed by a water torrent.

The Mysterious Mr. M—Universal; Lewis Collins and Vernon Keays; 13; 'Danger Downward': Grant's car falls down a shaft in a multi-storey carpark.

The Phantom Rider—Republic; Spencer G. Bennet and Fred Bannon; 12; 'Flaming Ambush': The Phantom Rider is left unconscious on a riderless, burning wagon.

The Scarlet Horseman—Universal; Ray Taylor and Lewis Collins; 13; 'Dry Grass Danger': Jim Bannion is left unconscious in a burning wagon.

Son of the Guardsman—Columbia; Derwin Abrahams; 15; 'Perils of the Forest': While attempting to avoid their pursuers, David and Louise fall off their horse and roll down a hill.

Notes

Introduction

1 'The Lost Jungle', *Motion Picture Daily*, 23 April 1934, p. 6.
2 It is described as 'both popular and profitable' in George E. Turner and Michael H. Price, *Forgotten Horrors: The Definitive Editions* (Baltimore: Midnight Marque Press, 1999), p. 130. Jack Mathis reports that it grossed $220,000 in the United States and $60,000 in England, with Mascot's worldwide share reaching an estimated $150,000: *The Valley of the Cliffhangers* (Northbrook, Illinois: Jack Mathis Advertising, 1975), p. 6.
3 A.D.S., 'Lions, Tigers and Mr Beatty', *New York Times*, 8 June 1934, p. 18.
4 Howard Berg, 'How Berg Did the Trick', *Motion Picture Herald*, 1 September 1934, p. 63.
5 'Chronicle of NBC, 1920–1951', *Broadcasting*, 26 November 1951, p. 129.
6 See, for instance, Bob Moak, 'H'wood Eyes Serial Cycle', *Variety*, 6 November 1940, p. 12. I use *Variety* to refer to the weekly edition, *Daily Variety* when I refer to the daily edition.
7 Alan Barbour, 'Complete List of Sound Serials', *Cliffhanger: A Pictorial History of the Motion Picture Serial* (New York: A & W Publishers, 1977), pp. 240–44.
8 Jack Mathis, *Republic Confidential, Vol. II. The Studio* (Northbrook, Ill.: Jack Mathis Advertising, 1999), p. 289.
9 *1947 Film Daily Year Book of Motion Pictures* (New York: Wid's Film and Film Folk, 1947), p. 55.
10 David Cook, *A History of Narrative Film*, 3rd edition (New York: Norton, 1996).
11 Jon Lewis, *American Film: A History* (New York: Norton, 2007), pp. 39–40.
12 Kristin Thompson and David Bordwell, *Film History: An Introduction*, 3rd edition (New York: McGraw-Hill, 2009), p. 50.

13 Jane Gaines's statement that 'Today, no scholar or silent-era cinephile would challenge the assertion that Pearl White was the first international American star celebrity' is quoted by Marina Dahlquist, 'Introduction: Why Pearl?' in Marina Dahlquist (ed.), *Exporting Perilous Pauline: Pearl White and the Serial Film Craze* (Urbana, Ill.: University of Illinois Press, 2013), p. 2. Ben Singer's discussion of the serial queen includes his *Melodrama and Modernity: Sensational Cinema and its Contexts* (New York: Columbia University Press, 2001): see in particular the chapter, 'Power and Peril in the Serial Queen Melodrama', pp. 221–62. See also Shelley Stamp, *Movie-Struck Girls: Women and Motion Picture Culture after the Nickelodeon* (Princeton, NJ: Princeton University Press, 2000).

14 Ben Singer, 'Serials', in Geoffrey Nowell-Smith (ed.), *Oxford History of World Cinema*, (Oxford: Oxford University Press, 1996), p. 110. See, however, Rudmer Canjels, *Distributing Silent Film Serials: Local Practices, Changing Forms, Cultural Transformation* (New York: Routledge, 2011).

15 Wayne Schultz's *The Motion Picture Serial: An Annotated Bibliography* (Metuchen, NJ: Scarecrow, 1992), covers the period up to the 1990s. For a serial on the serial see, for instance, *Favorite Westerns and Serial World* (1986–2004). For websites, see 'The Serial Squadron Cinema Cliffhanger Archive', www.serialsquadron.com or the currently more active (at the time of writing) 'Continued Next Week' section of the 'In the Balcony' message board: http://s13.zetaboards.com/In_The_Balcony/forum/7530/ [accessed 20 April 2015].

16 Jack Mathis, *The Valley of the Cliffhangers* and *Republic Confidential: Vol. 2, The Studio*.

17 William K. Everson, 'Introduction', Alan G. Barbour, *Saturday Afternoon at the Movies: Vol 1, Days of Thrills and Adventure* (New York: Bonanza Books, 1986), p. xiv.

18 Jim Harmon and Donald E. Glut, *The Great Movie Serials: Their Sound and Fury* (London: Woburn Press, 1973), p. xix.

19 Rob Allen and Thijs van den Berg (eds), *Serialization in Popular Culture* (London: Routledge, 2014).

20 Rafael Arnaldo Vela, 'With Parents Consent: Film Serials, Consumerism and the Creation of the Youth Audience, 1913–1938'. PhD diss., University of Wisconsin, Madison, 2000; Scott Higgins, *Matinee Melodrama: Playing with Formula in the Sound Serial* (New Brunswick, NJ: Rutgers University Press, 2016). The fact that Higgins' book appeared as this work was going to press has meant where I have drawn on his work it has been through his earlier publications, in particular 'Seriality's Ludic Promise: Film Serials and the Prehistory of Digital Gaming', *Euladomos: Journal for Computer Game Culture*, 8.1 (2014), pp. 101–13.

21 Barbour, *Cliffhanger*, pp. 240–44.

22 George E. Turner and Michael H. Price identify *The Voice from the Sky* as the first true sound serial: *Forgotten Horrors*, p. 24.

1 The Serial and the Cliffhanger: Definitions and Origins

1 Buck Rainey, *Serials and Series: A World Filmography, 1912–1956* (London: McFarland, 1999), p. 5.

2 Robert C. Allen, 'Introduction', in Robert C. Allen (ed.), *To Be Continued . . .: Soap Operas around the World* (London: Routledge, 1995), p. 17.

3 Linda Hughes and Michael Lund, *The Victorian Serial* (Charlottesville: University Press of Virginia, 1991), p. 275.

4 Alex Marlow-Mann, 'British Series and Serials in the Silent Era', in Andrew Higson (ed.), *Young and Innocent: The Cinema in Britain 1896– 1930* (Exeter: University of Exeter Press, 2002), p. 148.

5 Michelle Nolan, *Ball Tales: A Study of Baseball, Basketball and Football Fiction of the 1930s through the 1960s* (Jefferson NC: McFarland, 2010), p. 38.

6 See in particular Ben Singer, *Melodrama and Modernity: Sensational Cinema and its Contexts* (New York: Columbia University Press, 2001) and Scott Higgins, 'Suspenseful Situations: Melodramatic Narrative and the Contemporary Action Film', *Cinema Journal*, 47.2 (2008), pp. 74–96.

7 J. Randolph Cox, *The Dime Novel Companion: A Source Book* (Westport, Conn & London: Greenwood Press, 2000), p. 170.

8 Michael Denning, *Mechanic Accents: Dime Novels and Working Class Culture in America* (London: Verso, 1998), p. 205.

9 See Deirdre Johnson, 'Juvenile Publications', in Christine Bold (ed.), *U.S. Popular Print Culture 1860–1920* (Oxford: Oxford University Press, 2012), pp. 293–315.

10 Ibid., p. 4.

11 Reproduced in James M. Cain, 'The Man Merriwell', in Roy Hoopes (ed.), *60 Years of Journalism* (Bowling Green: Bowling Green State University Popular Press, 1985), p. 151 (first published in *Saturday Evening Post*, June 11, 1927). Jack Harkaway's adventures were first published in 1871.

12 Ryan K. Anderson, 'Merry's Flock: Making Something out of Educational Reform in the Early Twentieth Century', in Adam R. Nelson and John L. Rudolph (eds), *Education and the Culture of Print in Modern America* (Madison: University of Wisconsin Press, 2010), pp. 64–65.

13 Ibid., p. 61.

14 See the entry on Frank Merriwell in Cox, *The Dime Novel Companion*, pp. 170–73.

15 Jennifer Hayward, *Consuming Pleasures: Active Consuming Fictions: Audiences and Serial Fictions from Dickens to Soap Opera* (Lexington: University of Kentucky, 1997), p. 3.

16 Umberto Eco, *The Limits of Interpretation* (Bloomington, Ind.: Indiana University Press, 1990), p. 84 and p. 87.

17 Ruth Mayer, *Serial Fu Manchu: The Chinese Supervillain and the Spread of Yellow Peril Ideology* (Philadelphia: Temple University Press, 2014), p. 7.

18 See Lydia Cushman Schurman, 'The Librarian of Congress Argues Against Cheap Novels Getting Low Postal Rates', in Larry E. Sullivan and Lydia C. Schurman (eds), *Pioneers, Passionate Ladies and Private Eyes: Dime Novels, Series Books, and Paperbacks* (Binghampton, NY, Hawthorne Press, 1996), pp. 59–72.

19 *Smith v. Hitchcock*, 226 U.S. 53 (1912).

20 Ibid.

21 Ryan Anderson, '*Smith v. Hitchcock* (1912) and the Death of the Dime Novel', William M. Blount Symposium on Postal History, Smithsonian National Postal Museum, Washington D.C., 4 November 2006, https://*postalmuseum.si.edu/research/pdfs/Anderson.pdf* (accessed 21 January 2015), p. 12.

22 Christine Bold, *Selling the Wild West: Popular Western Fiction, 1860–1960* (Bloomington, Ind.: Indiana University Press, 1997), p. 7.

23 *Daily Times*, 14 November 1913, p. 7. I have found no other reference to a film called *Frank Merriwell's Schooldays*, and while its existence suggests a series I have seen no reference to other Merriwell films close to this date. There is a little more information on *Frank Merriwell in Arizona: The Mystery of the Mine* (to give the full title), and the film itself survives. It features a mine but no ring or father. It can be viewed at https://www.youtube.com/watch?v=wGO_2pZKTNM where it is described as an anti-alcohol drama, and dated as produced in 1910 though the 1913 advertising suggests the later date.

24 Ben Singer, 'Feature Films, Variety Programs and the Crisis of the Small Exhibitor', in Charlie Keil and Shelley Stamp (eds), *American Cinema's Transitional Era: Audiences, Institutions, Practices* (Berkeley and Los Angeles: University of California Press, 2004), p. 79.

25 Epes Winthrop Sargent, *Technique of the Photoplay* (New York: Moving Picture World, 1913), p. 122.

26 Ernest A. Dench, 'For the Photo-Play Writer', *Cinema News and Property Gazette*, 2 April 1913, p. 55.

27 J. Berg Esenwein and Arthur Leeds, *Writing the Photoplay* (Springfield, Mass.: Writers Library, 1913), p. 145.

28 *Motography*, 26 July 1913, p. 9.

29 J. Berg Esenwein and Arthur Leeds, *Writing the Photoplay* (Springfield, Mass.: Writers Library, 1919), p. 26.

30 Alfred A. Cohn, 'Harvesting the Serial', *Photoplay*, February 1917, p. 21.

31 *Motion Picture News*, 3 January 1914, p. 14. *The Chronicles of Cleek* was released between 1913 and 1914, *The Active Life of Dolly of the Dailies* in

1914, William Wadsworth's 'Wood B. Wedd' films between 1913 and 1915, *The Adventures of Andy Clark* in 1914, *The Adventures of Octavius* in 1914.

32 Ben Singer, *Melodrama and Modernity: Early Sensational Cinema and Its Contexts* (New York: Columbia University Press, 2001), p. 210.

33 'A Stupendous Undertaking', *Motography*, 6 September 1913, p. 181.

34 'Adventures of Kathlyn', *Motion Picture News*, 17 January 1914, p. 38.

35 James McQuade, '"The Adventures of Kathlyn" (Selig)', *Motion Picture News*, 21 February 1914, p. 926.

36 'Prince Umballah Again Triumphant', *Motography*, 7 March 1914, p. 158.

37 See, for instance, Ron Backer, 'Serial Sources', *Gripping Chapters: The Sound Movie Serial* (Albany, Geo.: Bear Manor Media, 2010), p. 135.

38 'If Customers Don't Cry, Producers Must: Hoke's Fancy Coast Revival', *Variety*, 3 September 1930, p. 2.

39 Harry Keller, 'Who Done "Whodunnit"?', letter to *New York Times*, 22 August 1937, section X p. 2; *Yorkshire Post and Leeds Intelligencer*, 19 August 1938, p. 6.

40 *Variety* 7 February 1933, p. 39 and 24 October 1933, p. 6.

41 'Metro Sees B.O. in Serials: May Do 'Em', *Variety*, 17 November 1937, p. 4.

42 Barrett C. Kiesling, *Talking Pictures: How They are Made and How to Appreciate Them* (London: Spon, 1937) p. 306.

43 Ashby Bland Crowder, 'Observations on the Crossing of Genres in the Nineteenth Century', *Aevum*, volume 51.5/6 (1977), pp. 541–47, p. 542.

44 William Makepeace Thackeray, *Vanity Fair* (New York and London: Norton, 1994), p. 152. Edgar F. Harden's 'The Discipline and Significance of Form in *Vanity Fair*', included in the Norton edition, details the material included in the serialised version: see p. 723.

45 Kathleen Tillotson, *Novels of the 1840s* (Oxford: Oxford University Press, 1954), p. 45. Robert McCrum identifies this as a cliffhanger in the *Guardian*, 23 December 2013, http://www.theguardian.com/books/2013/dec/23/william-thackeray-vanity-fair-100-best-novels.

46 Walter Clarke Phillips, *Dickens, Reade and Collins: Sensation Novelists* (New York: Columbia University Press, 1919), pp. 83–84.

47 Ibid., p. 85.

48 Wilkie Collins, *Armadale, Cornhill Magazine*, January 1865, p. 32. Phillips (p. 87) abbreviates this to '"The boat; the boat," he cried in a scream of horror. The boat was adrift' and Rob Allen does the same in his '"Pause You Who Read This": Disruption and the Serial Novel', in Allen and Berg, *Serialization in Popular Culture*, p. 41.

49 Esenwein and Leeds, *Writing the Photoplay*, 1913.

50 William Wallace Cook, *The Fiction Factory* (Ridgewood, NJ: Editor Company, 1912), p. 119.

51 Bruner, 'The Modern Dime Novel', p. 49.

52 *Motion Picture News*, 26 December 1914, p. 20.

53 *Motion Picture World*, 24 June 1916, pp. 2200–01.

54 *Motion Picture World*, 10 August 1918, p. 744; *Motion Picture News*, 10 April 1920, p. 3248–49. *The Hand of Vengeance* was the American title of the British serial, *Ultus: The Man from the Dead*.

55 Scott Higgins, 'Seriality's Ludic Promise: Film Serials and the Pre-History of Digital Gaming', *Euladamos: Journal for Computer Game Culture*, 8.1 (2014), pp. 101-02.

56 Singer, *Melodrama and Modernity*, pp. 41–42; Frank Leon Smith, 'The Man Who Made Serials', *Films in Review*, 7.8 (1956), p. 379.

57 *Exhibitors Trade Review*, 14 October 1922, p. 1295.

58 Frank Leon Smith, 'The Man Who Made Serials', p. 379.

59 Bruner, 'The Modern Dime Novel', p. 49.

60 Singer, *Melodrama and Modernity*, p. 13.

61 See Ron Backer, 'Serial Sources', *Gripping Chapters*, pp. 21–106.

62 See Rick Altman, 'Dickens, Griffith, and Film Theory Today', in Jane Gaines (ed.), *Classical Hollywood Narrative: The Paradigm Wars* (Durham, NC: Duke University Press, 1992), pp. 12–13.

63 Ben Brewster and Lea Jacobs, *Theatre to Cinema: Stage Pictorialism and the Early Feature Film* (New York: Oxford University Press, 1997), p. 213.

64 Joseph Arthur, *Blue Jeans* (New York: Samuel French, 1940), p. 87.

65 Shane Denson, 'The Logic of the Line Segment', in Allen and Berg, *Serialization in Popular Culture*, pp. 74–75.

66 A. Danson Michell, 'The Perils of Pauline', *Motion Picture News*, 13 June 1914, p. 108.

67 Edwin J. Brett, 'Three Modern Crusoes, or, Perseverance or Indolence', *Boys' Sunday Reader: A Magazine of Pure Literature*, 9 April 1879, p. 212.

68 Edwin J. Brett, 'Three Modern Crusoes, or, Perseverance or Indolence', *Boys' Sunday Reader: A Magazine of Pure Literature*, 16 April 1879, p. 226.

69 Scott Higgins, 'Suspenseful Situations', p. 87.

70 See Kristin Thompson, *Storytelling in the New Hollywood: Understanding Classical Narrative Technique* (Cambridge, Mass.: Harvard University Press, 1999).

71 'Serial Features', *Motography*, 22 August 1914, pp. 273–74.

72 Singer, *Melodrama and Modernity*, p. 210.

73 *Motography*, 5 September 1914, p. 14.

74 *Motion Picture News*, 23 March 1918, p. 1678.

75 *Motion Picture News*, 26 June 1915, no page number.

76 *Moving Picture World*, 24 February 1917, p. 1156; *Exhibitors' Trade Review*, 26 November 1921, p. 5.

77 Josh Lambert, '"Wait for the Next Pictures": Intertextuality and Cliffhanger Continuity in Early Cinema and Comic Strips', *Cinema Journal*, 48.2 (2009), p. 18.

78 *Exhibitors' Herald*, 3 January 1920, pp. 86–87.

79 Morgan Cox to Andy Sharick, on *Jungle Queen* (1945), Universal Collection, Cinematic Arts Library, University of Southern California, Los Angeles (hereafter USC), Box 184/4924, 11 December 1944.

80 'Continued Next Week', *New York Times*, 5 June 1938, p. 156.

81 William Roberts, 'Cliff-Hangers', *Los Angeles Times*, 20 October 1946: Section D, p. 12.

82 Ibid.

83 Lewis Herman, 'The Serial', *Practical Manual of Screen Playwriting*, (Cleveland and New York: World Publishing Company, 1952), pp. 50–53.

84 Singer, *Melodrama and Modernity*, p. 208.

85 William Lord Wright, 'Hints for Scenario Writers', *Picture-Play Magazine* (December 1918), p. 227.

2 Thursday Night at the Ritz: Exhibition, Audiences and Regulation

1 Alan Barbour, *Saturday Afternoon at the Movies*, 3 volumes (New York: Bonanza Books, 1986).

2 William Cline, *In the Nick of Time: Motion Picture Sound Serials* (London: McFarland, 1998), p. viii.

3 Ed Hulse, *Distressed Damsels and Masked Marauders: Cliffhanger Serials of the Silent-Movie Era*, (Morris Plains NJ: Murania Press, 2014), p. 1.

4 Richard M. Hurst, *Republic Studios: Between Poverty Row and the Majors*, Updated edition (Lanham, Maryland: Scarecrow Press, 2007), p. 271.

5 See, for instance, Richard Maltby's account of the 'Americanization' of his imagination in his 'Introduction: The Americanization of the World', in Melvyn Stokes and Richard Maltby (eds), *Hollywood Abroad: Audiences and Cultural Exchange* (London: British Film Institute, 2004), p. 2.

6 Yannis Tzioumakis, *American Independent Cinema: An Introduction* (Edinburgh: Edinburgh University Press, 2006), p. 76.

7 Jared Gardner, *Projections: Comics and the History of Twentieth-Century Storytelling* (Stanford: Stanford University Press, 2012), p. 29.

8 Ben Singer, 'Serials', in Geoffrey Nowell-Smith (ed.), *The Oxford History of World Cinema* (Oxford: Oxford University Press, 1996), pp. 110–11.

9 Roger Hagedorn, 'Doubtless to be Continued: A Brief History of Serial Narrative', in Robert C. Allen (ed.), *To be Continued . . .: Soap Operas Around the World* (London: Routledge, 1995), p. 34.

10 William K. Everson, 'The Silent Serial', *Screen Facts*, 1.1 (1963), p. 5.

11 Roy Kinnard, Tony Crnkovich and R.J. Vitone, *The Flash Gordon Serials, 1936–1940* (Jefferson NC and London: McFarland, 2008), p. 15.

12 J.P. Mayer, *The Sociology of Film; Studies and Documents* (London: Faber,

1946); Herbert Blumer, *Movies and Conduct* (New York: Macmillan, 1933). For more recent accounts see: Annette Kuhn, *An Everyday Magic: Cinema and Cultural Memory* (London: I B Tauris, 2002); Jeffrey Klenotic, '"Four Hours of Hootin' and Hollerin": Moviegoing and Everyday Life Outside the Movie Palace', in Richard Maltby, Melvyn Stokes and Robert C. Allen (eds), *Going to the Movies: Hollywood and the Social Experience of Cinema*, (Exeter: University of Exeter Press, 2007), pp. 130–154; Rafael Arnaldo Vela, 'With Parents Consent: Film Serials, Consumerism and the Creation of the Youth Audience, 1913–1938'. PhD diss., University of Wisconsin-Madison, 2000; Richard deCordova, 'The Child Audience, the Hays Code and Saturday Matinees', in Gregory A. Waller (ed.), *Moviegoing in America: A Sourcebook in the History of Film Exhibition* (Oxford: Blackwell, 2002), pp. 159–69.

13 Mayer, *The Sociology of Film*, pp. 160–61.

14 Herbert Blumer, *Movies and Conduct*, p. 121.

15 Scott Higgins, 'The Seriality's Ludic Promise: Film Serials and the Pre-History of Digital Gaming', *Eludamos: Journal for Computer Game Culture*, 8.1 (2014), p. 107.

16 See Garth Jowett, Ian C. Jarvie and Kathryn H. Fuller, *Children and the Movies: Media Influence and the Payne Fund Controversy* (Cambridge: Cambridge University Press, 1996), p. 237.

17 Sidney Bernstein, 'Attempts Made by the Film Trade to Meet the Problem and the Difficulties Encountered', *Report of the Conference on Films for Children*, 20 and 21 November 1936, British Film Institute, p. 33.

18 Universal Pictures, *How to Make Money with Serials: A Universal Text Book for the Use of Motion Picture Exhibitors* (New York: Universal Pictures Corporation, n.d.), p. 12.

19 Alan Wood, *Mr Rank: A Study of J. Arthur Rank and British Films* (London: Hodder and Stoughton, 1952), p. 173.

20 See Mary Field, *Good Company: The Story of the Children's Entertainment Film Movement in Great Britain 1943–1950* (London: Longman Green & Co., 1952).

21 'Ladies Attacking Sexless Serials as Too Moronic', *Variety*, 29 September 1931, p. 2.

22 *Daily Register*, Oelwein, Iowa, 1 February 1936.

23 On Autry's appeal, see Peter Stanfield, *Hollywood, Westerns and the 1930s: The Lost Trail* (Exeter: University of Exeter Press, 2001), pp. 82–87.

24 *Reel Life*, 17 October 1914, p. 34.

25 *Motion Picture News*, 21 October 1916, reproduced in Ben Singer, *Melodrama and Modernity: Early Sensational Cinema and Its Contexts* (New York: Columbia University Press, 2001), p. 225.

26 Singer, *Melodrama and Modernity*, p. 223.

27 Shelley Stamp, 'An Awful Struggle Between Love and Ambition: Serial

Heroines, Serial Stars and Their Female Fans', in Lee Grieveson (ed.), *The Silent Cinema Reader* (New York: Routledge, 2004), p. 211.

28   'Serial Breaking Records', *Variety*, 25 June 1915, p. 19.

29   Hulse, *Distressed Damsels and Masked Marauders*, p. 61.

30   Singer, *Melodrama and Modernity*, p. 216. See also Marina Dahlquist, 'Introduction: Why Pearl?' Marina Dahlquist (ed.), *Exporting Perilous Pauline: Pearl White and the Serial Film Craze* (Urbana: University of Illinois Press, 2013), p. 4, and Hulse's, *Distressed Damsels and Masked Men*, p. 137.

31   Singer appears to have missed the first page of the survey: see 'Popular Player Contest', *Motion Picture Magazine*, December 1916, pp. 14–15. In fact the final tally of votes was only published in February 1917, though White remained in fifth position, see 'Here are the Winners of the Great Popular Player Contest', pp. 126–28. In December 1918 she was again listed as the third most popular female star, as Singer notes: see 'Motion Picture Hall of Fame', p. 2, Singer, *Melodrama and Modernity*, p. 216.

32   H.A. Woodmansee, 'The New Tower of Babel', *Picture Play*, January 1931, p. 85.

33   Richard Abel, 'Early Motion Pictures and Popular Print Culture: A Web of Ephemera', in Christine Bold (ed.), *The Oxford History of Popular Print Culture*, Vol. 6 *U.S. Popular Print Culture 1860–1920* (Oxford: Oxford University Press, 2012), p. 201–02.

34   Singer, *Melodrama and Modernity*, p. 219; Frank V. Bruner, 'The Modern Dime Novel', *Photoplay*, June 1919, p. 118.

35   See Vela, 'With Parents Consent', p. 129. Vela goes on to say (p. 130) that serials booked by these chains were billed as 'first-run serials'. The only reference from this time to 'first-run serials' I have been able to locate is a report on the manager of the Family House in De Moines 'built up to a big paying theatre with second and third-run features and first-run serials', which implies that in this instance the first-run serial was equivalent to the second or third-run feature: 'De Moines will get two new houses', *Moving Picture World*, 29 May 1919, p. 1194.

36   'The Motion Picture News Chart', *Motion Picture News*, 22 May 1915, pp. 38–41.

37   'Where Serials Go Well', *Motion Picture World*, 23 January 1915, p. 528.

38   'Short Stuff', *Wid's Daily*, 1 June 1919, p. 24.

39   See Raphael Vela, 'With Parents Consent', pp. 135–47.

40   See Buck Rainey, *Serials and Series: A World Filmography 1912–1956* (Jefferson NC & London: McFarland, 1999), p. 4.

41   'Paul Burnett on the New Serial Policy', *Exhibitors' Trade Review*, 28 January 1922, p. 586.

42   'Serial's Importance Never Greater', *Exhibitors' Trade Review*, 15 April 1922, p. 1410.

43 Fred J. McConnell, 'Serial Peak in 1925', *Film Daily*, 15 March 1925, p. 33.

44 'Serials will build trade, says Showman', *Exhibitors' Herald*, 23 February 1924, p. 63.

45 'What the Picture Did For Me', D.A. White, Cosy Theatre, Checkotah, Okla., General Patronage, *Exhibitors' Herald*, 23 February 1924, p. 93.

46 Virginia Morris, 'We – Want – Hokum!' *Picture Play*, April 1927, p. 104.

47 'Chicagoans Fall for Mellers and Serials as Fad', *Motion Picture News*, 27 September 1930, p. 45.

48 *Gazette*, Xenia, Ohio, 7 September 1939.

49 *Afro-American*, 13 May 1939.

50 'What the Picture Did For Me', Orpheum Theatre, Oxford, *Motion Picture Herald*, 19 May 1934, p. 53.

51 'What the Picture Did For Me', Cedar Theatre, Cedartown, small town patronage, *Motion Picture Herald*, 14 May 1938, p. 64; Park Theatre, South Berwick, small town patronage, 4 December 1943, p. 48; Dirigo Theatre, Ellsworth, small town patronage, 27 April 1935, p. 60; Mission Theatre, Clayton, small town patronage, 2 March 1935, p. 75.

52 'What the Picture Did For Me', Mason Theatre, Mason, Mi., small town patronage, *Motion Picture Herald*, 29 January 1938, p. 79; Palace Theatre, Torrington, Conn., general patronage, 11 June 1938, p. 64.

53 'What the Picture Did For Me', Plaza Theatre, Tilbury, Ontario, general patronage, *Motion Picture Herald*, 3 June 1939, p. 69.

54 'What the Picture Did For Me', Owl Theatre, Lebanon, small town patronage, *Motion Picture Herald*, 30 March 1935, p. 65.

55 'What the Picture Did For Me', Liberty Theatre, Quinton, small town patronage, *Motion Picture Herald*, 4 May 1935, p. 68.

56 'What the Picture Did For Me', Orpheum Theatre, Tremonton, general patronage, *Motion Picture Herald*, 21 August 1936, p. 69.

57 'What the Picture Did For Me', Fox Theatre, Fertile, rural and small town patronage, *Motion Picture Herald*, 11 June 1938, p. 64.

58 'What the Picture Did For Me', Lyric Theatre, Hamilton, family patronage, *Motion Picture Herald*, 18 February 1939, p. 65.

59 'What the Picture Did For Me', Niles Theatre, Anamosa, general patronage, *Motion Picture Herald*, 12 August 1938, p. 66.

60 'What the Picture Did For Me', Strand Theatre, Suffern, general patronage, *Motion Picture Herald*, 23 April 1938, p. 59; Strand Theatre, Schroon Lake, small town patronage, 24 December 1938, p. 52.

61 *Motion Picture Daily*, 23 February 1938, p. 4; *Film Daily*, 16 February 1938, p. 7; *Motion Picture Herald*, 19 February 1938, p. 47.

62 'Serials Tossed Out of All F-WC Houses at Instigation of Femmes', *Variety*, 24 November 1931, p. 4.

63 Museum of the American West, Los Angeles, clipping from 'Buck Jones Scrapbook', GPCCOL; CCOL.U10.E10.

64 Lucie Nevile, '$250,000 Used to Make Some – Very Profitably', *Washington Post*, 6 March 1938, p. TS1.

65 Hubbard Keavey, 'Serials Still Pack Thrills', *Hartford Courant*, 17 August 1941, p. SM13.

66 'Serials are Still Popular Fare', *Motion Picture Herald*, 2 September 1944, p. 13.

67 Thomas Wood, 'The Sad State of the Serial', *New York Times*, 22 December 1946, p. 51..

68 Margaret Thorp, *America at the Movies* (London: Faber, 1946), p. 22.

69 Universal Pictures, *How to Make Money with Serials*, p. 59 and p. 31.

70 'For the Program', *The Perils of Pauline* pressbook. British Film Institute Pressbook Collection, BFI Reuben Library, London (hereafter BFI). Note that the pressbooks held by the British Film Institute cited here were designed for American exhibitors.

71 'Balaban & Katz Book Serials', *Universal Weekly*, 25 April 1936, p. 23.

72 'Go After the Kids', 'And the Adults', *The Galloping Ghost* pressbook (BFI).

73 'Go After the Men', *The Lost Jungle* pressbook (BFI).

74 'Use the Kids to Help Sell This Serial Made Principally for Their Amazement', *Undersea Kingdom* pressbook (BFI).

75 'Taboos for Serial Writer', and 'Specialize on Serial Production', *Dick Tracy vs. Crime Inc.* pressbook, Jack Mathis Papers, Howard B. Lee Library, Brigham Young University (hereafter BYU), MS2389 Box 50.

76 'Kids at Heart', *Overland with Kit Carson* pressbook (BFI).

77 'Contact Adults', 'Shirley Paterson', *Batman* pressbook (BFI).

78 'Lobby, Fronts, Tie-Ups', *The Desert Hawk* pressbook (BFI).

79 'See a Renewed Vogue for the Cliffhangers', *Variety*, 14 April 1937, p. 7.

80 *Film Daily*, 28 December 1936, p. 5; '"Captain Midnight" Rolls', *Showman's Trade Review*, 20 December 1941, p. 27.

81 'Universal Revamps Shorts for 1941–42', *Film Daily*, 25 June 1941, p. 7. See also 'Universal Pointing Up Serials' Adult Appeal', *Showman's Trade Review*, 5 April 1941, p. 24.

82 Avi Santo, 'Transmedia brand licensing prior to conglomeration: George Trendle and the Lone Ranger and Green Hornet brands, 1933–66'. PhD diss., University of Texas at Austin, 2006, p. 147; Avi Santo, email to the author, 13 April 2010.

83 Included in the anonymous unpublished manuscript, 'The Saga of Bringing the Lone Ranger to the Screen. Contracts, Production and the Aftermath Lawsuits', MS2389 Box 53, Folder 1 (BYU).

84 'Thrill of Serial Fare Knows No Age', *Perils of Nyoka* pressbook (BFI).

For a more detailed account of Republic's release of *The Lone Ranger* see the section on the film in Guy Barefoot, 'Who Watched That Masked Man? Hollywood's Serial Audiences in the 1930s', *Historical Journal of Film Radio and Television*, 31.2 (2011), pp. 179–83.

85 'Films Cut Absenteeism in War Plants', *Business Screen*, 5.1 (1942), p. 28; R.G. Yates, Memo to All Branches, 8 December 1950, MS2389 – Cabinet #1, Drawer 24A (BYU). The Memo also refers to Veterans playing serials over their 35mm circuit.

86 Shelley Stamp, *Movie-Struck Girls: Women and Motion Picture Culture after the Nickelodeon* (Princeton, NJ: Princeton University Press, 2000), p. 124.

87 'International Innovation', *Motography*, 3 June 1916, p. 1269.

88 'Got the Kids Coming to See Myra', *Moving Picture World*, 3 June 1917, p. 1731.

89 'The Young Picturegoer', *Pictures and the Picturegoer*, 29 January 1916, p. 418.

90 'Children Stage School Version of "Broken Coin"', *Motion Picture News*, 29 April 1916, p. 2510.

91 B.F. Barrett, 'What the Children Want in Pictures', *Motography*, 22 July 1916, p. 191.

92 B.F. Barrett, 'Has Studied Kiddies Likes and Dislikes', *Motion Picture News*, 3 March 1917, p. 1380.

93 Gardner, *Projections*, p. 33.

94 Vela, 'With Parents Consent', p. 193.

95 Ellis P. Oberholzer, 'What are the Movies Making of Our Children', in *Reference Shelf*, 2.1 (1923), p. 42.

96 'Ladies Attacking Sexless Serials as Too Moronic', p. 2.

97 'Serials Tossed Out of All F-WC Houses at Instigation of Femmes', p. 4.

98 Hazel Plate, Memo to Douglas Mackinnon, Aug 9 1938, *The Fighting Devil Dogs* Production Code Authority (hereafter PCA) File, Margaret Herrick Library, Academcy of Motion Picture Arts and Sciences, Los Angeles (hereafter MHL).

99 'New Policy of Serial Exploitation Adopted: Universal Planning to "Sell" its Chapter Plays to the Public', *Exhibitors' Herald*, 1 October 1921, p. 75.

100 'What the Picture Did For Me', *Exhibitors' Herald*, October 1922, p. 77; 14 October 1922, p. 80; 4 Nov 1922, p. 81; 6 January 1923, p. 102; 24 February 1923, p. 88.

101 'Comprehensive Exploitation Prepared for All "U" Shorts', *Film Daily*, 21 September 1930, p. 18.

102 'Selected Pictures Guide', *National Board of Review Magazine*, December 1930, p. 17.

103 'The Indians are Coming', *Educational Screen*, February 1931, p. 59.

104 'Macon's Matinee Mentor', *National Board of Review Magazine*, December 1931, p. 3.

105 '365 Films Picked for Special Use in Neighborhood, Small Towns', *Motion Picture Herald*, 18 November 1933, p. 46.

106 'The Indians are Coming', *Motion Picture News*, 23 August 1930, p. 57.

107 'Sound Shorts Keep Forging Ahead', *Film Daily*, 21 September 1930, p. 4.

108 'Serials Aiding In Luring Back Juvenile Trade', *Motion Picture News*, 25 October 1930, p. 26. See also '"Indian" Serial Brings Back Kids to Movies', *Motion Picture News*, 1 November 1930, p. 26.

109 'Exhibitors Clamoring for Serials', *Film Daily*, 30 September 1930, p. 1 and p. 8.

110 'Clubwomen Commend "Clancy"', *Universal Weekly*, 25 February 1933, p. 15.

111 Ibid.

112 'Bring the Kids Back', *Danger Island* pressbook (BFI).

113 Nat Levine, telegram to J.J. Milstein, 11 May 1936, MS2389 Box 40, File 5 (BYU).

114 *Lone Ranger* pressbook, MS2389 Box 50 (BYU).

115 *Dick Tracy vs. Crime Inc.* pressbook, MS2389 Box 50 (BYU).

116 See Robert J. Read, 'A Squalid-Looking Place: Poverty Row Films of the 1930s', PhD diss., McGill University, Montreal, 2010, p. 193.

117 'Special Preview Questionnaire', Box 238/7042, Folder 3, (USC).

118 'Special Preview Questionnaire', Box 238/7040, Folder 6 (USC).

119 *Film Daily*, 24 January 1945, p. 11.

120 'Serials in Marked Comeback: 50 N.Y. Loew Theatres Book 'em Sat. Mats', *Variety*, 6 March 1940, Clipping File, MS2389 Box 44 (BYU). See also 'Cliffhangers Would Woo Adult Film Fans with Maturer Plots', *Variety*, 9 September 1942, Clipping File, MS2389 Box 44 (BYU).

121 William Roberts, 'Cliff-Hangers', *Los Angeles Times*, 20 October 1946, p. 20.

122 'Speaking of Pearls', *Photoplay*, September 1917, p. 26.

123 On the distribution of American serials in Germany see Rudmer Canjels, *Distributing Silent Film Serials: Local Practices, Changing Forms, Cultural Transformation* (New York: Routledge, 2011), pp. 99–123.

124 Kristin Thompson, *Exporting Entertainment: America in the World Film Market 1907–1934* (London: BFI Publishing, 1985), p. 59.

125 'Specializing in Serial Pictures', *Moving Picture World*, 22 February 1919, p. 1089.

126 E.T. McGovern, 'Export Items', *Moving Picture* World, 14 July 1917, p. 223.

127 'Universal Obtains Markets For Film in South America', *Moving Picture World*, 4 September 1920, p. 64.

128 'The Foreign Outlook', *Film Daily Yearbook of Motion Pictures, 1922–23* (New York: (Wid's Films and Film Folk, 1923), 1923, p. 409, p. 422, p. 425.

129 Stephen Hughes, 'House Full: Silent Film Genre, Exhibition and Audiences in South India', *Indian Economic Social History Review*, 43.1 (2006), p. 38.

130 Ibid., pp. 43–44.

131 Ibid., p. 43.

132 See *Film India* advertisements, April 1938, p. 230, August 1946, p. 54, February 1946, p. 61.

133 James P. Cunningham, 'The World's Markets', *Film Daily*, 6 June 1926, p. 13.

134 J.P. Koehler, 'Problems in China', *International Motion Picture Almanac 1937–38* (New York: Quigley's Publishing Company, 1938), p. 1163.

135 'An International Survey of Motion Picture Markets', *The 1938 Film Daily Yearbook* (New York: Wid's Films and Film Folk, 1938), p. 1265.

136 'Favor Cliffers', *Variety*, 4 May 1938, p. 78.

137 Nathan P. Golden, 'Latin American Markets', *International Photographer*, November 1940, p. 18; 'Latin American Markets', *Business Screen Magazine*, 2.7 (1940), p. 28.

138 '15th Country Lost by Hollywood to Nazis', *Motion Picture Herald*, 18 May 1941, p. 54.

139 'Hollywood Inside', *Daily Variety*, 8 September 1941, p. 2.

140 'Hatton, Young, Jones Aid Trimming of Lone Ranger', *Daily Variety*, 27 October 1938, p. 4.

141 Thomas Wood, 'The Sad State of the Serial', *New York Times*, 22 December 1946, p. 51. In 'The Saga of Bringing the Lone Ranger to the Screen' it is identified as having been distributed in Algeria, Argentina, Australia, Bolivia, Brazil, Brussels, Burma, Central America, Ceylon, Chile, China, Colombia, Cuba, the Dutch East Indies, France, French Guiana, India, French Indo-China, Japan, Madagascar, Mexico, Morocco, New Zealand, Paraguay, Peru, the Philippines, Puerto Rico, Santo Domingo, Senegal, South Africa, the Straits Settlements, Tunisia, Uruguay, and Venezuela.

142 'A "Western" Film in Serial Form', *The Times*, 9 May 1939, p. 12; C.A. Lejeune, 'An Experiment in the Cinema', *Observer*, 7 May 1939, p. 21.

143 William Brass, *Sixth Annual Report* (London: British Film Institute, 1939), pp. 18–19.

144 Aside from the quote from *Pictures and the Picturegoer* given earlier, there is evidence of the popularity of the serial among children in a 1917 survey of 6,701 children: see National Council of Public Morals, *The Cinema: Its Present Position and Future Possibilities* (London: Williams and Norgate, 1917), pp. 272–74. Richard Ford provides a later perspective

on children and the film serial in his *Children in the Cinema* (London: Allen & Unwin, 1939). For evidence of the serial's presence on the regular programme at the beginning of the 1930s see Guy Barefoot, '"Always a Good Programme Here": The Records of the Tudor Cinema, Leicester, 1924–1932', *International Journal of Regional and Local History*, 8.1 (2013), pp. 26–39.

145 See Rudmer Canjels, *Distributing Film Serials*, pp. 83–87.
146 See the Cinema Context database, http://www.cinemacontext.nl/ [accessed 20 April 2015].
147 V.S. Naipaul, *The Middle Passage* (London: Andre Deutsch, 1962), p. 59.
148 *Daily Gleaner*, 16 June 1936, p. 4. Hughes also notes that in south India it was common to screen as many as six serial episodes at one sitting: 'House Full', p. 42.
149 Hortense Powdermaker, *Copper Town: Changing Africa* (New York: Harper & Row, 1962), p. 255.
150 Ibid.
151 Ibid, p. 261.
152 Charles Ambler, 'Popular Films and Colonial Audiences in Central Africa', in Maltby and Stokes (eds), *Hollywood Abroad*, p. 134.
153 Powdermaker, *Copper Town*, p. 259; Ambler, 'Popular Films and Colonial Audiences in Central Africa', p. 143.
154 Ambler, 'Popular Films and Colonial Audiences in Central Africa', p. 260.
155 Ibid. 'Jack', the name used to refer to cowboy heroes in general, was apparently taken from Jack Holt, star of numerous action-adventure feature films, and also of the 1942 serial, *Holt of the Secret Service*.

3 The Economy Chapter

1 'What the Picture Did For Me', Jackson Theatre, Flomaton, Alabama, general patronage, *Motion Picture Herald*, 25 March 1939, p. 76.
2 'What the Picture Did For Me', Baldwin Theatre, Baldwin, Michigan, small town patronage, 19 May 1934, p. 91.
3 Ben Taves, 'The B Film: Hollywood's Other Half', in Tino Balio, *Grand Design: Hollywood as a Modern Business Enterprise, 1930–1939* (Berkeley: University of California Press, 1995), pp. 317–29.
4 Yannis Tzioumakis, *American Independent Cinema: An Introduction* (Edinburgh; Edinburgh University Press, 2006), p. 76.
5 Ibid., p. 63.
6 See Eric Schaefer, 'The Style of Exploitation Films', *Bold! Daring! Shocking! True! A History of Exploitations Films, 1919–1959* (Durham and London: Duke University Press, 1999), pp. 75–95.
7 Ibid., for a discussion of *Lash of the Penitentes*, p. 284.

8   John Hall, 'Movie Making Throng', *Hollywood Filmograph*, 19 November 1932, p. 4.

9   Carl Laemmle, 'This Business of Motion Pictures', *Film History*, 3.1 (1989), p. 49 (excerpt from unpublished autobiography commissioned in 1927).

10 Douglas Gomery, *The Hollywood Studio System: A History*, revised edition (London: British Film Institute, 2005), p. 60.

11 Richard Ward, 'Extra Added Attractions: The Short Subjects of MGM, Warner Brothers and Universal', *Media History*, 9.3 (2003), p. 228.

12 '42 Features, 111 shorts from "U"', *Motion Picture Herald*, 1 July 1933, p. 34.

13 *Universal Weekly*, 3 June 1933, p. 8.

14 'Five Specials Among Universal's 55', *Film Daily*, 29 August 1945, p. 1 and p. 8.

15 *Motion Picture News*, 8 August 1946, p. 2.

16 See 'Universal Explains Complete Service Plan Just Launched', *Exhibitors' Trade Review*, 30 May 1925, p. 20.

17 'Exhibitors Divided on Merits of Universal "Complete Service Plan" Notes Reveal', *Exhibitors' Trade Review*, 11 July 1925, p. 23.

18 'Little Fellows Find Universal Service Plan Bridging Sound Picture Gap', *Universal Weekly*, 9 November 1929, p. 12.

19 'Complete Service Plan Continued by Universal', *Film Daily*, 12 July 1929, p. 7.

20 Maxine Garrison, 'When You Make Film Serials You Can't Dawdle Along! No Retakes, no Muffing of Lines Permitted—and Speed's the Rule', *Pittsburgh Press*, 17 March 1946, p. 39.

21 Roy Kinnard, Tony Crnkovich, and R.J. Vitone, *The Flash Gordon Serials, 1936–1940* (Jefferson, NC: McFarland: 2008), pp. 6–9.

22 Ibid.

23 Don Taylor, memo to Morgan Cox, 29 November 1944, Box 238/7040 Folder 3 (USC).

24 E.L. McEvoy to M.B. Cox, 29 June 1945, Box 239/7042 Folder 3 (USC).

25 M.B. Cox to E.L. McEvoy, 2 June 1945, Box 238/7042 (USC).

26 In *A History of Horror* (Rutgers University Press, 2010), Wheeler Winston Dixon describes *The Werewolf* (1913), directed by MacRae, as 'generally considered the first cinematic telling of the werewolf legend': pp. 7–8. MacRae directed *Miss Suwanna of Siam* in 1923: see Lisle Foote, *Buster Keaton's Crew: The Team Behind His Silent Films* (Jackson, NC: McFarland, 2013), p. 10.

27 Jon Tuska, *The Vanishing Legion: A History of Mascot Pictures 1927–1935* (Jefferson, NC: McFarland, 1982), p. 41.

28 Kalton C. Lahue, *Bound and Gagged: The Story of the Silent Serials* (New York: Castle Books, 1968), pp. 226–27.

29 See Charles Lee Jackson II, 'The Man Who Would be Serial King', *Filmfax* (1990), pp. 76–79, p. 87.

30 Kalton C. Lahue, *Continued Next Week: A History of the Motion Picture Serial* (Norman: Oklahoma: University of Oklahoma Press, 1964), pp. 151–52.

31 Guy Barefoot, 'Who Watched That Masked Man? Hollywood's Serial Audiences in the 1930s' *Historical Journal of Film, Radio and Television*, 31.2 (2011), pp. 170–71; Rudmer Canjels, *Distributing Silent Film Serials*, p. 241 n103; Raphael Vela, 'With Parents Consent: Film Serials, Consumerism and the Creation of the Youth Audience, 1913–1938'. PhD diss., University of Wisconsin-Madison, 2000, pp. 241–42. Vela identifies the Hays figures as almost certainly exaggerations: p. 272.

32 'BRING BACK THE KIDS and keep them coming with UNIVERSAL SERIALS' highlights *The Indians are Coming* as well as *Heroes of the Flames*, *The Spell of the Circus* and *Finger Prints*: *Exhibitors' Herald World*, 2 August 1930, p. 5.

33 D.W.C., 'That Hardy Perennial, The Serial', *New York Times*, 26 January 1936, section X p. 4; John Scott, 'Old Time Serial Thrillers Returning to Popularity', *Los Angeles Times*, 16 February 1936, p. 1 and p. 3.

34 'Back Stage in the Short Stops – Henry MacRae', *Showmen's Trade Review*, 6 December 1941, p. 30.

35 Frederic Othman, 'Gooseflesh Maestro', *Saturday Evening Post*, 27 March 1943, p. 76.

36 In *The Hollywood Story* (London: Mandarin, 1992), Joel Finler lists only eight films released in 1930 with rentals of a million dollars or more, including titles such *All Quiet on the Western Front* which actually made a loss, as did Universal that year: pp. 471–72.

37 Othman, 'Gooseflesh Maestro', 1943, p. 20.

38 Basil Dickey, 'TO HENRY MAC RAE Universal's Veteran Serial Producer', *Hollywood Filmograph*, 15 July 1932, p. 6.

39 'Studio Notables Attend MacRae Funeral Today', *Film Daily*, 5 October 1944, p. 2. Dickey's numerous screenwriting contributions stretched from the 1914 *The Perils of Pauline* to *Federal Agents vs. the Underworld* (1948).

40 Miguel de Zárraga, 'El medico del cinematógrafo', *Cinema Mundial*, March 1933, p. 166.

41 Kinnard, Crnkovich and Vitone, *The Flash Gordon Serials, 1936–40*, p. 6, p. 16.

42 William Wheeler Dixon, *Cinema at the Margins* (London and New York: Anthem Press, 2013), p. 23.

43 Larry 'Buster' Crabbe, interview, *Those Enduring Matinee Idols*, 2.4 (1971–1972), p. 193.

44 Jim Harmon and Donald F. Glut, *The Great Movie Serials: Their Sound and Fury* (London: Woburn Press, 1973), p. 29.

45 E.A. Tambert to Val Paul and Martin Murphy, 13 October 1937, Box 272283/9408 (USC).

46 'Picture Costs', 30 April 1938, Box 272283/9408 (USC).

47 'Early Serials', Box 820/26843 (USC).

48 Figures from USC, those for *Vanishing Shadow* and *Rustlers of Red Dog* come from a list of Universal Productions, 22 March 1935, Box 714, 23657, *The Spell of the Circus, Finger Prints, Battling with Buffalo Bill, Heroes of the Flames* and *Heroes of the West*, from Box 820/26843, for *The Phantom Rider* from Box 272/8663, *Secret Agent X-9* from Box 272/8661, for *Jungle Jim* from Box 272/8673, for *Ace Drummond* from Box 272 #784/08670.

49 '*Flash Gordon* in L.A. First Run', *Universal Weekly*, 7 March 1936, p. 8.

50 'Metro Sees B.O. in Serials: May Do 'Em', *Variety*, 17 November 1937, p. 4.

51 For a reference to *Riders of Death Valley* as a 'million dollar serial' see 'Hollywood Going Farther Afield and Oftener for Location Scenes', *Motion Picture Herald*, 4 January 1941, p. 17. The lower budget figure is given in Bob Moak, 'H'wood Eyes Serial Cycle', *Variety*, 6 November 1940, p. 21.

52 Quoted in Garrison, 'When You Make Film Serials You Can't Dawdle Along!' p. 39.

53 'Tidings from Talkie Town', *Talking Screen*, 14 June 1930, p. 432.

54 'The Indians are Coming', *Film Daily*, 4 November 1925, p. 2.

55 'Take Your Choice of These Titles!' *Film Daily*, 22 January 1926, pp. 4–5.

56 A letter to Filmcraft specifies that the agreement with Krellberg and Harris excludes the territories of Curacao and Aruba: Krellberg Papers, Library of Congress, Washington DC (hereafter LOC), Box 25, Folder 13, Richard B. Davis to Filmcraft, 20 January 1953. An earlier (1950) report indicates that Universal sold rights to *Flash Gordon* to Krellberg for $60,000 but subsequently paid $100,000 for seven years foreign rights to the *Flash Gordon* serial and the feature made from it: see David Pierce, '"Senile Celluloid": Independent Exhibitors, the Major Studios and the Fight over Feature Films on Television, 1939–1956', *Film History*, 10.2 (1998), p. 149.

57 Letter from Sherman Krellberg to HH Martin (LOC), Box 6 Folder 2, 23 November 1977.

58 See Tony Pipolo, 'The Spectre of *Joan of Arc*: Textual Variations in Key Prints of Dreyer's Film', *Film History*, 2.4, 1988, p. 305.

59 See 'Theatre Deals', *Film Daily*, 10 May 1944, p. 9.

60 'Court Orders Revolt of Zombies Title Dropped', *Independent Exhibitors Film Bulletin*, 1 July 1936, p. 9.

61 Coronet Pictures was established in 1936 to make films in Montreal: 'Production Plans of 64 Companies, Many Westerns are Promised', *Motion Picture Herald*, 9 May 1936, p. 15. The other companies come from

the Library of Congress's Finding Aid to their collection of Krellberg Papers.

62 'Six Features, Two Serials on Sam Katzman's Program', *Film Daily*, 6 July 1936, p. 1.

63 'Lesser Gets Jackie for "Peck's Bad Boy"', *Film Daily*, 6 February 1934, p. 1. In some accounts, Lesser's Principal Distribution Corporation is listed as the distributor for *The Lost City*: see, for instance, Michael R. Pitts, *Poverty Row Studios: 1929–40* (Jefferson NC and London: McFarland, 2005), p. 278. However this appears to be based on a confusion between Lesser's Principal Distribution Corporation and Krellberg's Principal Film Exchange.

64 'Krellberg to Finance Ten Features, 2 Serials', *Film Daily*, 20 March 1934, p. 1; 'Arrange Krellberg Financing', *Film Daily*, 12 June 1934, p. 6.

65 'Krellberg to Start New Serial', *Film Daily*, 30 March 1935, p. 3; 'Krellberg Signs Louis for Role in "Zombies" Serial', *Film Daily*, 2 April 1940, p. 6.

66 'New Incorporations', *Film Daily*, 22 June 1934, p. 3.

67 See George E. Turner and Michael H. Price, *Forgotten Horrors: The Definitive Edition* (Baltimore: Midnight Marquee Press, 1999), p. 171.

68 'Coming and Going', *Film Daily*, 16 January 1935, p. 2; 'Krellberg Coming East', *Film Daily*, 25 January 1935, p. 2. *Film Daily* reviewed *The Lost City* as an 'exciting serial' on 19 February 1935, p. 9. The *New York Times* review of *The Lost City* described it as a film that 'masquerades as a feature picture but actually is nothing more than about six-episodes of a twelve chapter serial, strung together with some sort of continuity, but hardly to be considered adult entertainment': 'F.S.N.', 21 February, p. 23.

69 Vincent G. Hart, letter to Joseph Breen, 10 April 1935; Vincent G. Hart, telegram to Joseph Breen, 8 April 1935, *Lost City* PCA File (MHL).

70 *Daily Variety*, 21 August 1935, *The Lost City* PCA File (MHL).

71 '*Lost City* at $14,683', *Motion Picture Daily*, 28 February 1935, p. 12; 'Deal for *Lost City*', *Motion Picture Daily*, 25 March 1935, p. 6.

72 'Lincoln Frees Some Coin for "Reckless" and "Tr. Saleslady"', *Variety*, 29 May 1935, p. 29.

73 'What the Picture Did For Me', Cozy Theatre, Winchester, Ind. General patronage, *Motion Picture Herald*, 24 August 1935, p. 69.

74 '*The Lost City*', *Film Daily*, 20 February 1935, p. 9.

75 'What the Picture Did For Me', Lyric Theatre, Hamilton, Ohio, family patronage, *Motion Picture Herald*, 30 May 1936, p. 82.

76 See, for instance, 'The Lost City', 'The Files of Jerry Blake', http://filesofjerryblake.com/2015/02/05/the-lost-city/#more-9137 [accessed 30 March 2015].

77 'Deals Closed on Serial', *Film Daily*, 1 September 1934, p. 3; 'Gets Serial For Orient', *Film Daily*, 25 July 1934, p. 13.

78 'U.A. Gets "Lost City" For Latin Countries', *Film Daily*, 25 March 1935, p.

4; Agreement with Regal Distribution, which provides a recap of existing agreements, Krellberg Papers, Box 26 Folder 3 (LOC), 15 July 1940.

79 'UA Handling 52 Foreign Features Abroad', *Film Daily*, 26 November 1935, p. 1 and p. 10.

80 'Arrange Krellberg Financing', *Film Daily*, 12 June 1934, p. 6. Hulse refers to eight and eleven reel feature versions released in 1935: 'The Lost City', *Blood n Thunder*, 41 (2014), p. 38. On 10 April 1935 *Independent Exhibitors Film Bulletin* published the following correction (p. 12): 'In our review of "The Lost City" in last week's issue, it was reported that eight two-reel episodes follow the feature. This is incorrect. The feature is *not* connected with the serial and there are twelve two-reel episodes in the chapter-play.'

81 Other accounts give a 1940 release date for *The City of Lost Men* but I have not identified screenings earlier than 1943: for instance it was advertised as playing with Fritz Lang's *M* at the Colony in Los Angeles, *Los Angeles Times*, 30 May 1943, p. C2. The Warner Bros. film *Castle on the Hudson* (1940) was at one point known as *The City of Lost Men*.

82 Schaefer, *Bold! Daring! Shocking! True!*, p. 64.

83 Ibid., pp. 96–99.

84 See Robert S. Birchard, *Cecil B. De Mille's Hollywood* (Lexington: University of Kentucky Press, 2004), p. 6. Revier took out full page advertisements for *The Penitentes Murder Case* in *Motion Picture Daily* which declared 'YOUR Exploitation HAS BEEN WRITTEN IN BLOOD BY SCREAMING HEADLINES OF THE NATION'S PRESS . . . ANOTHER BOX-OFFICE SENSATION FROM THE MAN WHO GAVE YOU 'THE LOST CITY' AND THE TARZAN SERIES: see 10 March 1936, p. 9. The 'Tarzan series' reference is to *The Son of Tarzan* (1920) and *The Revenge of Tarzan* (1920), probably the most successful films Revier directed.

85 'Last of the Pentitentes', Internet Movie Database, http://www.imdb.com/title/tt0029114/combined [accessed 30 March 2015]. Price's 'vagabond' credit appears at the beginning of a ten minute extract from the film available on YouTube: 'Lash of the Penitentes, directed by Roland Price & Harry Revier (1937) – excepts', https://www.youtube.com/watch?v=ddz0WM6AXN0 [accessed 30 March 2015].

86 Roland Barton, 'As I See Them', *Independent Exhibitors Film Bulletin*, 5 April 1935, p. 12; *Daily Chronicle* [Spokane, Washington], 27 Jan 1937, p. 9.

87 *Motion Picture Herald*, 9 March 1935, *The Lost City* PCA File (MHL).

88 *Variety*, 27 February 1935, p. 2.

89 Jon Tuska, *The Vanishing Legion: A History of Mascot Pictures 1927–1935* (Jefferson, NC: McFarland, 2000), p. 193.

90 See Read, 'A Squalid-Looking Place', p. 186.

91 Richard Maurice Hurst, *Republic Studios: Between Poverty Row and the Majors*, updated edition (Lanham, Maryland: Scarecrow Press, 2007).

92 See the budgets reproduced in Charles Flynn and Todd McCarthy, 'The Economic Imperative: Why was the B Movie Necessary', in Todd McCarthy and Charles Flynn (eds), *Kings of the Bs: Working Within the Hollywood System, an Anthology of Film History and Criticism* (New York: Dutton, 1975), pp. 26–29.

93 Hurst, *Republic Studios*, p. 93. Hurst's specific reference is to their work on *Mysterious Dr Satan* (1940).

94 Tziousmakis, *American Independent Cinema*, p. 75.

95 In addition to the information gathered from the Jack Mathis records at Brigham Young University, my main source on Republic's serials is Jack Mathis's discussion of the serial in his *Republic Confidential, Vol. 2, The Studio* (Northbrook, Ill.: Jack Mathis Advertising, 1999), pp. 288–99. I have also used Mathis's *Valley of the Cliffhangers* (Northbrook, Ill.: Jack Mathis Advertising, 1975), particularly for the information it has on individual serials.

96 Mathis, *Republic Confidential*, p. 180.

97 Ibid., p. 289.

98 Mathis, *Valley of the Cliffhangers*, 1975, p. viii.

99 Mathis, *Republic Confidential*, p. 122.

100 Quoted in Mathis, *Republic Confidential*, p. 123.

101 Inter-office memo, Saul N. Rittenberg to Legal, October 10 1952. Subject: 'KING OF THE ROYAL MOUNTED'—Stock Film Rights, Box 14, 1a (BYU).

102 Moak, 'H'wood Eyes Serial Cycle', p. 12.

103 Schaefer, *Bold! Daring! Shocking! True!* p. 56.

104 *1947 Film Daily Yearbook of Motion Pictures* (New York: Wid's Film and Film Folk, 1947), p. 55.

105 Moak, 'H'wood Eyes Serial Cycle', p. 12.

106 Thomas Doherty, '"This is Where We Came In": The Audible Screen and the Voluble Audience of the Early Sound Era', in Melvyn Stokes and Richard Maltby (eds), *American Movie Audiences: From the Turn of the Century to the Early Sound Era* (London: British Film Institute, 1999), p. 154.

4 The Second Chapter, 1930–46

1 Mathis, *Valley of the Cliffhangers*, (Northbrook, Illinois: Jack Mathis Advertising, 1975), p. vii. For a more recent version of this, see William Wheeler Dixon, '*Flash Gordon* and the 1930s and 40s Science Fiction Serial', *Cinema at the Margins* (London and New York: Anthem Press, 2013), p. 20.

2   Tzvetan Todorov, *The Fantastic: A Structural Approach to a Literary Genre* (Ithaca: Cornell University Press, 1975), p. 4.

3   Steve Neale, 'Questions of Genre', *Screen*, 31.1 (1990), p. 50 and p. 66. The Alan Williams quote comes from 'Is a Radical Genre Criticism Possible?' *Quarterly Review of Film Studies*, 9.2 (1984), p. 124.

4   Kristin Thompson, *Storytelling in the New Hollywood: Understanding Classical Narrative Technique* (Cambridge, Mass.: Harvard University Press, 1999), p. 13.

5   Ben Singer, *Melodrama and Modernity: Early Sensational Cinema and its Contexts* (New York: Columbia UP, 2001), p. 143.

6   See Rafael Arnaldo Vela, 'The Nature of Cliffhangers', 'With Parents Consent: Film Serials, Consumerism and the Creation of the Youth Audience, 1913–1938'. PhD diss., University of Wisconsin-Madison, 2000, pp. 279–87.

7   'Robinson Crusoe of Clipper Island', *Variety*, 22 September 1937, p. 19.

8   'What the Picture Did For Me', Myrtle Theatre, Detroit, Mich., neighborhood patronage, *Motion Picture Herald*, 8 May 1937, p. 63. The same page includes a further complaint about the same serial: 'Levine takes unbelievable liberties. Last week the ending clearly showed an airplane (carrying the hero, of course) crashing into the ocean; this week that shot was omitted and the airplane never got within 100 feet of the water. Levine kills his hero every week and then revives him in the next by changing the story. Even the kids give it the ha-ha . . .': Elted Theatre, Absarokee, Mont. Rural patronage.

9   'What the Picture Did For Me', Flomaton, Alabama, general patronage, *Motion Picture Herald*, 12 June 1937, p. 90.

10 For a more recent variation on this, see *The Twilight Saga: Breaking Dawn Part 2* (2012).

11 I am continuing the practice here of using character names: just as Clyde Beatty played Clyde Beatty in *The Lost Jungle*, in *The Phantom Empire* Gene Autry played Gene Autry.

12 For a discussion of the reality of the injuries depicted in a Hollywood film, see Lauren Hansen, 'Diagnosing the *Home Alone* Burglars' Injuries: a Professional Weighs In', *This Week*, 20 December 2012, http://theweek. com/article/index/238037/diagnosing-the-home-alone-burglars-injuries-a-professional-weighs-in?cmpid=?tw [accessed 12 April 2015].

13 John Tuska, *The Vanishing Legion: A History of Mascot Pictures 1927–1935* (Jefferson, NC: McFarland, 2000), pp. 43–44.

14 Lewis Herman, *A Practical Manual of Screen Playwriting: For Theater and Television Films* (Cleveland and New York: World Publishing Company, 1952), p. 53.

15 See the review of the film published in *Motion Picture News*, 20 December 1937, p. 3.

16 Singer, *Melodrama and Modernity*, p. 144.

17 Ibid., p. 210–11.

18 See Herman, *A Practical Manual for Screenplay Writing*, pp. 50–53, but also Mathis, *Valley of the Cliffhangers*, p. vii.

19 Scott Higgins, 'Republic Lands the Punch: Art of the Serial Dust-Up', 'Thinking Cinematically: Conjecture, Convictions and Other Unsubstantiated Ideas', http://shiggins.blogs.wesleyan.edu/2013/08/23/republic-lands-the-punch-art-of-the-serial-dust-up/, 23 August 2013 [accessed 1 April 2015].

20 For William Witney's own version of this story see his autobiography: *In a Door, Into a Fight, Out a Door, Into a Chase* (Jefferson, NC and London: McFarland, 1996), pp. 94–95.

21 'Teaser Thrillers', 2 April 1940, p. 6; unidentified source, 'Serials' clipping file, New York Library for the Performing Arts, Lincoln Centre, New York.

22 Tuska, *The Vanishing Legion*, p. 92.

23 On the serial and the marriage plot, see Robyn Warhol, 'Making "Gay" and "Lesbian" into Household Words: How Serial Form Works in Armistead Maupin's *Tales of the City*', *Contemporary Literature*, 40.3 (1999), pp. 378–402.

24 Singer, *Melodrama and Meaning*, p. 294.

25 Ibid., pp. 293–94.

26 Ibid., p. 295.

27 Chis Baldrick and Robert Mignall, 'Gothic Criticism', in David Punter (ed.), *A New Companion to the Gothic* (Chichester: Wiley-Blackwell, 2012), p. 280 (emphasis on 'generic obligation' in the original).

28 Singer, *Melodrama and Modernity*, pp. 143. The Vicinus quote comes from her 'Helpless and Unfriended: Nineteenth-Century Domestic Melodrama', *New Literary History*, 13.1 (1981), p. 128.

29 Singer, *Melodrama and Modernity*, p. 233.

30 Ibid., p. 145.

31 See Tuska, *The Vanishing Legion*, p. 31.

32 Ibid., pp. 31–32. To be accurate, Mascot employed two Rin-Tin-Tins in its serials, the first appearing in *The Lone Defender* and *The Lightning Warrior* (1931), while Rin-Tin-Tin Jr. was in *The Wolf Dog*, *The Law of the Wild* and *The Adventures of Rex and Rinty*.

33 The phrase was used in 'Chatter', *Variety*, 27 November 1935, p. 61. Ray Wise, known also as Ray Mala, or just Mala, had a Russian-Jewish father and a native Alaskan mother. 'Eskimo' is in part a reference to the 1933 MGM film of that name, also known as *Mala the Magnificent*.

5 Four Serials and a Feature, 1932–38

1   J.P. Mayer, *Sociology of Film: Studies and Documents* (London: Faber, 1946), pp. 53–54.

2   Kristin Thompson, *Storytelling in the New Hollywood: Understanding Classical Narrative Technique* (Cambridge, Mass.: Harvard University Press, 1999), p. 28.

3   Ibid., p. 43.

4   Ibid., p. 21.

5   William Lord Wright, *Photoplay Writing* (New York: Falk Publishing, 1920), p. 109.

6   Ibid, p. 115.

7   Kristin Thompson, *Breaking the Glass Armor: Neo-Formalist Film Analysis* (Princeton NJ: Princeton University Press, 1988), pp. 49–86.

8   Arthur Conan Doyle, *The Conan Doyle Stories* (London: John Murray, 1929), p. 559.

9   Thompson, *Breaking the Glass Armor*, p. 62.

10 Ibid., pp. 53–70.

11 Ibid., p. 55.

12 Aristotle, *Poetics*, trans. Malcolm Heath (London: Penguin, 1996), p. 12.

13 Ibid., p. 13.

14 Lewis Herman, *Practical Manual of Screen Playwriting*, (Cleveland and New York: World Publishing Company, 1952), p. 53.

15 Jim Harmon and Donald F. Glut, *The Great Movie Serials: Their Sound and Fury* (London: Woburn Press, 1973), p. 341.

16 'Langdon's Serial', *Variety*, 29 November 1932, p. 12.

17 Thompson, *Breaking the Glass Armor*, p. 61.

18 For more on the Death Ray in films of this time see William J. Fanning Jr., 'The Historical Death Ray and Science Fiction in the 1920s and 1930s', *Science Fiction Studies*, 37.2 (2010), pp. 253–74.

19 Bill Slater, 'Weekend Serials of Silent Era: Loved Brawls, Not Sex 'Mush'; Recall Nat Levine, Sam Bischoff', *Variety*, 5 January 1977, p. 4.

20 Thompson, *Breaking the Glass Armor*, pp. 58–59.

21 On the use of plans and maps in the traditional detective story, see Julian Symons, *Bloody Murder: From the Detective Story to the Crime Novel: A History* (Harmondsworth: Penguin, 1974), p. 118.

22 See Richard Koszarski, 'Coming Next Week: Images of Television in Pre-War Motion Pictures', *Film History*, 10.2 (1998), pp. 128–40.

23 William Lord Wright, 'Hints for Scenario Writers', *Picture Play*, 9.4 (1918), p. 226.

24 Gary Don Rhodes, *Lugosi: His Life in Films, on Stage, and in the Hearts of Horror Lovers* (Jefferson, NC: McFarland, 1977), p. 147.

25 'Jungle Jim' pressbook, Universal Pressbook Collection, (USC).

26 See Guy Barefoot, 'Recycled Images: *Rose Hobart, East of Borneo* and *The Perils of Pauline*', *Adaptation*, 5.2 (2012), pp. 152–68.

27 Richard Dyer, 'White', *Screen*, 29.4 (1988), p. 46.

28 Ibid., p. 53.

29 '*The Whispering Shadow*', *Motion Picture Herald*, 26 December 1936, p. 56.

30 '*Daredevils of the Red Circle*', *Showman's Trade Review*, 10 June 1939, p. 31.

31 Jack Mathis identifies the shot of the list as one of Republic's occasional 'visual inconsistencies': *Valley of the Cliffhangers* (Northbrook, Illinois: Jack Mathis Advertising, 1975), p. 112.

Aftermath and Conclusion

1 Richard Maurice Hurst, *Republic Studios: Between Poverty Row and the Majors*, updated edition (Lanham, Maryland: Scarecrow Press, 2007), p. 145.

2 Jim Harmon and Donald F. Glut describe Katzman at Columbia (though without identifying a source) as making serials 'cheaper than anybody had ever produced union-made theatrical movies': *The Great Movie Serials: Their Sound* (London: Woburn Books, 1973), p. 270.

3 See Blair Davis, 'Small Screen, Smaller Pictures: Television Broadcasting and B-Movies in the Early 1950s', *Historical Journal of Film Radio and Television*, 28.2 (2008), pp. 219–38.

4 *Broadcasting* identified the screening of *The Lost Jungle* on 23 August 1939 as the first episode of a serial telecast: 'Chronology of NBC: 1926–1951', p. 137.

5 'CBS-TV To Lead Daytime Race; DuMont on Heels', *Billboard*, 6 August 1950, p. 6.

6 David Pierce, '"Senile Celluloid": Independent Exhibitors, the Major Studios and the Fight over Feature Films on Television, 1939–1956', *Film History*, 10.2 (1998), p. 154 and p. 150.

7 'Hypo Gets 31 Serials From Universal in $1½-Mil. Deal' *Billboard*, 14 July 1956, p. 7.

8 Advertisement in *Broadcasting Telecasting*, 8 April 1957, p. 77.

9 'Hygo's U-I Serials Sell to 14 Thus Far', *Billboard*, 15 September 1956, p. 9.

10 See Jack Mathis, *Republic Confidential, Vol. 2: The Studio* (Northbrook, Ill.: Jack Mathis Advertising, 1999), p. 296.

11 *Ocala Star Banner*, 1 November 1980, p. 23.

12 *Kentucky New Era*, 8 April 1983, p. 3.

13 *Nashua Telegraph*, 1 May 1982, p. 4.

14 *Sumter Daily Item*, 20 July 1985, p. 5A (no details of the show provided).

15 See Joseph McBride, *Steven Spielberg*, 2nd Edition (Jackson: University

of Mississippi Press, 2010), p. 79; Garry Jenkins, *Empire Building: The Remarkable Real Life Story of* Star Wars (London: Simon & Schuster, 1997), p. 2.

16   Bob Thomas, 'Serials May Come Back', *Kentucky New Era*, 28 February 1966, p. 6.

17   Brian Patten, 'Where Are You Now Batman?' Adrian Henri, Roger McGough, Brian Patten, *The Mersey Sound* (Harmondsworth: Penguin, 1967), p. 97.

18   Brian Patten, 'Where are you now, Superman?' in Edward Lucie-Smith (ed.), *The Liverpool Scene* (London: Donald Carroll, 1967), pp. 26–27.

19   Roger McGough, 'Goodbat Nightman', Adrian Henri, 'Batpoem', in *The Liverpool Scene*, pp. 27–28.

20   Alan Moore interviewed by Pádraig Ó Méalóid, 'Boy from the Boroughs', *3.AM Magazine*, 17th March 2011, http://www.3ammagazine.com/3am/boy-from-the-boroughs/ [accessed 20 April 2015].

21   At the time of writing a further *Tarzan* film, directed by David Yates, is scheduled for release in 2016. The most recent *Lone Ranger* film appeared in 2013; it was described as a 'costly misfire': Andrew Stewart and Rachel Abrams, 'Bomb Summer Casualties: Epic Fail Dissecting the Disasters', *Variety*, 15 July 2013, p. 48. *The Legend of Zorro* (2005) is the most recent big-budget Zorro film. Thomas S. Hischak reports that the spoof Broadway musical, *Frank Merriwell, or Honor Challenged*, closed after its first night: *American Literature on Stage and Screen: 525 Works and Their Adaptations* (Jefferson, NC: McFarland, 2012), p. 74.

22   *Film Society Programmes 1925–1939*, intro by Dr George Amberg (Arno Press, New York, 1972).

23   *Sight and Sound*, 7.27 (1938).

24   'Museum of Modern Art to Conclude its Cycle of 500 Films with Old and New Serial Thrillers, Films for Latin America, and American Defence Films', 20 January 1942, available at http://www.moma.org/docs/press_archives/765/releases/MOMA_1942_0008_1942-01-20_42120-6.pdf?2010 [accessed 20 April 2015].

25   Ibid.

26   See 'Program Notes Theodore Huff Memorial Society, http://www.nyu.edu/projects/wke/byseries/huff_index.php [accessed 12 April 2015]

27   For instance William K. Everson, 'Serials with Sound Have Steadily Declined in Quality and Quantity', *Films in Review*, 4.6 (1953), pp. 269–76.

28   'An Interview with Kenneth Anger', *Film Culture*, 40 (1966), p. 69.

29   J. Berner to Goodwill, 7 December 1972; Clyde Jeavons to Sherman Krellberg, 20 December 1972; 'Certificate of Destruction for *Don Winslow of the Coast Guard*', 19 February 1973 (LOC), Box 19, Folder 2.

30   See William Wheeler Dixon, '*Flash Gordon* and the 1930s and 40s Science

Fiction Serial', *Cinema at the Margins* (London and New York: Anthem Press, 2013), pp. 19–30.

31 See Blair Davis, 'Singing Sci-Fi Cowboys: Gene Autry and Generic Amalgamation in *The Phantom Empire* (1935)', *Historical Journal of Film Radio, and Television*, 33.4 (2013), pp. 552–75.

32 See Lawrence Alloway, *Violent America: The Movies 1946–1964* (New York: Museum of Modern Art, 1971) and Francis M. Nevins, 'Ballet of Violence: The Films of William Witney', *Films in Review*, 25 (1974), pp. 523–45.

33 See Jeffrey Sconce, '"Trashing" the Academy: Taste, Excess, and an Emerging Politics of Cinematic Style', *Screen*, 36.4 (1995), pp. 371–93.

34 William K. Everson, 'Introduction', Alan G. Barbour, *Saturday Afternoon at the Movies: III, Days of Thrills and Adventure* (New York: Bonanza Books, 1986), p. xv. See also, for instance, Noah William Isenberg, *Edgar Ulmer: A Filmmaker on the Margins* (Berkeley: University of California Press, 2013), one of several recent books on Ulmer. For Sconce's discussion of Wood, see '"Trashing" the Academy', pp. 387–89.

35 See, for instance, 'Serials Released Since 1920', *The 1945 Film Daily Yearbook of Motion Pictures* (New York: Wid's Films and Film Folk, 1945), pp. 419–23.

36 Buck Rainey, *Serials and Series: A World Filmography, 1912–1956* (Jefferson NC: McFarland, 1999).

Bibliography

Collections

BFI Reuben Library, London
Cinematic Arts Library, University of Southern California, Los Angeles
Howard B. Lee Library, Brigham Young University, Provo, Utah
Library of Congress, Washington DC
Margaret Herrick Library, Academy of Motion Picture Arts and Sciences, Los
    Angeles
Museum of the American West, Los Angeles
New York Library for the Performing Arts, Lincoln Centre, New York
Theatre Art Library, University of California at Los Angeles, Los Angeles

Trade Journals

Billboard
Broadcasting
Broadcasting Telecasting
Business Screen
Cinema Mundial
Cinema News and Property Gazette
Exhibitors' Herald
Exhibitors' Trade Review
Film Daily
Film India
Hollywood Filmograph
Independent Exhibitors Film Bulletin
International Photographer
Motion Picture Daily
Motion Picture Herald

Motion Picture News
Motography
National Board of Review Magazine
Picture Play
Pictures and the Picturegoer
Reel Life
Showman's Trade Review
Talking Screen
Universal Weekly
Wid's Daily

Magazines

Boys' Sunday Reader
Tip Top Weekly

Newspapers

Afro-American [Baltimore]
Daily Chronicle [Spokane, Washington]
Daily Times [Beaver, Pennsylvania]
Daily Register [Oelwein, Iowa]
Gazette [Xenia, Ohio]
Guardian [UK]
Hartford Courant
Kentucky New Era
Los Angeles Times
Nashua Telegraph [New Hampshire]
New York Times
Ocala Star Banner [Florida]
Pittsburgh Press
Sumter Daily Item [South Carolina]
Yorkshire Times and Leeds Intelligencer [UK]

Year Books

British Film Institute Annual Report
Film Daily Year Book of Motion Pictures
International Motion Picture Almanac

Books and Articles

Abel, Richard, 'Early Motion Pictures and Popular Print Culture: A Web of Ephemera', in Christine Bold (ed.) *The Oxford History of Popular Print Culture*, Vol. 6 *U.S. Popular Print Culture 1860–1920* (Oxford: Oxford University Press, 2012) pp. 191–209.

Allen, Rob, '"Pause You Who Read This": Disruption and the Serial Novel', in Rob Allen and Thijs van den Berg (eds) *Serialization in Popular Culture* (London: Routledge, 2014) pp. 33–46.

Allen, Rob and Berg, Thijs van den (eds), *Serialization in Popular Culture* (London: Routledge, 2014).

Allen, Robert C., 'Introduction' in Robert C. Allen (ed.) *To Be Continued . . . Soap Operas Around the World* (London: Routledge, 1995) pp. 1–26.

Alloway, Lawrence, *Violent America: The Movies 1946–1964* (New York: Museum of Modern Art, 1971).

Altman, Rick, 'Dickens, Griffith, and Film Theory Today', in Jane Gaines (ed.) *Classical Hollywood Narrative: The Paradigm Wars* (Durham, NC: Duke University Press, 1992) pp. 9–47.

Ambler, Charles, in Richard Maltby and Melvyn Stokes (eds), *Hollywood Abroad: Audiences and Cultural Exchange* (London: BFI Publishing, 2004) pp. 133–57.

Anderson, Ryan K., 'Merry's Flock: Making Something Out of Educational Reform in the Early Twentieth Century' in Adam R. Nelson and John L. Rudolph (eds) *Education and the Culture of Print in Modern America* (Madison: University of Wisconsin Press, 2010) pp. 59–80.

Anderson, Ryan K., '*Smith v. Hitchcock* (1912) and the Death of the Dime Novel', William M. Blount Symposium on Postal History, Smithsonian National Postal Museum, Washington DC, 4 November 2006, available at http://postalmuseum.si.edu/research/pdfs/Anderson.pdf (accessed 21 January 2015).

Anger, Kenneth, 'An Interview with Kenneth Anger', *Film Culture*, 40 (1966) pp. 68–75.

Aristotle, *Poetics*, trans. Malcolm Heath (London: Penguin, 1996).

Arthur, Joseph, *Blue Jeans* (New York: Samuel French, 1940).

Backer, Ron, *Gripping Chapters: The Sound Movie Serial* (Albany, Ge.: Bear Manor Media, 2010).

Baldrick, Chris and Robert Mignall, 'Gothic Criticism', in David Punter (ed.), *A New Companion to the Gothic* (Chichester: Wiley-Blackwell, 2012) pp. 267–87.

Barbour, Alan G., *Cliffhanger: A Pictorial History of the Motion Picture Serial* (New York: A. & W. Publishers, 1977).

Barbour, Alan G., *Saturday Afternoon at the Movies: III: Days of Thrill and Adventure* (London: Collier, 1970).

Barefoot, Guy, '"Always a Good Programme Here": The Records of the Tudor Cinema, Leicester, 1924–1932', *International Journal of Regional and Local History*, 8.1. (2013) pp. 26–39.

Barefoot, Guy, 'Recycled Images: *Rose Hobart*, *East of Borneo* and *The Perils of Pauline*', *Adaptation*, 5.2 (2012) pp. 152–68.

Barefoot, Guy, 'Who Watched That Masked Man? Hollywood's Serial Audiences in the 1930s', *Historical Journal of Film, Radio and Television*, 31.2 (2011) pp. 167–90.

Bernstein, Sidney, 'Attempts Made by the Film Trade to Meet the Problem and the Difficulties Encountered', *Report of the Conference on Films for Children*, British Film Institute, 20–21 November 1936.

Birchard, Robert S. *Cecil B. De Mille's Hollywood* (Lexington: University of Kentucky Press, 2004).

Blumer, Herbert, *Movies and Conduct* (New York: Macmillan, 1933).

Bold, Christine, *Selling the Wild West: Popular Western Fiction, 1860–1960* (Bloomington, Ind.: Indiana University Press, 1987).

Brewster, Ben and Jacobs, Lea, *Theatre to Cinema: Stage Pictorialism and the Early Feature Film* (New York: Oxford University Press, 1997).

Bruner, Frank V., 'The Modern Dime Novel', *Photoplay* (January 1919) pp. 32–33, 118.

Cain, James M., *Sixty Years of Journalism*, Roy Hoopes (ed.), (Bowling Green: Bowling Green State University Popular Press, 1985).

Canjels, Rudmer, *Distributing Silent Film Serials: Local Practices, Changing Forms, Cultural Transformation* (New York: Routledge, 2011).

Cline, William C., *In the Nick of Time: Motion Picture Sound Serials* (London: McFarland, 1998).

Cohn, Alfred A., 'Harvesting the Serial', *Photoplay*, February 1917, pp. 19–26.

Collins, Wilkie, *Armadale*, Book the Second, Chapters 2 and 3, *Cornhill*, January 1865, pp. 1–32.

Cook, David, *A History of Narrative Film*, 3rd edition (New York: Norton, 1996).

Cook, William Wallace, *The Fiction Factory* (Ridgewood, NJ: Editor Company, 1912).

Cox, J. Randolph, *The Dime Novel Companion: A Source Book* (Westport, Conn & London: Greenwood Press, 2000).

Crowder, Ashby Bland, 'Observations on the Crossing of Genres in the Nineteenth Century', *Aevum*, 51.5/6 (1977) pp. 541–47.

Dahlquist, Marina, 'Introduction: Why Pearl?' in Marina Dahlquist (ed.) *Exporting Perilous Pauline: Pearl White and the Serial Film Craze* (Urbana, Ill.: University of Illinois Press, 2013) pp. 1–23.

Davis, Blair, 'Singing Sci-Fi Cowboys: Gene Autry and Generic Amalgamation in *The Phantom Empire* (1935)', *Historical Journal of Film Radio, and Television*, 33.4 (2013) pp. 552–75.

Davis, Blair, 'Small Screen, Smaller Pictures: Television Broadcasting and

B-Movies in the Early 1950s', *Historical Journal of Film, Radio and Television*, 28.2 (2008) pp. 219–38.

deCordova, Richard, 'The Child Audience, the Hays Code and Saturday Matinees', in Gregory A. Waller (ed.) *Moviegoing in America: A Sourcebook in the History of Film Exhibition* (Oxford: Blackwell, 2002) pp. 159–69.

Denning, Michael, *Mechanic Accents: Dime Novels and Working Class Culture in America* (London: Verso, 1998).

Denson, Shane, 'The Logic of the Line Segment: Continuity and Discontinuity in the Serial-Queen Melodrama', in Rob Allen and Thijs van den Berg (eds) *Serialization in Popular Culture* (London: Routledge, 2014) pp. 65–79.

Dixon, William Wheeler, *Cinema at the Margins* (London and New York: Anthem Press, 2013).

Dixon, Wheeler Winston, *A History of Horror* (Rutgers University Press, 2010).

Doherty, Thomas, '"This is Where We Came In": The Audible Screen and the Voluble Audience of the Early Sound Era', in Melvyn Stokes and Richard Maltby (eds) *American Movie Audiences: From the Turn of the Century to the Early Sound Era* (London: British Film Institute, 1999) pp. 143–63.

Doyle, Arthur Conan, *The Conan Doyle Stories* (London: John Murray, 1929).

Dyer, Richard, 'White', *Screen*, 29.4 (1988) pp. 44–65.

Eco, Umberto, *The Limits of Interpretation* (Bloomington, Ind.: Indiana University Press, 1990).

Esenwein, J. Berg and Leeds, Arthur, *Writing the Photoplay* (Springfield, Mass.: Writers Library, 1913).

Esenwein, J. Berg and Leeds, Arthur, *Writing the Photoplay* (Springfield, Mass.: Writers Library, 1919).

Everson, William K., 'Serials with Sound have Steadily Declined in Quality and Quantity', *Films in Review*, 4.6 (1953) pp. 269–76.

Everson, William K., 'The Silent Serial', *Screen Facts*, 1.1 (1963) pp. 1–14.

Fanning Jr., William J., 'The Historical Death Ray and Science Fiction in the 1920s and 1930s', *Science Fiction Studies*, 37.2 (2010) pp. 253–74.

Field, Margaret, *Good Company: The Story of the Children's Entertainment Film Movement in Great Britain 1943–1950* (London: Longman Green & Co., 1952).

Film Society Programmes 1925–1939, introduced by Dr George Amberg (Arno Press, New York, 1972).

Finler, Joel, *The Hollywood Story* (London: Mandarin, 1992).

Flynn, Charles and McCarthy, Todd, 'The Economic Imperative: Why Was the B Movie Necessary', in Todd McCarthy and Charles Flynn (eds) *Kings of the Bs: Working Within the Hollywood System, an Anthology of Film History and Criticism* (New York: Dutton, 1975) pp. 13–43.

Foote, Lisle, *Buster Keaton's Crew: The Team Behind His Silent Films* (Jackson, NC: McFarland, 2013).

Ford, Richard, *Children in the Cinema* (London: Allen & Unwin, 1939).

Gardner, Jared, *Projections: Comics and the History of Twentieth-Century Storytelling* (Stanford: Stanford University Press, 2012).

Gomery, Douglas, *The Hollywood Studio System: A History*, revised edition (London: British Film Institute, 2005).

Hagedorn, Roger, 'Doubtless to be Continued: A Brief History of Serial Narrative', in robert C. Allen (ed.), *To be Continued . . .: Soap Operas Around the World* (London: Routledge, 1995) pp. 27–48.

Hansen, Lauren, 'Diagnosing the *Home Alone* Burglars' Injuries: a Professional Weighs In', *This Week*, 20 December 2012, http://theweek.com/article/index/238037/diagnosing-the-home-alone-burglars-injuries-a-professional-weighs-in?cmpid=?tw

Harden, Edgar F., 'The Discipline and Significance of Form in *Vanity Fair*', in William Makepeace Thackeray, *Vanity Fair* (New York and London: Norton, 1994) pp. 710-30.

Harmon, Jim and Donald F. Glut, *The Great Movie Serials: Their Sound and Fury* (London: Woburn Press, 1973).

Hayward, Jennifer, *Consuming Pleasures: Active Consuming Fictions: Audiences and Serial Fictions from Dickens to Soap Opera* (Lexington: University of Kentucky, 1997).

Henri, Adrian, Roger McGough, Brian Patten, *The Mersey Sound* (Harmondsworth: Penguin, 1967).

Herman, Lewis, *Practical Manual of Screen Playwriting*, (Cleveland and New York: World Publishing Company, 1952).

Higgins, Scott, *Matinee Melodrama: Playing with Formula in the Sound Serial* (New Brunswick NJ: Rutgers University Press, 2016).

Higgins, Scott, 'Seriality's Ludic Promise: Film Serials and the Prehistory of Digital Gaming', *Euladomos: Journal for Computer Game Culture*, 8.1 (2014) pp. 101–13.

Higgins, Scott, 'Suspenseful Situations: Melodramatic Narrative and the Contemporary Action Film', *Cinema Journal*, 47.2 (2008) pp. 74–96.

Higgins, Scott, 'Thinking Cinematically: Conjecture, Convictions and Other Unsubstantiated Ideas', http://shiggins.blogs.wesleyan.edu/2013/08/23/ [accessed 20 April 2015].

Hischak, Thomas S., *American Literature on Stage and Screen: 525 Works and Their Adaptations* (Jefferson, NC: McFarland, 2012).

Hughes, Linda and Lund, Michael, *The Victorian Serial* (Charlottesville: University Press of Virginia, 1991).

Hughes, Stephen, 'House Full: Silent Film Genre, Exhibition and Audiences in South India', *Indian Economic Social History Review*, 43.1 (2006) pp. 31–62.

Hulse, Ed, *Distressed Damsels and Masked Marauders: Cliffhanger Serials of the Silent-Movie Era* (Morris Plains NJ: Murania Press, 2014).

Hulse, Ed, '*The Lost City*', *Blood 'n' Thunder*, 41 (2014) pp. 28–38.

Hurst, Richard Maurice, *Republic Pictures: Between Poverty Row and the Majors*, updated edition (Lanham, Maryland: Scarecrow Press, 2007).

Isenberg, Noah William, *Edgar Ulmer: A Filmmaker on the Margins* (Berkeley: University of California Press, 2013).

Jackson III, Charles Lee, 'The Man Who Would be Serial King', *Filmfax* 20 (1990) pp. 76–79, 87.

Jenkins, Garry, *Empire Building: The Remarkable Real Life Story of* Star Wars (London: Simon & Schuster, 1997).

Johnson, Deirdre, 'Juvenile Publications', in Christine Bold (ed.) *U.S. Popular Print Culture 1860–1920* (Oxford: Oxford University Press, 2012) pp. 293–315.

Jowett, Garth S., Ian C. Jarvie and Kathryn H. Fuller, *Children and the Movies: Media Influence and the Payne Fund Controversy* (Cambridge: Cambridge University Press, 1996).

Kiesling, Barrett C., *Talking Pictures: How They Are Made and How to Appreciate Them* (London: E. & F.N. Spon, 1937).

Kinnard, Roy, Crnkovich, Tony and Vitone, R.J., *The Flash Gordon Serials, 1936–40* (Jefferson, NC: McFarland, 2008).

Kinnard, Roy, *Science Fiction Serials: A Critical Filmography of the 31 Hard SF Cliffhangers* (London: McFarland, 1998).

Klenotic, Jeffrey, '"Four Hours of Hootin' and Hollerin": Moviegoing and Everyday Life Outside the Movie Palace', in Richard Maltby, Melvyn Stokes and Robert C. Allen (eds) *Going to the Movies: Hollywood and the Social Experience of Cinema* (Exeter: University of Exeter Press, 2007) pp. 130–54.

Koszarski, Richard, 'Coming Next Week: Images of Television in Pre-War Motion Pictures', *Film History*, 10.2 (1998) pp. 128–40.

Koszarksi, Richard, *An Evening's Entertainment: The Age of the Silent Feature Picture, 1915–1928* (Berkeley and Los Angeles: University of California Press, 1990).

Kuhn, Annette, *An Everyday Magic: Cinema and Cultural Memory* (London: I.B. Tauris, 2002).

Laemmle, Carl, 'This Business of Motion Pictures', *Film History*, Vol. 3 No. 1 (1989 [1927]), 47–71.

Lahue, Kalton C., *Bound and Gagged: The Story of the Silent Serials* (New York: Castle Books, 1968).

Lahue, Kalton C., *Continued Next Week: A History of the Motion Picture Serial* (Norman: Oklahoma: University of Oklahoma Press, 1964).

Lambert, Josh, '"Wait for the Next Pictures": Intertextuality and Cliffhanger Continuity in Early Cinema and Comic Strips', *Cinema Journal*, 48.2 (2009) pp. 3–25.

Lewis, Jon, *American Film: A History* (New York: Norton, 2007).

Lucie-Smith, Edward (ed.), *The Liverpool Scene* (London: Donald Carroll, 1967).

McBride, Joseph, *Steven Spielberg*, 2nd edition (Jackson, Miss,: University of Mississippi Press, 2010).

McKernan, Luke, 'Tied to the Tracks', *The Bioscope*, 3 November 2010, http://thebioscope.net/2010/11/23/tied-to-the-tracks/ [accessed 5 April 2015].

Maltby, Richard, 'Introduction: The Americanization of the World', in Richard Maltby and Melvyn Stokes (eds.) *Hollywood Abroad: Audiences and Cultural Exchange* (London: BFI Publishing, 2004) pp. 1–20.

Marlow-Mann, Alex, 'British Series and Serials in the Silent Era', in Andrew Higson (ed.) *Young and Innocent: The Cinema in Britain 1896–1930* (Exeter: University of Exeter Press, 2002) pp. 147–61.

Mathis, Jack, *Republic Confidential: Vol. 2, The Studio* (Northbrook, Ill.: Jack Mathis Advertising, 1999).

Mathis, Jack, *Valley of the Cliffhangers* (Northbrook, Illinois: Jack Mathis Advertising, 1975).

Mayer, J. P., *Sociology of Film: Studies and Documents* (London: Faber, 1946).

Mayer, Ruth, *Serial Fu Manchu: The Chinese Supervillain and the Spread of Yellow Peril Ideology* (Philadelphia: Temple University Press, 2014).

Naipaul, V.S., *The Middle Passage* (London: Andre Deutsch, 1962).

National Council of Public Morals, *The Cinema: Its Present Position and Future Possibilities* (London: Williams and Norgate, 1917).

Neale, Steve, 'Questions of Genre', *Screen*, 31.1 (1990) pp. 45–66.

Nevins, Francis M., 'Ballet of Violence: The Films of William Witney', *Films in Review*, 25 (1974) pp. 523–45.

Nolan, Michelle, *Ball Tales: A Study of Baseball, Basketball and Football Fiction of the 1930s through 1960s* (Jefferson NC: McFarland, 2010).

Oberholzer, Ellis P., 'What are the Movies Making of Our Children?' *Reference Shelf*, 2.1. (1923) pp. 36–47.

Ó Méalóid, Pádraig, 'Boy from the Boroughs', *3.AM Magazine*, 17 March 2011, http://www.3ammagazine.com/3am/boy-from-the-boroughs/ [accessed 20 April 2015].

Othman, Frederic, 'Gooseflesh Maestro', *Saturday Evening Post*, 27 March 1943, pp. 20–21, 74, 76.

Phillips, Walter Clarke, *Dickens, Reade and Collins: Sensational Novelists* (New York: Columbia University Press, 1919).

Pierce, David, '"Senile Celluloid": Independent Exhibitors, the Major Studios and the Fight over Feature Films on Television, 1939–1956', *Film History*, 10.2 (1998) pp. 141–164.

Pipolo, Tony, 'The Spectre of *Joan of Arc*: Textual Variations in Key Prints of Dreyer's Film', *Film History*, 2.4 (1988) pp. 301–23.

Pitts, Michael R., *Poverty Row Studios, 1929–1940* (London: McFarland, 1997).

Powdermaker, Hortense, *Copper Town: Changing Africa* (New York: Harper & Row, 1962).

Rainey, Buck, *Serials and Series: A World Filmography 1912–1956* (Jefferson NC & London: McFarland, 1999).

Read, Robert J., 'A Squalid-Looking Place: Poverty Row Films of the 1930s', PhD diss., McGill University, Montreal, 2010.

Regester, Charlene, 'Movies and the Marginalised' in Ina Ray Hark (ed.) *American Cinema of the 1930s: Themes and Variations* (New Brunswick, NJ: Rutgers University Press, 2007) pp. 117–38.

Rhodes, Gary Don, *Lugosi: His Life in Films, on Stage, and in the Hearts of Horror Lovers* (Jacksonville and London: McFarland, 1997).

Santo, Avi, 'Transmedia Brand Licensing Prior to Conglomeration: George Trendle and the Lone Ranger and Green Hornet Brands, 1933–66. PhD diss., University of Texas at Austin, 2006.

Sargent, Epes Winthrop, *Technique of the Photoplay* (New York: Moving Picture World, 1917).

Schaefer, Eric, *Bold! Daring! Shocking! True! A History of Exploitation Films, 1919–1959* (Durham and London: Duke University Press, 1999).

Schatz, Thomas, *The Genius of the System: Hollywood Filmmaking in the Studio Era* (London: Simon & Schuster, 1988).

Schultz, Wayne, *The Motion Picture Serial: An Annotated Bibliography* (Metuchen, NJ: Scarecrow Press, 1992).

Schurman, Lydia Cushman, 'The Librarian of Congress Argues Against Cheap Novels Getting Low Postal Rates', in Larry E. Sullivan and Lydia C. Schurman (eds) *Pioneers, Passionate Ladies and Private Eyes: Dime Novels, Series Books, and Paperbacks* (Binghampton, NY, Hawthorne Press, 1996) pp. 59–72.

Sconce, Jeffrey, '"Trashing" the Academy: Taste, Excess, and an Emerging Politics of Cinematic Style', *Screen*, 36.4 (1995) pp. 371–93.

Singer, Ben, 'Feature Films, Variety Programs, and the Crisis of the Small Exhibitor', in Charlie Keil and Shelley Stamp (eds) *American Cinema's Transitional Era: Audiences, Institutions, Practices* (Berkeley: University of California Press, 2004) pp. 76–100.

Singer, Ben, *Melodrama and Modernity: Early Sensational Cinema and its Contexts* (New York: Columbia UP, 2001).

Singer, Ben, 'Serials', in Geoffrey Nowell-Smith (ed.) *The Oxford History of World Cinema* (Oxford: Oxford University Press, 1996) pp. 105–11.

Smith, Frank Leon, 'The Man who Made Serials', *Films in Review*, 7.8 (1956) pp. 375–83.

Stamp, Shelley, 'An Awful Struggle Between Love and Ambition: Serial Heroines, Serial Stars and Their Female Fans', in Lee Grieveson (ed.) *The Silent Cinema Reader* (New York: Routledge, 2004) pp. 210–25.

Stamp, Shelley, *Movie-Struck Girls: Women and Motion Picture Culture after the Nickelodeon* (Princeton, NJ: Princeton University Press, 2000).

Stanfield, Peter, *Hollywood, Westerns and the 1930s: The Lost Trail* (Exeter: University of Exeter Press, 2001).

Stedman, Raymond William, *The Serials: Suspense and Drama by Instalment* (Norman, Oklahoma: University of Oklahoma Press, 1971).

Symons, Julian, *Bloody Murder: From the Detective Story to the Crime Novel: A History* (Harmondsworth: Penguin, 1974).

Taves, Brian, 'The B Film: Hollywood's Other Half', in Tino Balio, *Grand Design: Hollywood as a Modern Business Enterprise, 1930–1939* (Berkeley: University of California Press, 1995) pp. 313–50.

Thackeray, William Makepeace, *Vanity Fair: An Authoritative Text, Backgrounds and Content Criticism* (New York: Norton, 1994) [first published 1847–48].

Thompson, Kristin, *Breaking the Glass Armor: Neo-Formalist Film Analysis* (Princeton, NJ: Princeton University Press, 1988).

Thompson, Kristin, *Exporting Entertainment: America in the World Film Market 1907–1934* (London: BFI Publishing, 1985).

Thompson, Kristin, *Storytelling in the New Hollywood: Understanding Classical Narrative Technique* (Cambridge, Mass.: Harvard University Press, 1999).

Thompson, Kristin, and Bordwell, David, *Film History: An Introduction*, 3rd edition (New York: McGraw-Hill, 2009).

Thorp, Margaret Farrand, *America at the Movies* (London: Faber, 1946).

Tillotson, Kathleen, *Novels of the 1840s* (Oxford: Oxford University Press, 1954).

Todorov, Tzvetan, *The Fantastic: A Structural Approach to a Literary Genre*, trans. Richard Howard (Ithaca: Cornell University Press, 1975).

Turner, George E. and Price, Michael H., *Forgotten Horrors: The Definitive Edition* (Baltimore: Midnight Marque Press, 1999).

Turner, Mark W., 'The Unruliness of Serials in the Nineteenth Century (and the Digital Age)', in Rob Allen and Thijs van den Berg (eds) *Serialization in Popular Culture* (London: Routledge, 2014).

Tuska, Jon, *The Vanishing Legion: A History of Mascot Pictures 1927–1935* (Jefferson, NC: McFarland, 2000).

Tzioumakis, Yannis, *American Independent Cinema: An Introduction* (Edinburgh: Edinburgh UP, 2006).

Universal Pictures, *How to Make Money with Serials: A Universal Text Book for the Use of Motion Picture Exhibitors* (New York: Universal Pictures Corporation, n.d.).

Vela, Rafael Arnaldo, 'With Parents Consent: Film Serials, Consumerism and the Creation of the Youth Audience, 1913–1938', PhD diss., University of Wisconsin-Madison, 2000.

Ward, Richard, 'Extra Added Attractions: The Short Subjects of MGM, Warner Brothers and Universal', *Media History*, 9.3 (2003) pp. 221–44.

Warhol, Robyn, 'Making "Gay" and "Lesbian" into Household Words: How Serial Form Works in Armistrad Maupin's *Tales of the City*', *Contemporary Literature*, 40.3 (1999) pp. 378–402.

Witney, William, *In a Door, Into a Fight, Out a Door, Into a Chase* (Jefferson, NC and London: McFarland, 1996).

Wood, Alan, *Mr Rank: A Study of J. Arthur Rank and British Films* (London: Hodder and Stoughton, 1952).

Wright, William Lord, *Photoplay Writing* (New York: Falk Publishing, 1920).

Index